# Three East European Plays

### THE HORSE
*Julius Hay*
TRANSLATED BY
PETER HAY

·

### TANGO
*Slawomir Mrozek*
TRANSLATED BY
NICHOLAS BETHELL AND
TOM STOPPARD

·

### THE MEMORANDUM
*Václav Havel*
TRANSLATED BY
VERA BLACKWELL

PENGUIN BOOKS

Penguin Books Ltd, Harmondsworth, Middlesex, England
Penguin Books Inc., 7110 Ambassador Road, Baltimore, Maryland 21207, U.S.A.
Penguin Books Australia Ltd, Ringwood, Victoria, Australia

—

Introduction copyright © Martin Esslin, 1970

—

*The Horse*
Translated from the Hungarian by Peter Hay
Originally published in German under the title *Das Pferd*
Copyright © Julius Hay and Rowohlt Verlag GmbH,
Reinbek bei Hamburg, 1964
Translation copyright © Peter Hay, 1970

*Tango*
This translation first published in Great Britain
by Jonathan Cape Ltd, 1968
Translation copyright © Nicholas Bethell and Tom Stoppard, 1968

*The Memorandum*
This translation first published by Jonathan Cape Ltd, 1967
Translation copyright © Vera Blackwell, 1967

Published in Penguin Books 1970

—

Made and printed in Great Britain by
C. Nicholls & Company Ltd
Set in Monotype Baskerville

# CONTENTS

# INTRODUCTION

THE theatre holds a very special place in the cultural life of the nations of Eastern Europe: in their long-drawn struggles to preserve and re-assert their nationhood against the overwhelmingly powerful tides of Germans and Russians (in the case of Poland), Austrians and Turks (in the case of Hungary and the Southern Slavs) or Austrians and Germans (in the case of the Czechs) these fanatically proud nations clung to their language and literary traditions with far greater fervour and deliberate devotion than more fortunate peoples. At times when the political independence, and therefore the political *identity* of these nations seemed lost, they had to cling to their cultural identity with redoubled tenacity; for if that too had perished in the face of German, Russian or Austrian efforts to impose their own language and culture, all hope of ever regaining nationhood would have been swept away for ever.

The poets and thinkers of these nations therefore became, of necessity, rallying points of their national aspirations. But the theatre held a particular importance: being a collective art, requiring the presence of an audience, a cross-section of the nation-in-being, it could give *living* proof of its continued vitality; indeed, it could play the part of a visible rallying point, a true sounding board for national sentiment, even a substitute for the suppressed parliaments and solemn mass ceremonials of independent nations: for on the stage, and in the living response of the audience, the moral and political issues of the day could be aired – in however guarded language, in the guise of historical or mythological subject matter – and publicly debated. The plays of Mickiewicz (the suppression to please the Russians of his drama *Dziady*, written around 1830, led to the Warsaw student riots of

7

1968!) and Krasinski in Poland, of Vörösmarlty, Madách and Arany in Hungary, the patriotic operas of Dvořák and Smetana in Czechoslovakia, are thus more than just literary or musical classics: they are sacred manifestations of the national personality, embodiments of its enduring spirit.

It is against this background that we must see the role of theatre and of playwrights in Poland, Czechoslovakia and Hungary in the period which followed the Second World War.

During the period of Stalinism great efforts were made to use the theatre as a powerful weapon of indoctrination and propaganda: even at a time of economic hardship the theatres were heavily subsidized and actors and playwrights given a privileged position in the community. Yet the glut of Soviet propaganda plays which spread across the stages of Eastern Europe after the war failed to make the desired impact. For even in a strictly planned and controlled economy the theatre remains, to a certain extent, an area in which the free play of the market, supply and demand, continues to operate. If dull plays are offered, audiences will stay away. In highly subsidized theatres this does not lead to bankruptcy or the closure of the plays concerned; the managements could go on indefinitely playing to empty houses. But the optical effect remains highly unfortunate. Efforts can be made to fill the theatres by giving away tickets, or by forcing trade unions and other mass organizations to buy them and distribute them to their members. But even then the public could vote with their feet by not making use of the tickets that have been thrust upon them.

The theatres were, therefore, urged to please the public *somehow*. (Even in the Soviet Union, where the audience has been far more thoroughly conditioned over a very long period, non-political operettas and musicals lead all popularity contests.) And theatre managements had to find plays that would attract a willing and eager audience. The great national classics always did the trick, so did Western plays, insofar as they were permitted and became available. Even more enthusiastically received, however, were those plays which made their own topical and relevant comment on the contemporary scene although, outwardly, they might appear to be dealing with some quite different subject matter. The first night of Mrozek's *Police* on 27 June 1958, for example, was considered an event of sensational significance in Poland at that time. The author insisted in a programme note that 'this play contains nothing apart from that which it contains; that is to say: no hints at anything and no metaphors. Between its lines there is nothing: to try to read between them, therefore, is love's labour lost.' Yet to tell this to an audience just emerging from ten years of savage Stalinist terror is simply an additional sly irony, when the play they are seeing is about a police state in which the police have been so successful that all opposition has been wiped out; with the result that, lest they become totally superfluous and therefore lose their jobs, the police themselves have to be ordered to commit political crimes.

The theatre had played its part in preparing the thaw by providing evidence of the true feelings of the population. After 1956 in Poland it briefly enjoyed an upsurge of relative freedom. When I visited Poland in 1965 a high official in the Ministry of Culture told me how things had changed: under Stalinism, he said, 'we tried to tell the theatres what to perform; nowadays we merely tell them what they may *not* perform'.

In Czechoslovakia this thaw came much later than in Poland – not till the early nineteen sixties: Václav Havel's play *The Garden Party* was produced at the Theatre at the Balustrade in 1963 and became, with Ionesco's *The Lesson*, Beckett's *Waiting for Godot* and Jarry's *King Ubu*, one of the mainstays of the repertoire of that daringly experimental little theatre. This theatre was originally founded as the home of Ladislas Fialka's brilliant mime troupe, who were later joined by Jan Grossman, an equally brilliant director of straight plays. In the brief period between 1963 and 1968 Czech drama reached an astonishing flowering with the work of playwrights like Josef Topol, Milan Uhde, Ladislav Smoček, Ivan Klima, Václav Havel and – in Slovakia – Peter Karvas.

In Hungary the revolt of the intellectuals came earlier, more violently and more briefly, in 1956. After the suppression of the popular rising which it had triggered off there was a relapse into a far less permissive atmosphere in the arts. But here also a return to Stalinism proved a practical impossibility; gradually the theatre reflected the popular mood, with more productions of foreign plays (from Peter Weiss to Arthur Miller) and the guarded discussion of the more burning local issues by Hungarian playwrights.

Julius Hay's *The Horse*, although it has had a performance in Czechoslovakia, has not as yet reached the Hungarian stage. Hay, the oldest of the playwrights represented in this volume, is one of the great – and typical – figures of East European left-wing literature. His life story reflects the problems and dilemmas of a whole generation of intellectuals.

Hay was born on 5 May 1900 in Abony. His father was an engineer. While still at school, during the Frst World War, he was involved in the pacifist protest movement against the war. When Hungary was briefly under a Communist government in 1919 he became a youth propagandist in the Ministry of Education. (The minister was George Lukács, the great Marxist theoretician.) After the collapse of the Communist régime he fled the country, studied architecture in Germany and became a stage designer. In Berlin he met Brecht, who belonged to the same generation and whose political development followed parallel lines. In 1932 Hay had two plays running in Berlin theatres, a comedy *The New Paradise* and a historical drama, *God, Emperor and Peasant*, in

Reinhardt's famous *Deutsches Theater*. As it turned out, this was the last première in Reinhardt's theatre. Nazi storm-troopers invaded the auditorium and demanded the suppression of the play. A few weeks after it opened, Hitler came to power. Hay, who had joined the Communist party, had to flee from Germany, and settled in Vienna. (I remember him as a frequent visitor in my father's flat there. I was fourteen years old at the time and deeply impressed by the handsome, dark, soft-spoken man with burning eyes, who appeared to me as the embodiment of my own dream of a true hero, who was both a fighter for freedom and a great writer.) After the violent suppression of the Socialists in Austria in February 1934, Hay again had to move. He was briefly under arrest in Vienna, went to Paris, then Zurich and finally accepted an invitation to Moscow. He lived in the Soviet Union until 1945. After the war he returned to his native Hungary, a celebrated writer and a hero of the new Communist régime. At last his plays could be performed – at least for a time. For soon it became clear that even writers of Hay's merit and record could not work freely. Hay gradually became one of the leaders of the intellectuals' fight against the Stalinist Rákosi régime. In the brief period of liberalization in 1956 Hay became Vice-President of the Writers' Union which led the movement for greater freedom. After the Russians put an end to the country's bid for freedom, Hay was arrested and sentenced to six years' imprisonment. After having served three years of this sentence he was amnestied. It was at this time – 1960 – that he started work on *The Horse*. Although his plays remained banned in Hungary, they now were widely produced abroad, in Czechoslovakia, Switzerland, Austria and Western Germany. *The Horse* had its first performance at the Salzburg Festival in 1964. Having obtained a passport, Hay decided to settle outside Hungary. He now lives in Ascona, Switzerland.

Like Brecht's, Hay's path led from hatred of war to radical socialist ideas, from opposition to the mad, militarist aspirations of Hitler to support of the only political force that seemed energetic enough to offer effective opposition to Hitler, the Soviet brand of Communism. Brecht never settled in the Soviet Union; Hay spent ten years there and witnessed the period of the purges, but also the heroism of the war years. It was only after the war that, in his own country – now at last liberated from the reactionary, feudalist régime of landowners which had driven him into exile – that disillusionment with totalitarian Soviet methods set in. The radical Marxists and pacifists of Brecht's and Hay's generation became Communists because they stood for *freedom*. Hence, when the 'liberation' led to anything but freedom, they, of necessity, logically, had to continue their fight for free expression, free thought, free movement. And so inevitably they again came into conflict with authority.

*The Horse*, based on a true incident in the life of the Roman Emperor Caligula (whom Camus also used as a metaphor for problems of our own time), is a lighthearted satire and yet it expresses a lifetime's bitter experience. The process by which people under a totalitarian régime train themselves to accept every absurd whim of their rulers as rational and wise may be a grotesquely funny spectacle, but it is also one of the most tragic phenomena of our time: the voluntary abdication of reason. In this light, satirical play, as in his great historical dramas and his social tragedies, Hay shows himself a master of the scrupulously constructed, brilliantly carpentered 'well-made play'. He is a consummate craftsman in the manner of Ibsen, Hauptmann and Shaw.

The two other East European playwrights in this volume – who belong to a much younger, post-war, generation – follow a completely different tradition: their work clearly shows the influence of Beckett and Ionesco, of the Theatre of the Absurd.

It is no coincidence that the cultural thaw both in Poland and Czechoslovakia should have been marked by performances of Ionesco and Beckett. These writers who had been under persistent attack in Western Europe, particularly in France, for being unpolitical and socially uncommitted, revealed themselves as highly political dramatists in the completely different atmosphere of an Eastern Europe just emerging from Stalinism and the dreary cult of 'social realism'. *Waiting for Godot*, with its description of a pointless and painful existence kept going by the vain promise of a vague salvation which obviously cannot and will not come, suddenly exploded into topicality in a country like Poland where, indeed, the population eked out a joyless existence, waiting for the fulfilment of an ever elusive promise of freedom to come. *The Lesson*, with its authoritarian, sadistic professor who drains his pupil's vitality by forcing her to repeat nonsensical phrases, also assumed immediate and obvious relevance in an environment poisoned by nonsensical propaganda forced down the nation's throat with threats of violence. Yet, at the same time, the non-realistic, dreamlike atmosphere of these plays, their technique of suggestion by symbol and metaphor, gave them a certain immunity from the most obvious objections of the censors. In other words: the 'non-political' Theatre of the Absurd turned out to be the ideal form of political theatre in Eastern Europe.

Slawomir Mrozek (born 26 June 1930) is only one among a number of Polish playwrights who saw the value of the absurdist style. A master of the grotesque (he began his professional career as a cartoonist on a football weekly), he starts out with seemingly ordinary situations which, developing with scrupulous and relentless logic, lead to the wildest paradox. In one of his short stories a man acquires a sheepdog: the dog is a good sheepdog, so he must *act* as a good sheepdog; in the end, we find the master on all fours eating grass in a corner of his garden, jealously watched by the good sheepdog fulfilling his sheepdog's duty. It is with the same rigorous logic that the basic situation in *Tango*, Mrozek's hitherto most successful full-length play, is pursued to its utmost consequence.

The starting point of *Tango* is the paradox of rebellion: if rebellion is, in itself, a positive attitude – and how else could it appear in a society proud of having emerged from a revolution? – then the victory of the rebels along the whole line creates a grave problem for the next generation: what are they to rebel against, once every aim of rebellion has been reached, total permissiveness has been established, all rules and standards have been destroyed? With acute insight Mrozek has seen that the problem of revolution must, therefore, also be a problem of generations. Hence his use of the form of the traditional family comedy to deal with a subject which, ultimately, amounts to an anatomy, a dialectic, of the process of revolution itself.

The parents of the family in *Tango* were cultural, aesthetic rebels: they fought for freedom in the arts, for experiment, for the destruction of traditional rules. With the rules of conduct and of art, all other standards have also toppled. The brutish, half-human barbarian, Eddie, has been taken into the household and has become the mother's lover. Arthur, the son, a latter-day Hamlet, has nothing to rebel against, so he longs for the restoration of old-world standards and manners. When he gets hold of his father's gun he forces the family to return to tidiness and Victorian standards of propriety so that he can marry his cousin, Ala, in a proper white wedding. But, on the eve of the wedding day, he realizes that all that can be restored by such compulsion are the outward trappings of respectability; the substance has been destroyed once and for all. In his despair he comes to the conclusion that in such a moral desert the only yardstick left is that of brute force, pure, nihilistic terror. But, Arthur, being an idealist and an intellectual, may have reached such a conclusion in theory, in practice he is not brute enough to exercise a true régime of terror in all its savage cruelty. And so, by the logic of Arthur's own conception, his theory can be put into practice only by Eddie, who alone is insensitive and brutal enough. Eddie kills Arthur with a savage blow and dances the tango over his corpse; the tango, which, in the far off-days when the fight for permissiveness was started, was regarded as so lewd a dance that progressives had indulged in it as a symbol of defiance.

When *Tango* was first performed in Warsaw in 1964 it understandably produced a violent reaction: the audience interpreted the play's message as a sardonic comment on Stalinism and its totalitarian structure of terror. But the play made an equally strong impact in Western Germany and other countries in non-Communist Europe. The destruction of standards and the problems of permissiveness are just as topical in the West, even though they do not manifest themselves in the same outward trappings of open, physical brutality: the growth of arbitrary bureaucratic power, the erosion of political ideals and the consequent pursuit of power for its own sake by otherwise undistinguishable parties, led by crude, uncultured careerists, might also, after all, turn out to be a feature of such 'advanced' Western societies as the United States, France or even Britain.

Although Mrozek's work clearly shows the influence of Ionesco and Beckett, it also owes much to the rich tradition of surrealist and experimental art indigenous in Poland itself, above all to Stanislaw Witkiewicz (1885–1939), painter, playwright and novelist, who developed his own brand of surreal theatre which anticipated much of the avant-garde work of the nineteen fifties in France.

Václav Havel, born 5 October 1936, the youngest of the three playwrights represented in this volume, is also deeply rooted in his own country's tradition. Franz Kafka and Jaroslav Hašek, two seemingly irreconcilable worlds, of brooding, metaphysical anguish on the one hand, and of genial, low-life clowning on the other, seem strangely fused in Havel's plays. The common denominator between them might perhaps be found in the fact that both Kafka and Hašek derive much of their atmosphere from that peculiarly Austrian kind of bureaucracy which is raised to the status of a malignant cosmic power in Kafka's *Trial* or *Castle*, while it is mercilessly derided and exposed in Hašek's *Good Soldier Schweik*. The fact that the Habsburg monarchy's bureaucracy provided, at its worst, a mild foretaste of the vast machinery of modern totalitarianism, clearly makes these great classics of the literature of Prague peculiarly fruitful models for latter-day satirists. (Another important Czech play of the period of liberalization in the mid-sixties, Ivan Klíma's *The Castle*, openly bases itself on Kafka's novel of the same title and projects it into contemporary terms.) Havel, who has worked for some years as resident playwright and literary manager of the Theatre at the Balustrade (where Beckett, Jarry and Ionesco were performed) also, of course, has felt the influence of these pioneers of meta-physical tragi-comedy. Beyond that he has a philosophical bent of mind (shown in a number of brilliantly argued essays) and is at home with modern structural linguistics and Wittgenstein's language games.

Havel's first success, *The Garden Party*, presented a bureau-cratic structure in the grip of a linguistic dilemma: a totalitarian country which has undergone a change of heart wants to get rid of its most negative ministry, the Ministry of Liquidation, and entrusts its most positive Ministry, the Ministry of Inauguration, with the task of liquidating the Ministry of Liquidation. But this, by all rules of logic and language, must clearly be an impossibility. The Ministry of Liquidation can argue, with great conviction, that it alone is entitled to undertake liquidations, it alone can be entrusted with the task concerned – and consequently, in order to carry out its own liquidation, it must be kept in being rather than liquidated. The young hero of the play, making use of the opportunities offered by this problem, rises to dizzy heights in his career, for it is just on problems of this nature and such subtle intricacy that the true-born bureaucrat must thrive. The situation remains deadlocked, but our young man has his life's work cut out for him.

In *The Memorandum* Havel's insights into structural linguistics and communications theory give rise to an even more deadly probing of the power structure of a society based on the interpretation of incomprehensible but sacred texts. Whoever can substantiate a claim, or even pretend, to be able to translate these texts into everyday language, automatically holds the keys of power. This is a situation which can be found in the history of the Church as well as that of societies based on the sacred texts of Marxism. New men come to power by imposing the use of a new language which only they can manipulate and understand. Their rule collapses when it is found that they did not, in fact, know the new language themselves and had turned the message conveyed to them in that language into its own opposite. But – and this is the crowning irony of the play – even those who get innocently involved in the illusory conflicts arising out of such battles about the interpretation of undecipherable sacred texts, suffer irreparable damage to their characters: their trust in reason, in themselves and in the ultimate victory of the light, is so deeply undermined that they turn into sycophantic cowards, concerned only with getting by with a minimum of trouble. That is the fate of Gross, the hero of *The Memorandum*. When faced with the ultimate test he takes refuge in fine phrases about humanitarianism and justice; by using these concepts to camouflage his moral surrender, he has made them as useless as the gibberish vocabulary of the nonsense language he himself has exposed as a fraud. Yet – and this is a further brilliant twist of irony – the girl, whom he is letting down and betraying, is herself so dazzled by this display of meaningless verbosity that she fails to realize the meanness and perfidy of Gross's refusal to help her and departs with the words: 'Nobody ever talked to me so nicely before'.

Again, as in the case of Mrozek, this is theatre of acute political insight and relevance. Havel does not deny that his theatre, theatre in general, is politically relevant. In an essay contributed to the *Times Literary Supplement* in September 1967, he cogently argued that the theatre, which can only exist on the stage at the moment of performance, is *bound* to be political in the widest sense of the term. But, 'the essential politicality of the theatre does not, of course, mean that there exists any particularly friendly relationship between the theatre and practical politics, or between the theatre and politicians. Paradoxical as it may sound, quite the reverse is true.... The theatre shows the truth about politics not because it has a political aim: politics itself is the aim. The theatre can depict politics precisely because it has no political aim. For this reason it seems to me that all ideas of a so-called "political theatre" are mistaken ...'

Havel's attitude reflects the disillusionment of dramatists in the Communist world with the manipulated drama of the Stalinist period, when playwrights were ordered to write to propagate specific ideas: the need to beware of Western spies, or to grow more turnips. Young dramatists of Mrozek's and Havel's generation did much, in the period of the thaw, to re-establish the theatre as a forum for the genuine discussion of real issues and as an instrument designed to search for deeper truths.

With the spread of a much more intolerant, anti-semitic

attitude among those in power in Poland, with the Russian occupation of Czechoslovakia, the prospects for this type of witty, vital and penetrating drama may seem far bleaker. Yet, ultimately, the development embodied in the work of Hay, Mrozek and Havel must prove irreversible. Audiences which have experienced the intellectual exhilaration of *Tango* or *The Memorandum*, the pleasure of responding to the subtle play of allusion and allegory, of discovering layer after layer of satire, irony and deeper meanings, such audiences will prove even more allergic to the predictable obviousness of crude propaganda. And so the theatre in Eastern Europe will, undoubtedly, remain a sensitive seismograph of popular feeling and an area of relative freedom even in the – it is to be hoped, brief – period of reduced independence that started in 1968.

# THE HORSE

*A Comedy by Julius Hay*

TRANSLATED BY PETER HAY

The translator gratefully acknowledges
the many people – and principally Mr
Robin Ackland and Mr Robin Kirkpatrick
– for their helpful reading and criticisms of
his version of the play.

All inquiries concerning performing
rights in the English language should be
addressed to Peter Hay, c/o Casa Elga
Maria, Brissago, Switzerland.

# CHARACTERS

CALIGULA *the Emperor*

EGNATIUS *the Consul*

MACRO *Commander of the bodyguards*

LOLLIA *Macro's wife*

SELANUS *a young man from the country*

FUFICIUS *a banker*

VALERIA *his wife*

AMEANA *their daughter*

SUFFENUS  
THALLUS } *Senators*  
COMINIUS

LENTULUS  
VERANIUS } *Young men about town*  
FABULLUS

CLODIA  
JULIA } *Senators' daughters*  
TULLIA

PYRALLIS *an elderly whore*

ERIA *her daughter, in the same trade*

TAVERNER

DRUNK SAILOR

FIRST TEUTON  
SECOND TEUTON } *of the bodyguards*  
THIRD TEUTON

Senators, citizens, whores, young men about town, young maidens from the best families, sailors, day-labourers, porters, Teuton bodyguards

Set in Rome, the first century of our era.

# ACT ONE

## SCENE ONE

*Tavern at night.*

*In the background, whores dancing, playing the flute, striking the lyre and singing, with Pyrallis and Eria among them.*

*In the foreground a game of dice is in progress. Throwing in the middle is a man made unrecognizable by a shaggy false beard; his companion is disguised with a bushy moustache. Between the two is a finely built, well-dressed and handsome looking young man:* SELANUS. *He has evidently been travelling and has come as a stranger to mix in this company. They are surrounded by a few young men about town:* LENTULUS, VERANIUS, FABULLUS *and others, along with a motley crowd of dirty day-labourers, sailors and porters.*

*The* TAVERNER *serves drinks and makes some attempt at order.*

*Everyone makes a distinct effort to be rude to the man with the false beard, who evidently requires this in token of the fact that nobody has recognized him. The one exception is* SELANUS, *who really knows nobody here.*

SELANUS *has already lost all his money. He is just casting his last pieces of jewellery on to the table. A throw: the young man loses again.*

SEVERAL: He's lost! Lost again! He's lost everything!

SELANUS [*beside himself*]: I've got a horse . . .

BUSHYBEARD: A horse! What d'you expect me to do with a horse? Chop him up for sausages!

SELANUS: My friends! My fellow gamblers! I've got a horse. This'll be my last bet. A dapplegrey. . . . Worth all the gold in the world!

BUSHYBEARD and MOUSTACHED MAN: Chop him up for sausages.

23

SELANUS: Take a look! At least take a look at him! There he stands tied to that post. Does anybody want to see him? – You've never seen a horse like him.

DRUNK SAILOR: Ch ... chop him up f ... for sausages!

THE PLAYERS [*in chorus*]: Chop-him-up-for-sausages!

[*They laugh and no one looks at the horse.*]

SELANUS: Listen to me! I am a stranger in Rome! You have turned my pockets inside out. My ring, my armlet – you have taken the lot. The cloth I brought for an outfit, you have won that too. And now – why won't you take my last bet? [*Beats his heels.*] I want to play! I want to win! I stake my horse! My dapplegrey!

TAVERNER: My good lad, do you expect favours from them? From these bedraggled brigands? From this bearded bandit? Eh?

[*Resounding laughter.* BUSHYBEARD *evidently enjoys the insult. The* TAVERNER *provides his taunts with emphatic readiness, though he accompanies them with a slight bow – subconsciously.*]

SELANUS: He's a dapplegrey! A stallion! No horse like him has ever trod Roman cobbles!

TAVERNER: Are you trying to move this heartless, hirsute gorilla?

LENTULUS: Sooner the stones in the Forum!

VERANIUS: The sand in the Sahara!

FABULLUS: The lava in Etna's belly!

TAVERNER [*with a deep bow*]: In all his divine majesty the emperor Caligula's endless realms, you won't find such another [*accompanying each epithet with a kick towards* BUSHYBEARD] merciless marauder ... soulless slaughter-man ... sneaking pickpocket ...

LENTULUS: Such a bloodsucker!

VERANIUS: Such a highwayman!

FABULLUS: Such a head-shrinker!

MOUSTACHED MAN: No, my boy, compassion and kindheartedness are not my dear companion's strong points.

SELANUS: It's not compassion I want! I don't give a damn for your kind hearts! I want to play ...! Dice I want! I want to give fortune, that whore, one last chance to put right what she has done to me today!

ERIA [*young whore, goes up to* SELANUS]: Leave the dice for today, handsome. You've gambled the roof away from over your head! Come to me, I will squeeze some room for you.

PYRALLIS [*elder whore*]: Not bloody likely! This is my daughter, I give the orders in her bed. You won't get her free, dear sir! This body, this pair of thighs, these breasts ... my only daughter whom I bore on a bed of pain – her, free? Get away from here, Eria ... my daughter, my little dove! For nothing, handsome young man, the best you can do is me.

SELANUS: God rot your souls, try to understand ... it's my only ... yes, I want to stake my last remaining, but priceless, treasure against a few lousy bags of gold and your gaudy, tinkling trinkets – my horse!

BUSHYBEARD. Your nag?

SELANUS: What did you say? What did you dare say against my dapplegrey?

TAVERNER: Come, come, not so fast young man! In my tavern rudeness is compulsory, but fighting forbidden.

BUSHYBEARD: Enough, let's go! Put today's catch in the bag.

MOUSTACHED MAN: Have a good night's rest, penniless lad!

SELANUS [*cools down*]: I didn't want to hurt anyone. I am Selanus, my father is Marcus. I come from a decent country family, from a gentry home. I set out for Rome to try my luck. I am my father's seventh son. . . . I was also a bit bored at home. . . . But for all that, I didn't go about the world penniless, as you've seen. . . . Well, no matter! –

Now I am almost ashamed that in the heat of the moment I could think of wagering Italy's finest horse, my most loyal friend. My dapplegrey Incitatus.... That's what he is called. That's his name – Incitatus ...! – He was still in his mother's belly when I sensed he had got a great future. A fortune-teller predicted it: no horse has ever had such a shining career as awaits my Incitatus.... Pity, the prophecy goes on to say he won't have a long life ...

DRUNK SAILOR: Because ... you'll ch ... chop him up f... for s ... sausages ...

SELANUS: I looked after him myself, I broke him in myself. I fed him on honeyed oats. Never has another's hand brushed him or scrubbed him ...

MOUSTACHED MAN: We're sick to death with your horse, Empty-purse.

YOUNG MEN: We're sick to death!

SELANUS: Yes, I must apologize to my horse, to my dearest companion, for ever mentioning his name in front of people who probably can't tell a mule from a camel!

BUSHYBEARD: Heard you that, Rome? Heard you, Germania, Britannia? That I ... I ... I mean that, this unknown fellow with the beard.... I don't know about horses?

SELANUS [*shouts outside*]: Hey, my horse, my lovely horse, hey, Incitatus, forgive me for ever wanting to stake you, my only friend, for the amusement of rogues. Will you forgive your poor master, Incitatus?

[*A stallion's fine, powerful and tuneful whinny is heard outside. All ears are strained.*]

SELANUS: Thank you, Incitatus!

TAVERNER [*surprised*]: I say, he's got a voice!

PYRALLIS [*in rapture*]: What a voice! It makes you swoon.

ERIA: Oh, Mummy, I've never heard the like of it!

[*A number of mares answer from varying distances.*]

26

SELANUS: Aha! The mares of Rome!

BUSHYBEARD [*admiringly*]: What kind of a stallion has a voice like that?

[*He presses his way to the entrance, to take a look outside. Many push after him.*]

BUSHYBEARD [*stunned*]: Is this a horse? This a horse? I know what a horse is! This is a vision! Magic! A dream ...!

MOUSTACHED MAN: No horse like this has ever trod the Roman cobbles.

[*Elongated, emotional bray of a she-ass is heard.*]

TAVERNER: Haha! Even my dear old she-ass has found an appetite to make mules.

DRUNK SAILOR: Hehehe.... You are ... all d ... drunk! There isn't a h ... horse like this in the whole wide world!

SELANUS [*shouts out*]: Hey, boy, walk the dapplegrey around once!

[*Complete silence inside, while the clatter of hooves on the stones rings through.*]

LENTULUS: Look, what legs ...!

VERANIUS. Look at that rump swaying ...!

FABULLUS: What a swing ...!

TAVERNER: Well, boy, why didn't you say you had a horse like this?

SELANUS: Are you deaf, all of you? I've been telling you all this time.

ERIA: Mother dear, in all my life, I have never seen such beauty ...

PYRALLIS: You'd better not gape too much. He'll be with you in your dreams!

BUSHYBEARD: All right then. I'll accept your bet. Mine's this bag of gold.

SELANUS: I don't want it now. I'm ashamed it entered my head.

BUSHYBEARD: More gold.... Have this too ...

SELANUS: No.

BUSHYBEARD [*throws up money, jewels, the cloth*]: Have your jewels back! Take back everything!

SELANUS: No.

BUSHYBEARD [*taking and tearing off chains and bangles*]: And this! And this! And this!

SELANUS: No! No! No!

BUSHYBEARD [*tearing off jewels from his moustached friend*]: And this – the lot!

SELANUS: No.

BUSHYBEARD [*tearing off the young men's jewels*]: Here you are! And this! I'm staking the whole lot! For your horse! Come on! Come on! What else do you expect in return for one dapplegrey?

SELANUS: Nothing, I am not playing.

BUSHYBEARD [*pulling off his pearl-studded anklets, emptying his hidden pockets*]: Well, that's that! I've turned myself inside out: You've got everything there!

[SELANUS *shakes his head.*]

BUSHYBEARD: Taverner! Bring the cash-box! I want every penny from everybody in here! Guards, anyone trying to escape is to be put to death!

DRUNK SAILOR: You are dr ... dr ... drunk!

[BUSHYBEARD *tears the golden ear-ring off the* DRUNK SAILOR's *ear. The* DRUNK SAILOR *yells. All, terrified, put down their valuables.*]

BUSHYBEARD [*to the whores*]: Hey, you sluts there! Let's have all your knick-knacks!

[*The whores rush to hand over their jewels. Pieces which one or two try to hide are recovered and set down by the others.*]

BUSHYBEARD: No more? All for the horse!

[*Since* SELANUS *makes no reply,* BUSHYBEARD *digs out from a hidden fold a marvellous pearl, which he has kept hidden up to now. He rubs to make it glitter, then throws it among the rest. Everybody gapes at it.*]

BUSHYBEARD: Take it now?

[*Pause.*]

SELANUS [*shouts outside*]: Incitatus, my good and faithful horse, shall we risk it?

[*Brief whinny.*]

SELANUS: All right then. [*Seized by a sudden idea.*] That is – if you add one thing more to your stake.

BUSHYBEARD: What?

SELANUS: This mangy false beard.

[*General horror.*]

MOUSTACHED MAN: That's impossible, man!

SELANUS: And you take off that false moustache too!

TAVERNER: Leave it at that, my good lad, leave it …

SELANUS [*pettishly*]: Then I won't play. [*To* BUSHYBEARD] You must be somebody, man, to hide your face behind so much fur. When I'm losing all my money I want to know who I'm losing it to!

BUSHYBEARD [*vehement*]: Eh, who cares, have it!

[*He throws off the false beard, the other his moustache: the emperor* CALIGULA *and* MACRO, *commander of the bodyguard.*]

ERIA [*screams*]: The emperor …!

ALL [*with feigned astonishment but genuine fear*]: The emperor.…! His divine majesty, the emperor …!

[*They all fall on their knees prostrate,* SELANUS *alone stands hesitantly.*]

SELANUS: The emperor …?

CALIGULA: I haven't the time! Worship me when I'm not busy! The dice!

[*The* EMPEROR *throws amidst dead silence, followed by* SELANUS, *still giddy.* SELANUS *wins. Small screams of surprise, shouts, then all freeze in silence.*]

DRUNK SAILOR: If he w … won it, let him t … take it!

SELANUS [*gradually recovering his senses*]: I've won … I've won …! I've won …!!!! I've won …!!!! Incitatus! We've won the lot, we've won everything!

[*The horse gives a brief whinny.* SELANUS *hurriedly gathers up his winnings.*]

MACRO [*shouts outside*]: Guards! Litter-bearers!

[*Flourish outside.*]

CALIGULA [*completely sunk into himself, whimpering*]: I'm ill.... Macro ... my faithful captain.... Call your wife.... Let her nurse me ...

MACRO: My Lollia gives her prostrate thanks to my divine lord. Me too.

CALIGULA: Hold me up, Macro ...

[CALIGULA, MACRO *and the young men exit.*]

SELANUS [*still dizzy, with a large sachet of winnings across his arm*]: Was that really the emperor?

TAVERNER: What a simple lad you are! There isn't a man in Rome who can't recognize his divine majesty's false beard or commander Macro's false moustache. But we have to play the game night in night out, because that gives him pleasure.

SELANUS: And what's going to happen to me now?

TAVERNER: If I knew that ...?!

SCENE TWO

*A street.*

[*Enter from one side* AMEANA, *and her three friends from the other:* CLODIA, JULIA *and* TULLIA.]

AMEANA: It's about time! I don't think I could have waited a minute longer.

CLODIA: Ameana ... when we were hurrying ever so much ...

JULIA: We are out of breath ...

TULLIA: We ran as fast as we could ...

AMEANA: And why don't you speak now you're here? What did you find out? How you torture me, really!

CLODIA: We've found out everything.

AMEANA: But what? But what?

TULLIA: He doesn't live here. He's from the country.

AMEANA: Oh, there's nothing more wonderful than healthy country life!

JULIA: But it seems now he's going to stay in Rome.

AMEANA: Oh, the loveliest city! Rome, heart of the world!

CLODIA: He's taken up lavish lodgings. They say he's loaded.

AMEANA: I can't stand poverty.

JULIA: But he's a gambling addict.

AMEANA: Well, better than being bored.

TULLIA: Many's the time he has been left without a penny.

AMEANA: The heart is fuller on empty pockets, the saying goes.

CLODIA: And you know what else he's got?

AMEANA: No. . . . I can't guess what you mean . . .

THE THREE GIRLS: He's got a horse!

AMEANA: A horse? Everyone's got a horse.

TULLIA: Ameana, personally I don't know too much about horses, but they say . . .

JULIA: My brother is a great horse expert, Ameana, and he says . . .

CLODIA: I heard the men saying . . .

THE THREE GIRLS [*in chorus*]: That this horse . . .

[*SELANUS comes and greets the girls with deep respect.*]

SELANUS: Beautiful ladies . . .

[*The girls burst into a short squeal and bow in return. Then the three girls run out, leaving AMEANA on her own.*]

SELANUS: Charming young lady. . . . All morning I've been following you along Rome's streets . . .

AMEANA: Really? I hadn't even noticed.

SELANUS: Afterwards, when I'd lost sight of you, along came your girl friends talking to all sorts of people — always about me.

AMEANA: No, really? My girl friends? What could have possessed them?

SELANUS: And then they ran back to you – to report.

AMEANA: Report? I can't think what about.

SELANUS: And I followed them.

AMEANA: Oh, dear stranger, perhaps you're attracted by one of them?

SELANUS: Young lady, they are no doubt all precious stones on the splendid diadem of Rome – queen of the world. But my eyes cannot see, for all their glitter is eclipsed by the mysterious radiance of a single pearl ...

AMEANA: Which is? Which is?

SELANUS: Young lady, I am a stranger in Rome ...

AMEANA: Which is a fault, noble youth. My mama and papa don't allow me to converse with anyone whom they have not chosen for me ...

SELANUS: Your father – is he high up?

AMEANA: A banker, and most distinguished.

   [*Two windows open.* FUFICIUS *and* VALERIA *call out to the street.*]

FUFICIUS ⎱
VALERIA ⎰ Ameana!

SELANUS [*repeats the name in ecstasy*]: Ameana ...

AMEANA: Oh, my parents ... [*Aloud*] I'm coming, papa! Right away, mama ...!

SELANUS: Then just answer me one question. [*Whispers*] But make it loud so they'll think we've been talking about it the whole time. [*Loud*] Young lady, in which house, if you please, does his excellency, the consul Egnatius live?

AMEANA [*Loud*]: Knock on that door there, sir. [*Exits.*]

   [SELANUS *knocks on* EGNATIUS' *door.*]

EGNATIUS [*appears on the balcony above the door*]: Who's there? Who's knocking?! Where are you ... where are you all, knocking on my door?

SELANUS: I am by myself, my lord.

EGNATIUS: Oh, alone? And who are you, boy? Who sent you, on what errand?

SELANUS: For his excellency, Egnatius ...

EGNATIUS: Egnatius? That's me.

SELANUS: ... I've brought countless greetings from my father, Marcus Selanus.

EGNATIUS: Immortal gods, Marcus, my old friend ...!

SELANUS: I am his son: the seventh.

EGNATIUS: Step inside, my friend. Or rather, wait, till I come down to you. Wait for me there, out there, where there's no tree, no bush, no window, no pillar near you. [*Disappears within.*]

SELANUS [*alone*]: Amazing old man. No tree, no bush, no window, no pillar.... I wonder why?

  [EGNATIUS *comes.*]

SELANUS: My lord consul ...

EGNATIUS: Call me uncle: that I can be while I live. But who knows how long I shall be either consul or a lord ...? – Your dear father, how is he? Living, still firm on his feet?

SELANUS: Nothing wrong with him, uncle.

EGNATIUS: Rare news nowadays.

SELANUS: But I, uncle, arrived in Rome only yesterday and I'm already mixed up in trouble.

EGNATIUS: That sounds more like it. What trouble?

SELANUS: I robbed the emperor.

EGNATIUS: Eh ...?!

SELANUS: I stripped his divinity, the Roman emperor, Caligula, of his last penny.

EGNATIUS: And do they know it was you?

SELANUS: Of course they know, uncle. He was wearing the false beard, not me.

EGNATIUS: But how did you do it? Waylaid him? Stole into the palace? Cut open his purse? Massacred his bodyguard? You didn't knock him down, did you?

SELANUS: Really uncle! The emperor?! We played at dice and I won.

EGNATIUS: Oh, so it's you, is it? The news reached me this morning. And what are you afraid of, my son? His divine majesty recognizes only one power higher than himself: that of dice. That's why if somebody robs him at dice, he won't dare to avenge himself in a hurry.

SELANUS: You've rolled a rock off my chest, uncle! I'd have had to be afraid. To search my heart – and somehow I didn't feel like it. My mind is on other things.

EGNATIUS: What, my son?

SELANUS: My gracious uncle, lord consul! I've had one lucky break in Rome. I've got a second one in mind. Will you help me – teach me the ropes? What if, just for an example, I wanted to marry ... someone ... anyone ... let's see whom.... Well, let's say the daughter of some distinguished, wealthy banker ...

EGNATIUS [*smiling*]: Someone ... like – Ameana? Daughter of Fuficius?

SELANUS: Ameana? ... I don't know.... Are there girls called that in Rome?

EGNATIUS [*after brief thinking*]: Rumour is also spreading about a marvellous horse, which appeared in the city yesterday ...

SELANUS: Dapplegrey? That's my horse. Incitatus.

EGNATIUS: Hm ... in that case I might have an idea.... But come inside my house, have something to eat and drink. As long as we are only discussing horses, perhaps not even I, the consul, need be afraid of ears listening. ... Step inside ...

[*They enter the house.*]

*The emperor's palace.*

CALIGULA [*comes in alone*]: I am emperor. I am god! I
worship myself! I roll about in the dust in front of my
feet! – What?! Me, in the dust? I, the emperor? The
god? – But who else then, if not I? Should the devotion
of human wretches magnify me? Oho! I deserve divine
devotion. But the only indisputable divinity is me....
Yes, I, and I alone am worthy of worshipping Myself, and
again on the other hand, worthy am I alone to give
Myself worship.... Yes! No!... Well, that much is clear
anyway.... – If I ascend my throne there [*he does it*], and
receive ... receive graciously ... receive benevolently ...
receive sternly ... receive with my annihilating divine
wrath the homage ... the prostrate homage ... the
annihilated homage ... of whom? ... Of whom ...?! –
Because if I go down to the foot of my throne ... [*he does
it*] ... and lift my eyes to gaze at the divine Me.... By
my own transcendent greatness I'm struck down to the
dust ... [*he does it*] ... in front of Myself ... and I
reverence ... and wheedle ... and whine ... and grovel
... and I am at the sight of my infinite greatness annihilated.... Sight? ... But I don't see a thing.... No!
Up ... Up ...! [*Springs on his feet.*] Just now a god was
sitting up there. In greatness, in splendour, in wisdom
unsurpassable. Who was he? Me! Where has he got to?
Where have I got to ...? Where has the Me got to?! Has
the god failed his votary? Have I deserted myself? Have I
deserted the Me? No! [*Shouts*] Hey, Macro! Hey,
Captain!

MACRO [*rushes in*]: Yes, holy god?!

CALIGULA [*returns to his throne, solemnly*]: I, Caius, the divine
Caesar, also called Caligula, hereby make known my new
divine decree ...

MACRO: New divine decree ...?

CALIGULA: No, not new! New decrees are dangerous. They accustom the earthly rabble to draw distinction between decree and decree. A new age-old decree! The sacred decree of the emperor Augustus. What, to hell with Augustus! King Romulus's own! In other words, the emperor Caligula's, who on his deification became the sum total of past and future, and god of that sum total ...

MACRO: I hear you, great god!

CALIGULA: This is it then: I am not I because I am that I am! I alone am worthy of Myself, since I alone make myself me, and on the contrary, I make me Myself ...! I am a twin being. – Oho, this is just becoming clear. ... Rare moment! – I am My own twin brother. I am Pollux to Castor, and again, I am also Castor to Pollux. [*Whispering mysteriously*.] This the world hasn't heard yet. I was born at the same time with Myself! By one and the same mother ... it's even possible ... also from one and the same father ... [*In a voice of command*] Captain!

MACRO: Yes, my god?

CALIGULA: In the temple of Castor and Pollux ...

MACRO: Yes, my god ...

CALIGULA: ... the statue of the Heavenly Twins ...

MACRO: Yes, my god ...

CALIGULA: ... the masterpiece of Praxiteles ...

MACRO: Yes, immortal god ...

CALIGULA: ... have both the heads knocked off!

MACRO [*aghast*]: Oh my god ... most high!

CALIGULA: And on their necks have my head stuck.

MACRO: Y.... Yes, divine god ...!

CALIGULA: This is my order. Got it? Clear?

MACRO: As the glint in your eyes, O god of wisdom!

CALIGULA: Run! Proclaim it! See to it!

MACRO: At once, divine god!

[MACRO *rushes off*.]

CALIGULA [*alone*]: This'll be good. . . . Good. . . . – No, no, it won't be good! God omnipotent! Most high Me! Again I am left alone to be both the worshipped and the worshipper! [*On the verge of tears.*] In all my limitless realm, is there no one, really no one who is worthy to grovel in the dust before me? [*Calls*] Lollia! Lollia!

[*Enter* LOLLIA.]

LOLLIA: What's the matter, godling?

CALIGULA: Grovel in the dust before me.

LOLLIA: I've got a new dress on.

CALIGULA: Well, at least lie down before me!

LOLLIA: Look, little godling, am I to waste my precious strength on things like this?

CALIGULA: Don't you dare fall down before me! Don't you dare! A mortal wench is not worthy.

LOLLIA: Mortal wenches have been found useful for a number of things by the heavenly gods. By you too, Caligula, little godling.

CALIGULA [*whispering*]: I had the heads of Castor and Pollux knocked off. Dreadful, no?

LOLLIA [*yawning*]: Not dreadful at all.

CALIGULA: No, it isn't dreadful enough! Call your husband back. My godheads are still pondering.

LOLLIA [*calls out in a bored voice*]: Call back his honour, the captain. His wife wants him . . .

CALIGULA: His wife?!

LOLLIA: . . . and the god.

CALIGULA [*on the verge of tears*]: Once more I've found nothing and no one worthy to utter a prayer to me . . . !

LOLLIA: Little godling, your divine love has lifted me high above mere mortal women. [*Yawns.*] I will utter a prayer to you, at least until you think of something better.

CALIGULA: Good, good, you pray to us. I've now become a twin-headed deity: for look, here's Castor's head, and here again is Pollux's head – let me conjure up with one of my brains something which will be remembered to the world's end for its brilliance!

[MACRO *rushes in.*]

MACRO: Infinitely wise godhead ...?

LOLLIA: Both infinitely wise godheads are still pondering. My dear, go and give orders to have the small altar decked for tonight. I shall be uttering a prayer to the little godling.

MACRO: The consul is here with the senators.

LOLLIA: Let them wait.

[MACRO *exits.*]

CALIGULA: Will there be incense too?

LOLLIA: When? Where?

CALIGULA: On the small altar tonight?

LOLLIA: You want it?

CALIGULA: Yes.

LOLLIA: There won't be. The constant stench of incense has driven all the nightingales from my garden. In the boredom of my sleepless nights my only solace was to listen to the nightingales warbling. [*She whistles a nightingale imitation.*]

CALIGULA [*whimpering*]: I want incense ...!

LOLLIA: Let me have the consul Egnatius's orchard. It's still packed with nightingales.

CALIGULA: And what about Egnatius?

LOLLIA [*yawning*]: His is the head you should knock off, not the statues'.

CALIGULA: But who would be my consul then?

LOLLIA: Whomsoever your divine whim appoints consul – he will be consul.

CALIGULA: Not so simple! The scarcer money becomes in the state treasury, the cleverer must the consul be. And Egnatius is the best brain in Rome.

LOLLIA: A consul has only as much brain as your unbounded divine wisdom is pleased to loan him. – Don't you want incense tonight?

CALIGULA: I do!

LOLLIA: Egnatius's orchard . . .! [*Nightingale whistle.*]

CALIGULA and LOLLIA [*with the gesture of beheading*]: Snip-snip . . .! [*Both exit.*]

[EGNATIUS *and* SELANUS *come.*]

EGNATIUS: Take a good look around, my son: you are standing in the Roman Emperor's palace.

SELANUS: Aha. – And when is the chariot race?

EGNATIUS: From here the course of the world is guided.

SELANUS: Good. – Just don't forget to tell your bailiff to provide enough oats.

EGNATIUS: The drop of a pin here could mean the fate of nations.

SELANUS: I see. – And no one is to lay hands on Incitatus except myself. He can't bear strangers.

EGNATIUS: The Senate of Rome holds council here today. The senate and the emperor.

SELANUS: You can rely on me and my horse. – Where shall I wait?

EGNATIUS: There, beyond those pillars. Better go now, my son . . .

SELANUS: Only don't drag it out too long, uncle. I cannot stand to be kept waiting.

EGNATIUS: My child, in Rome today everyone has learnt to do things they once thought they could never bear to do. It's a wonder we still exist: both the empire and its citizens. . . . But how long will this miracle last . . . ? Well, go my son, go beyond those pillars.

SELANUS: One more question, uncle: these chariot races . . . do young ladies turn out for them too?

EGNATIUS: Anyone who's anyone goes. Young ladies too.

SELANUS: All's well then! [*Exits.*]

EGNATIUS [*alone*]: Marcus, my good friend. . . . It won't be an easy task in this Rome to look after your son. . . . And in the meanwhile, who is going to look after me . . . ? !

[*Enter the three Senators.*]

SUFFENUS [*draws aside* EGNATIUS, *while* THALLUS *and* COMINIUS *whisper among themselves*]: Consul, beware: Thallus and Cominius are plotting your downfall. But you can count on me, old Suffenus won't let you down.

EGNATIUS: Thank you, Suffenus.

THALLUS [*draws* EGNATIUS *aside, while* SUFFENUS *whispers with* COMINIUS]: Egnatius, be alert: Suffenus and Cominius thirst for your blood. You have but one supporter left, who will keep by your side. And that's me, Thallus.

EGNATIUS: Accept my gratitude, Thallus.

COMINIUS [*draws* EGNATIUS *aside;* THALLUS *whispers with* SUFFENUS]: My friend, a monstrous conspiracy is afoot against you: Thallus and Suffenus are after your property. But I, I Cominius, will be your defence!

EGNATIUS: Most noble of you, my Cominius.

[*Procession of* CALIGULA, *in ceremoniat dress, with* MACRO *and bodyguards. Leaning on* EGNATIUS' *shoulder he ascends the throne and occupies his seat.* LOLLIA *sits on the steps. The Senate falls prostrate to greet the* EMPEROR. *Complete silence.*]

CALIGULA [*after slight pause, throws a letter in the senators' midst*]: There! There, read it! Another three of my legions gone!

[*Movement: the Senate quietly wails.*]

CALIGULA [*throws further letters into their midst*]: Here! . . . Have it. . . . Another two legions. . . . Another four. . . . Another one . . . ! These – wiped out, these – routed, these – traitors, these – dispersed. . . . And why? I'll tell you: because there's no money! Read each one of them: send money! Money, always money!

[*Movement. The Senate wails louder.*]

CALIGULA: What says the consul to all this?

[*Silence.* EGNATIUS *steps forward, still pondering.*]

LOLLIA: [*nightingale whistle*]

CALIGULA: Consul! Wise Egnatius! Spotless Egnatius! Rich Egnatius! ... [*Pleading*] Won't you save the state treasury, please ...!

LOLLIA: [*nightingale whistle*]

CALIGULA [*ominously*]: Consul of Rome! Since my divine capacity will bear no contradiction, by all the wrath of the heavens, I ask you ...

LOLLIA: [*nightingale whistle*]

CALIGULA [*yelling*]: ... I order you to save, in a twinkling of an eye, the state treasury!

EGNATIUS [*after pause*]: My lord, you are worshipped by humankind as the god of might. As the god of wisdom. As the god of strength and valour. Favour undeserving mankind by revealing to it yet another aspect of your divine being, which it has pleased you to keep hidden until now ...

CALIGULA [*with curiosity*]: And what's that? What's that?

EGNATIUS: Rome's money and Rome's blood are drained into one and the same stream. My lord! Manifest yourself to us as the god of peace!

CALIGULA: Or in other words?

EGNATIUS: Make peace with all your enemies!

[*Movement.*]

CALIGULA [*tamely*]: Egnatius, do you play at dice?

EGNATIUS: Never, divine lord.

CALIGULA: Then you don't know what it's like when a man is out to have his money's worth. If there were peace from tomorrow, my money wouldn't go on wars, true enough. But then neither could a lucky break bring me in a single battle all the treasures of Britannia, Gallia, and Judaea!

LOLLIA: [*nightingale whistle*]

CALIGULA [*yelling*]: And why don't I have any luck either

41

at dice or war? Because the nightingales keep escaping from my garden and take my luck away with them! And where, where are the nightingales gathering in larger and larger crowds? In the consul's orchard!

THE SENATORS [*whispering among themselves*]: Fishy! Fishy! Fishy!

SUFFENUS: Imperial god! I beg the favour to be allowed to whisper a secret in your ear!

CALIGULA [*gravely*]: The chief source of imperial wisdom is from whispers in the ear. Come on!

SUFFENUS [*approaches, the* EMPEROR *bends down,* SUFFENUS *whispers*]: My god, there's a plot afoot against you! Egnatius is hatching it with Thallus and Cominius.

CALIGULA [*grimly*]: Aha!

SUFFENUS [*returning to his place, half aloud to* EGNATIUS]: I've put in a good word for you, Egnatius.

EGNATIUS: Thank you.

THALLUS: Merciful god ... a secret.... May I be permitted to whisper ...

CALIGULA [*more grimly*]: Whisper!

THALLUS [*whispers*]: My lord god, be alert. Suffenus and Cominius with Egnatius ...

CALIGULA: Aha!

THALLUS [*on his way back, half aloud*]: I've helped you in your trouble, Egnatius ...

EGNATIUS: Thank you.

COMINIUS: God most high ... your ear ...

CALIGULA [*very grimly*]: Who with whom?

COMINIUS [*whispering*]: Egnatius with Suffenus and Thallus.

CALIGULA: Aaaaaah!

COMINIUS [*on his way back, half aloud*]: Egnatius! I've settled it!

EGNATIUS: Thank you.

CALIGULA [*descends half the steps from his throne, grabs*

EGNATIUS' *cloak at his chest, shakes him, yelling*]: Traitor!
Traitor! Traitor!

THE SENATORS: Traitor! Traitor! Traitor!

CALIGULA: You've sold me, betrayed me, bartered me!
You are not my consul any more ...!

THALLUS, SUFFENUS, COMINIUS [*all at once*]: And who's to
be your new consul, my lord?

CALIGULA: I confiscate all your wealth ...!

THE SENATORS: Beggar! Out with you!

CALIGULA: Off with his head!

THE SENATORS: Off with it!

[*Silence.* LOLLIA *gives forth a quiet nightingale whistle.*]

EGNATIUS [*pale and broken*]: My lord, on this wide earth,
you are the sole master of life and death. If the interests
of the Empire demand it, take my life. Could greater
honour be conferred on a Roman citizen than to be permitted to die for Rome ... whatever Rome has become ...

THE SENATORS [*whisper in a hiss*]: Traitor! ...

EGNATIUS: But will my own death, I wonder, will the con-
fiscation of all my property cure the treasury's malady?
Everybody knows quite well, I have hardly any wealth in
cash. By the time you've converted my estates, houses and
nightingale orchard into cash, your whole army will be
in tatters.

CALIGULA: Hm ...

THE SENATORS: Hm ...

EGNATIUS: My lord, you've stripped me of my consular
rank: I'm not asking it back, I wouldn't have it back for
anything. But advance my life to me on loan, while I give
you one last piece of good advice ...

CALIGULA: On your word: never played dice?

EGNATIUS: Never.

CALIGULA: Any other game? Horse racing, chariot
racing?

EGNATIUS: Never.

CALIGULA: A virgin hand brings luck! Let's hear your advice!

EGNATIUS: But for your ears alone, my lord! Send everybody out.

CALIGULA: Clear out, all of you! [*To* LOLLIA *who wants to remain*] You too! [*To* MACRO] You too! [*To the three senators who try pushing their way through to him*] And you!

[*All exit, the* EMPEROR *remains alone with* EGNATIUS.]

CALIGULA: Speak on your borrowed life!

EGNATIUS: My lord, allow me to bring a man into your presence, whom you've seen already ...

CALIGULA: Who is it?

EGNATIUS [*calls*]: Selanus!

[SELANUS *runs in, goes down on one knee.*]

SELANUS [*half aloud*]: Uncle, don't make me late for feeding time!

CALIGULA: What do you want with this lad ...?!

EGNATIUS: Allow young Selanus, the son of Marcus, to take part with his horse, Incitatus, in today's chariot race. And – under the colour blue.

CALIGULA: Under blue? You ought to know I always back green!

EGNATIUS: All Rome backs green since she knows that your colour alone can win. That's why your divine share of winnings is steadily becoming less and less. My lord, back today, as usual, the green and let all Rome follow suit.

CALIGULA: Well, what then?

EGNATIUS: And let me, enjoying my life only on loan, lay a bet on the race for the first and last time; since any winnings would now be due to you, my lord. Let me back this young man's colour, blue ...

SELANUS: And since Incitatus will win, let's make sure we get every penny in Rome.

EGNATIUS: All for you, my lord!

CALIGULA: Haha! Are you so sure what you are about, lad?

SELANUS: My lord, you have seen Incitatus. [*Calls*] Incitatus! Are we sure what we're about?

[*A brief whinny is heard from Incitatus.*]

CALIGULA: All right, let's try it! [*Shouts*] Lollia!

[LOLLIA *hurries in.*]

LOLLIA: Great god ...? [*Notices* SELANUS.] Great god! Oh, and who's he? Who are you, handsome fellow?

SELANUS: Driver to Incitatus.

CALIGULA: Take that blue ribbon off.

LOLLIA: Anything you ask for, good god!

CALIGULA: And tie it round the arm of this young chariot-eer.

LOLLIA: Blue? No matter, I'll do that too, with pleasure!

CALIGULA: Egnatius, I advance your life on loan until the chariot race is over. Your property remains mine.... And whoever compels my fleeting fortune to return to me, whoever he may be, I'll make him my consul in your place. [*Calls out*] I declare the session of the Senate adjourned! Trumpets! Chariot race!

[*Flourish of trumpets. Music.*]


SCENE FOUR

*Near the race course. The chariot race nearing its end.*
*Music.*

[SUFFENUS, THALLUS *and* COMINIUS *come.*]

SUFFENUS: Damned blue! I put everything on green!

THALLUS: Blue's winning, it's blue! Nothing can keep it back now! Oh lord!

SUFFENUS: The emperor backed green, as always. How could I think of betting on blue?

COMINIUS: That schemer Egnatius ... and that fury-ridden horse ..

45

THALLUS: The dapplegrey!

SUFFENUS: Who has ever seen a horse like this!

[*The deafening roar of sports-fans' admiration signifies the end of the race.*

*The banker* FUFICIUS *comes with* VALERIA, *his wife, and* AMEANA, *his daughter.*]

FUFICIUS: Oh, oh, is this the reward for my loyalty to the emperor?

VALERIA: I told you so ...

FUFICIUS: What did you tell me? You've never ever told me anything in advance, always afterwards, you always begin: 'Didn't I tell you so?'

VALERIA: You've gambled away all the money we could lay our hands on ...!

FUFICIUS: Hark, who's talking? I only just managed to hold you back: You'd have staked all your paternal inheritance on green!

[*A large crowd dashes in led by the* TAVERNER, *the* DRUNK SAILOR, *the whore and others, whom we have seen in the tavern.*]

TAVERNER: The race's over, blue has won!

DRUNK SAILOR: Blue has won. ... I ... I ... Incitatus has won!

CROWD: Incitatus won!

AMEANA: Did you lose a lot, father?

FUFICIUS: Oh don't ask, my daughter.

AMEANA: I've won back a little for you.

VALERIA: How?

AMEANA: I secretly put some of the pin-money I'd saved on blue.

FUFICIUS: What a girl! A wonderful girl! However did you think of it!

AMEANA: Well ... when I saw among the blues ... that ... that horse ...

FUFICIUS: The gods do love my little daughter ...

VALERIA: But what's that compared with our losses!
  [*Vast roar of triumph.*
  *Enter the young layabouts.* LENTULUS, VERANIUS *and*
  FABULLUS *bring* SELANUS *on their shoulders.* AMEANA'S
  *girlfriends strew flowers.*]

YOUNG MEN [*with triumph*]: Incitatus! Incitatus! Incitatus!

LENTULUS [*ardently*]: I've lost my tunic on today's race!

VERANIUS: So have I, but who cares!

FABULLUS: Rome has never seen a horse like this.

THE CROWD: Incitatus! Incitatus! Incitatus! . . .!

SELANUS: Egnatius! Where's Egnatius?
  [EGNATIUS *enters followed by servants who bring the*
  *winnings in bags and on plates.*]

SELANUS [*embraces* EGNATIUS]: Uncle, the victory is ours!

EGNATIUS: It's yours and the emperor's . . . but what will I
  get out of it . . .?!
  [*Enter* CALIGULA, LOLLIA, MACRO, *the senators, and*
  *bodyguards.*
  *Silence.*]

CALIGULA: Hear, Senate of Rome, hear Roman people! I,
  the emperor, I, the twin-headed deity, my own twin
  brother, Pollux to Castor, and again Castor to Pollux, I
  command . . .

THE CROWD: Hear, hear!

CALIGULA: . . . that Egnatius, sometime consul, who has
  today forfeited his head and property . . .

THE CROWD: The traitor!

CALIGULA: . . . will now hand the measureless winnings he
  made on today's chariot race – over to me.
  [*The crowd approves. At the bidding of* EGNATIUS, *the*
  *winnings are placed at the* EMPEROR's *feet.*]

CALIGULA: All his remaining property, lands, numerous
  houses, cattle – are also mine . . .

LOLLIA: [*nightingale whistle*]

CALIGULA: . . . including his nightingale orchard.

[*Murmur of approbation.*]

LOLLIA [*to* CALIGULA]: Reward, great god, the one who achieved this triumph for you. What a fellow! Deserves every prize!

CALIGULA [*to* MACRO]: Trumpets!

[*At* MACRO's *bidding, flourish of trumpets.*]

CALIGULA: And to the vacant consular office I appoint ...

SUFFENUS, THALLUS, COMINIUS [*pressing forward, breaking in upon one another's words*]: My lord ... imperial majesty ... my god ... don't forget my deserts ... remember your most loyal servant. ... Grovelling in the dust I beg you ...

CALIGULA: I appoint him, to whom my thanks for today's victory are due ...

AMEANA: Oh how happy it makes me ...

ERIA: Oh, Mummy, we've never had such a smart consul before!

LOLLIA: Be brave, let's have it, my dear god! What if he's young, or stupid or unschooled! I'll take care of that.

CALIGULA: ... I appoint him who, after a lengthy run of misfortune, has at last brought luck and money to the house ... [*With a side glance at* LOLLIA] I appoint consul of the Roman Empire him in whom a spark of my infinite and divine greatness is incarnate; I appoint the new consul of the Roman Empire, his excellency ... the strong and handsome ... the great and wise ... the victorious and insuperable ...

SUFFENUS, THALLUS, COMINIUS [*whispering*]: My lord ... majesty ... my god ...

CALIGULA: ... the one surpassing all human worth – his lordship Incitatus, the dapplegrey stallion!

LOLLIA: Little godling ...!

[*After stunned silence:*]

SUFFENUS, THALLUS, COMINIUS [*in piping voices*]: Long live his excellency, the consul Incitatus!

[*Another brief silence.*]

DRUNK SAILOR: L ... long live I ... Incitatus, his excellency, the c ... consul!

[*General outburst of cheers.*]

EGNATIUS [*indignant*]: My lord, kill me rather than bring this shame on Rome ...!

CALIGULA: To his lordship the consul's side, I appoint as his chief equerry, his groom and fodderer, to feed, scratch, scrub, walk and ride him – the youth Selanus, son of Marcus.

[*Cheering.*]

EGNATIUS: Rome, what will they do to you!

SELANUS [*to* CALIGULA]: My lord, so far so good.... But now his excellency, the lord consul Incitatus wishes to make a request too!

CALIGULA: Let him!

SELANUS: May he appoint as his chief purveyor of fodder, lord Egnatius, since he's never tasted oats so good as those which came from his granary.

CALIGULA: Is that his lordship the consul's request?

[LOLLIA *lets out a very brief jeer.*]

CALIGULA: Anything else?

SELANUS: Yes, there is. And let Egnatius, that honourable purveyor of fodder, live henceforth in the nightingale orchard, in the mansion, where until now Egnatius the ex-consul has lived. And next to it, let a splendid marble stable be built for his lordship the new consul ...

LOLLIA: [*brief jeer.*]

THE SENATORS: [*brief jeer*]

CALIGULA [*threateningly*]: Who dare jeer when the emperor and god is listening to propositions submitted by the Roman consul? – Lord Equerry! I promote your master his consular excellency's suggestions to the status of imperial-divine decrees! Whosoever breaks them, shall die!

EGNATIUS [*moved*]: My friend Marcus has a good and

brave son. . . . But all the same I won't survive this disgrace.

CALIGULA [*to* MACRO]: Trumpets!

[*Flourish.*]

CALIGULA: Let the ceremony of inauguration begin.

[*Music.*]

SELANUS [*calls out*]: Hey, groom! Lead in his excellency the consul . . .

[*From outside the clatter of hooves and Incitatus' whinny is heard.*

*Thundering cheers. Music.*

*Then suddenly complete silence. Something is taking place off stage, which they all watch with the greatest admiration. Those present exchange looks of approbation.* FUFICIUS *purses his lips to show his exceptional ecstasy.* SUFFENUS *and* THALLUS *take a broom each,* COMINIUS *grabs a dust pan, and all three, fully conscious of their importance, form a solemn procession towards the lora consul.*

*A shattering long whinny.*]

CURTAIN

# ACT TWO

*In front of the emperor's palace.*

[MACRO *enters.*]

MACRO: New bodyguard to his excellency, the consul
Incitatus – quick march!

[*Teuton music.*

*The Teuton bodyguards march in. They salute* MACRO *with
a swing of their arms. They speak only Teutonic.*]

MACRO: All right. Stop, halt there, you needn't come so
close. – Teutons! Bodyguards! Men of our divine and
imperial home guard! By order of our god and emperor,
as from today you will guard the exalted person of his
excellency, the consul Incitatus! Understood?

FIRST TEUTON [*steps forward*]: Henkertochtersschnabel-
wetzer!

TEUTONS [*swinging their arms*]: Eins! Zwei! Drei!

MACRO: All right, all right ...! According to our god and
emperor's latest ancient decree, his lordship the consul
Incitatus's person is divine, because a spark of the
imperial divinity in him has become flesh, and again on
the other hand, because in him has become flesh his
imperial divinity's spark. Is that clear?

SECOND TEUTON [*steps forward*]: Schneckenfresserraben-
futter!

TEUTONS [*swinging their arms*]: Eins! Zwei! Drei!

MACRO: That's enough ... enough ... Teuton bodyguard!
On your shoulders rests the fabric of the Empire. If
Teuton bodyguards like you did not exist, neither could
such a divine emperor, nor even a consul of divine nature
exist! Do you feel your sacred responsibility, Teutons?

THIRD TEUTON [*steps forward*]: Scheibeschiesserreden-scheisser!

TEUTONS [*swinging their arms*]: Eins! Zwei! Drei!

MACRO: Dismiss!

[*Teuton music. The Teuton guards march out.*]

MACRO [*alone*]: Einz, zvy, dry.... Well, that seems to be settled.... Right.... Einz. But we still have to do the zvy, the dry and more. Macro, Macro, never in your life have you had so much to do.... [*Takes out a list.*] His divine majesty's command: get the best sculptor brought from Greece to execute an artistic statue of his excellency the consul ... an equestrian statue ... and then get that duplicated in a thousand copies, and set it up at every cross-road.... The command of his divine majesty: let the chief priests work out special rites and liturgy for the glorification of the divine and imperial spark indwelling in his lordship Incitatus, the consul.... The orders of Selanus, chief consular equerry: from Asia have special bedding-straw brought for his lordship.... From Syria have special shoes brought for his lordship.... From Thrace have special curry-combs brought for his lordship.... The command of my dear love, Lollia: catch five sackfuls of nightingales in the consul's orchard and let them loose in the imperial gardens – they might like it and stay.... – Hey, Macro, Macro, you aren't the man for all this work.... Never before have you had so lofty a position, Macro! Never have you walked so close to snip-snip, Macro! ... The command of his divine majesty: special police inspectors should be on guard at every public and private place, lest anyone openly doubts or questions the spark of deity that dwells in his excellency the consul.... Special police inspectors on guard, to prevent mass betting on blue at the next chariot race, which might decrease the rate of imperial winnings.... And finally: special police squads to guard the roads, and prevent anyone from daring to bring an even finer horse to Rome, than the divine lord Incitatus. . . . Einz and zvy and . . .

[*The restless, insistent whickering of Incitatus is heard.*]

MACRO: Heavens! And the insatiable, standing order of his lordship Incitatus: Ihahahahaha. . . . Bring me mares! Mares, mares and more mares. . .! All the mares of Rome can't satisfy him. And, of course, it falls to me to pick out the more distinguished ones for him . . .

[*Incitatus' whickering is repeated.*]

MACRO: Coming, at once! Poor Macro. . . . Ihahahaha . . .

[*He turns to go, but the three senators appear from three different directions:* SUFFENUS, THALLUS *and* COMINIUS.]

SUFFENUS: Worthy Macro, let me have a word with you . . .

THALLUS: Commander . . . give me a private hearing . . .

COMINIUS: Oh, my most honoured friend, Macro, just for one second . . .

MACRO: My dear lord senators, I have no time for exchanging whispers . . .

SUFFENUS [*has already taken him by the hand and led him aside*]: My friend, I've got a mare, real Arab thoroughbred. . . . Ever since I had the singular honour of acquaintance with his consular lordship, the excellent stallion. . . . I wouldn't shrink even from a slight material sacrifice. . . . [*Gives* MACRO *some money.*]

THALLUS [*grabs* MACRO *for himself*]: Noble Macro! You know my team of three: all milk-white mares, I bought them at the auction of the queen of Cappadocia . . . [*gives him money.*] It means money for you, and pleasure for his lordship Incitatus. . . . We've fixed it then?

COMINIUS [*drags* MACRO *aside, presses money into his hand*]: Here, have it! I shall have my whole herd chased up from my estate. They're all thoroughbred mares. . . . Let's leave the rest to his lordship . . .

[*The three place their fingers on their lips and go out in three different directions.*]

MACRO: Einz, zvy, dry.... Ihahaha.... [*He hurries off.*]

[*Enter the youth of Rome gaily and noisily.* LENTULUS, FABULLUS, VERANIUS, CLODIA, JULIA *and* TULLIA *are among them. Their conduct has undergone change in every respect; they walk as children playing at horses, they whinny, toss their heads wildly and paw the ground with their feet. The girls are sporting their new pony-tails.*]

LENTULUS: Youth of Rome! At last you've someone to adore.

FABULLUS: Here's a hero for us, at long last!

THE YOUNG MEN: Incitatus!

THE GIRLS: Ihahaha!

CLODIA: Come and look, girls, at my new hairstyle: pony-tails!

JULIA, TULLIA: I've got it too, I've got one too ...!

TULLIA: Lord Incitatus will like this!

VERANIUS: Long live the idol of the youth of Rome!

THE GIRLS: Incitatus!

ALL: Ihahahaha!

FABULLUS: Ladies and gentlemen! What a sublime moment. Never in the history of Rome or her barbarians has there been such a hero for us to worship!

CLODIA: At last Roman virgins will have someone to dream about!

LENTULUS: The most Roman of Romans!

TULLIA: The most manly of Romans!

ALL: Ihahahaha!

VERANIUS [*tossing his head, paws the ground with his foot in front of* JULIA]: Julia, will you come with me ...?

JULIA: To dance?

VERANIUS: Dance? My dear Julia, who dances nowadays? Horse-play!

LENTULUS [*to* CLODIA]: Oh my dear Clodia, how I yearn to lay my neck across yours, scrunching hay in reveries of romance ...

VERANIUS: If only I could be as handsome as his excellency the consul ...

FABULLUS: I'd career around the course, faster than fleet-footed Mercury ...!

LENTULUS: If only I had firm sinewy legs like lord Incitatus ...!

TULLIA: But four of them! Four of them!

VERANIUS: Shod ...

CLODIA: With shoes ...

FABULLUS: With hooves of sparkling steel ...!

JULIA: With a silvered harness on my body ...!

LENTULUS: Oh, if only I could be dapplegrey!

FABULLUS: Be kind to me, Tullia. See how I whinny and paw with impatience.

TULLIA: You are prancing?

FABULLUS: I am prancing!

TULLIA: You are snorting fire through your nostrils?

FABULLUS: I am snorting fire through my nostrils!

TULLIA: I myself am rearing to go, as you see. [*They whinny.*]

[*Enter the* TAVERNER, *followed by whores, sailors, porters and day-labourers.*]

TAVERNER: Here's the latest Roman fashion, ladies and gentlemen! Miniature snaffle-bits, gold or silver, to suit every pocket. Incitatus snaffle-bits!

ALL [*stunned with admiration*]: Incitatus snaffle-bits ...!

TAVERNER: From now on everybody will be champing snaffle-bits in Rome! The impatient man champs his snaffle-bit! The disgruntled man grits his snaffle-bit! Ihaha! Ihaha! The contented man shall chew his snaffle-bit; he who dreams licks his snaffle-bit.... The bold man and determined bites his snaffle-bit!

YOUNG MEN, GIRLS: Here, give me one! Let's have one! Give me an Incitatus snaffle-bit . . .!

TAVERNER: Here, have it! Here's one more! Going cheap. . . . Incitatus snaffle-bits . . .

YOUNG MEN [*to their ladies*]: Here. . . . Allow me. . . . Accept this little snaffle-bit from me . . .

THE GIRLS: Oh, thank you. . . . How kind. . . . I'll start champing straightaway . . .

DRUNK SAILOR: Ro. . . . Rome . . . champ your b . . . bit. . . . Ihaha. . . . All Ro. . . . Rome is just one b . . . big whinny! . . . Ihahahaha!

ALL: Ihahahaha! [*They all go off, playing at horses and champing bits.*]

[*On the balcony of the emperor's palace,* CALIGULA *appears, in the company of* MACRO *and* LOLLIA.]

CALIGULA: I can't have this, I won't have this, this is just too much!

LOLLIA: What's wrong, little godling?

MACRO: What's your wish, majestic deity?

CALIGULA: I wish all Rome had one single neck, so I could roll it off at a snip. Snip-snip.

LOLLIA: Snip-snip! And why?

CALIGULA: It really is quite unbearable that all Rome should be grovelling at Incitatus's hooves. Everything is Incitatus, always Incitatus! Ihaha and Incitatus and on the other hand Incitatus and Ihaha! How often do I hear them crying these days, 'Long live Caligula'? All Rome is crying 'long live' to that beast. Oh, if only my wars and triumphal processions could do without the money from those chariot races . . .

MACRO: Just wait, my lord, till the first taxes are decreed under his name!

LOLLIA: Nonsense, godling! Get a wife for Incitatus, and the adulation will stop immediately.

CALIGULA: Get a wife for Incitatus?

LOLLIA: At the moment all Rome clamours: the consul! The consul! Just plant a wife at the consul's side, and he'll go out of fashion at once.

CALIGULA: Get a wife for Incitatus? Woman, there's something in what you say! I shall discuss this with my closest servant and adviser, with that wheedling, snivelling bootlicker whom in my greatness and wisdom I exceed immeasurably ...

MACRO: With me, most gracious god?

CALIGULA: With you? Haha! With Jupiter!

[*All exit.*]

### SCENE TWO

*In the house of the banker,* FUFICIUS.

[FUFICIUS *enters from one door,* AMEANA *from another.*]

FUFICIUS: It's you I am looking for, my daughter. What are you up to?

AMEANA: Nothing, father! Oh dear, my days are so empty nowadays. My girl friends won't come to play ball with me or strike the lyre.... I don't really understand why not.... They have new, wild games ...

FUFICIUS: My dear, you are too old for ball games. You should start thinking about getting married.

AMEANA: Really? – Oh, Papa, how you frighten me ...

FUFICIUS: From now, you must live like a marriageable girl.... That is exactly what I came to discuss with you. ... Why are you being so backward, my darling? Why don't you go along with the others ... to play at horses? Why don't you wear your hair in a pony-tail? Why don't you champ a snaffle-bit? You will never get a suitor this way, my daughter! You know I've had certain set-backs lately.... Your dowry has decreased too.... Ameana! My darling! Why haven't I ever heard you, never even once ... whinny?

AMEANA: I can't, father!

FUFICIUS: You should learn! Try practising! Whinny, Ameana!

AMEANA: No.

FUFICIUS [*threateningly*]: Ameana, whinny!

AMEANA [*tries*]: Ihaha ...

FUFICIUS: Again! More freely, with more self-confidence!

AMEANA: Ihahaha ...

FUFICIUS: Once more! Put more youth into it, try it more seductively with still more innocence! Well?

AMEANA: I can't ...

FUFICIUS: My darling, my sweetheart, my little angel ... Daddy's begging you for just one nice whinny for him!

AMEANA [*crying*]: I won't ...

FUFICIUS [*threateningly*]: Ameana ...!

AMEANA [*desperately*]: Ihahahahahaha ...

[VALERIA *entering hears the last whinny.*]

VALERIA: Splendid, excellent, first class, my darling! I'm glad your father has so much sense today for once! I'm glad you're being my sensible daughter.... It seems, you've heard the great news already.

FUFICIUS: What news? I haven't heard a thing.

VALERIA: That's more like your true self again. – Ameana, leave the room!

[AMEANA *turns to go.*]

VALERIA: Watch your step! Like a horse, please!

[AMEANA *leaves in a bitter gallop.*]

FUFICIUS: What's happened? Some trouble?

VALERIA: There's but one trouble I have, and that's your empty head. – Haven't you heard his divinity's latest order yet?

FUFICIUS: Not me. Oh dear ...

VALERIA: Nothing to moan about. His divinity's searching for a wife for the lord consul!

FUFICIUS: What's the use to me? My mares aren't up to that.

VALERIA: Mares? You don't really imagine that Rome's consul will be married to a horse?

FUFICIUS: What, then?

VALERIA: To a maiden! To Rome's loveliest, purest, best-brought up and most respectable virgin. That's what his divinity is seeking for his consul. He's seeking, but I've found her!

FUFICIUS: Oh dear.... Who is it, woman, whom have you found?

VALERIA: The one I've found is called ...

FUFICIUS: Oh no ...

VALERIA: ... Ameana!

FUFICIUS [*stuttering*]: No ... no ... it's impossible!

VALERIA [*grandly*]: I feel an unbounded talent to become a divine consul's mother-in-law!

FUFICIUS: But your daughter ... your daughter is human! You can't give her to ... to a beast!

VALERIA: Well, and when they gave me to you?

FUFICIUS: Minotaur! Is our dear consul a Minotaur that we should sacrifice maidens to him? ... Such a marriage ... entails all sorts of things.... My poor child's frail body...! But when.... [*He whispers into* VALERIA'*s ear.*]

VALERIA: Still better than ... [*whispers into* FUFICIUS' *ear*] ... So! That much I can tell you from experience.

[AMEANA *dashes in, excited.*]

AMEANA: Mama.... Papa! Visitors are coming! Neighbour Egnatius and ... and ... that young gentleman.... I think he's called Selanus.... I.... I can't think why they are coming ...!

VALERIA: The chief consular equerry's coming ...? And the chief purveyor of the fodder...? My darling daughter ...! What! Have you still that old hairdo ...?

Husband! Support me with your strong arm! I can't bear this dreadful suspense . . .

[*Enter* EGNATIUS *and* SELANUS.

FUFICIUS *and* VALERIA *greet them whinnying and pawing;* AMEANA *stands in the background with her eyes cast down.*]

EGNATIUS: Peace and good health to this house . . .

FUFICIUS and VALERIA: Ihaha . . .

EGNATIUS: Beg your pardon?

SELANUS: Much happiness to the master, mistress and daughter of this house.

FUFICIUS and VALERIA: Ihahaha . . .

EGNATIUS: What? – And the young gentleman here, whom you'd know by sight anyway, is Selanus, the son of my friend Marcus.

FUFICIUS: Pleased to meet you, ihaha.

VALERIA: Extremely pleased, ihaha. – Darling Ameana, step forward and greet the new friend of our house.

AMEANA [*steps forward, quietly*]: I greet the new friend of our house.

FUFICIUS: Not like that! Do it properly, the way I taught you.

[AMEANA *shakes her head.*]

SELANUS: I wish you much happiness in your life, lady Ameana.

AMEANA [*her eyes fixed on the ground*]: I wish you the same happiness, my lord Selanus.

FUFICIUS [*playing the master of the house*]: Woman! Food and drinks!

VALERIA: You'll excuse me, my lords. . . . Plod after me, my little Ameana.

[VALERIA *gallops out.* AMEANA *runs after her with ordinary steps.*

*Long silence.*]

FUFICIUS: Good yield of hay this year. . . . Oats too are extremely promising . . .

EGNATIUS: If the weather holds, even people might have enough to eat.

[VALERIA *and* AMEANA *return, laden with wine and cakes.*]

FUFICIUS: Our dear guests, have this meagre fodder to munch.

EGNATIUS: How d'you call it? Thank you, thank you.

VALERIA: My daughter baked it: my little filly ...

SELANUS: Never have I tasted anything quite so good ... lady Ameana ...!

AMEANA: May you eat much more like it yet ... my lord Selanus!

[*Brief silence.*]

EGNATIUS: Dear neighbours, perhaps you have already guessed why I have come to see you in the company of this excellent young man ...

FUFICIUS: We have our pleasant surmises ...

VALERIA: Our pleasant and uplifting surmises ...

EGNATIUS: You may well ask, just as I ask myself too: I, who am indebted only to a horse, as long as I am permitted to be indebted, for my life ...

FUFICIUS: Oh, we all feel that we are creatures of the divinely bestowed lord consul ...!

VALERIA: Iha ... iha ...

EGNATIUS: What was that? – Well, be that as it may, dear Marcus is a true and good friend of mine; for his son's sake I'd rise up from my grave ...

VALERIA: Marcus ...?

EGNATIUS: The father of my young friend, Selanus ...

FUFICIUS [*explaining to* VALERIA]: The lord equerry's father ...

VALERIA: Aha ... aha ... iha ...

EGNATIUS: Life will be life, young folk will marry ...

VALERIA: Quite! Quite!

EGNATIUS: And ageing people like you want grand-children.... Isn't that so?

FUFICIUS [*suddenly*]: That's it! Grandchildren ...! Woman, tell me, how are we going to get them – in the given circumstances ...?

VALERIA: Really, stop bickering! If someone's got power, he's got everything. Grandchildren too!

EGNATIUS: But why shouldn't there be grandchildren? Ameana, though she may be tenderly formed, appears to be strong as a horse.

VALERIA: Oh, she is up to anything! I can vouch for her!

EGNATIUS: And my friend Marcus has twelve strong and healthy sons. My young friend here is the seventh.

FUFICIUS: Marcus?

VALERIA [*explaining to* FUFICIUS]: The lord equerry's dear father.

FUFICIUS: Iha.

VALERIA: The only point I don't get, good neighbour, is why you are harping on that worthy gentleman Marcus all the time.

EGNATIUS: Well, after all it's him I'm representing.

VALERIA: In what?

EGNATIUS: In the suit.

VALERIA: And what has Marcus to do with that?

EGNATIUS: He's the father.

VALERIA: Whose?

EGNATIUS: The bridegroom's.

VALERIA: The lord consul's?

SELANUS: Whose?!

[*They stare at each other amazed.*]

SELANUS: Uncle, as I see it, we've come to the wrong place.

AMEANA: Oh dear me ...

EGNATIUS: Whom then did you think I was seeking your daughter for?

VALERIA: And whom did you think I was seeking for her?

Young man, aren't you ashamed of yourself, coming to a noble house in Rome to pay suit on a day when the divinely endowed consul himself is looking for a spouse from among Rome's maidens?

AMEANA: I will never survive this disgrace ...!

SELANUS: Oh, you honourable old matron, and you aged, good sir! Have your heads too been turned by this mad wind whirling through Rome? What the devil does his lordship the consul care about Rome's maidens! His lordship is a horse! My horse! He's for me to use, not me for him! I like the man who cares for his favourite pet, but if mine goes lame, I'll chop him up for sausages! Would you want to marry your daughter off to this beast?

FUFICIUS: Young man ... in my house ... really ...

VALERIA: Ameana! My snaffle! Give me my snaffle, I want to check myself ...!

EGNATIUS: Perhaps we should come back some other time?

SELANUS: Oh, is there a single spark of human sense left in Rome?

AMEANA: Let me die!

FUFICIUS: Woman, they are only putting us through a test! Young friend, you can report: Fuficius and his wife Valeria are crawling in the dust in front of our divine emperor's feet, as well as in front of our divinely bestowed lord consul's hooves.

VALERIA and FUFICIUS: Ihahahaha ...!

VALERIA: Whinny, Ameana!

AMEANA: Sooner be struck by lightning and die here on the spot ...!

SELANUS: Devil take it! Will you listen to me ...

MACRO [*his voice from outside*]: Selanus! Sela-a-anus!

SELANUS: Who's that? What's up?

[MACRO *almost falls through the door.*]

MACRO: Selanus! Lord Chief Equerry! I've been looking

for you everywhere. . .! The emperor wants you. . . . The god. . . . As chief expert. . . . A bride must be chosen for the lord consul . . .

SELANUS: To hell with the lot of you . . .!

MACRO: The chief purveyor of the fodder is to come too . . .

EGNATIUS: My son, we must obey.

MACRO: And you, Fuficius, prepare and get your daughter ready . . . make her beautiful and desirable. . . . Ah, there's vast competition. . . . Hurry to the imperial palace!

EGNATIUS: The gods watch over you, neighbours.

SELANUS: Lady Ameana . . .

[MACRO, EGNATIUS *and* SELANUS *exit.*]

VALERIA [*to* FUFICIUS]: Run and catch up with them. Promise money to Macro if the choice falls on our daughter.

FUFICIUS: I am off! And in the meantime trim and dress our little filly . . .

[FUFICIUS *rushes after* MACRO.]

VALERIA: Come, my daughter, let me harness you.

AMEANA: Strangle me first, mother!

[VALERIA *leads* AMEANA *off.*]


SCENE THREE

*The emperor's palace.*

[SUFFENUS, THALLUS *and* COMINIUS *wait about for decisions being taken behind closed doors. Each has his daughter at his side:* CLODIA, JULIA *and* TULLIA.]

CLODIA [*to* SUFFENUS]: Daddy, the lord consul will choose me, won't he?

SUFFENUS: Well, he won't choose any upstart impostor's brat, I can tell you!

JULIA [*to* THALLUS]: Father, I'll simply die if he doesn't choose me!

THALLUS: And I'd break every bone in your body if the daughter of some sworn intriguer got there before you!

TULLIA [*to* COMINIUS]: Father, touch wood quickly, father cast spells on me.... Father, I've crossed my fingers and put my underwear on inside out ...

COMINIUS: Don't worry, my daughter. Surely you can't be outstripped by the daughter of an infamous trouble-maker!

JULIA: It's quite amazing! Some of the thick-legged types who have dared to turn up here!

CLODIA: And the things that some of them have the cheek to call pony-tails! Haha!

TULLIA [*snorting, stamping*]: They reek of cheap stables! Pooh!

[MACRO *enters with a list; he ticks each name he calls out. He has evidently made secret promises to each one of the fathers in return for presents from each.*]

MACRO: Clodia, daughter of Suffenus!

CLODIA: Iha ...

MACRO: Julia, daughter of Thallus!

JULIA: Ihaha ...

MACRO: Tullia, daughter of Cominius!

TULLIA: Ih ... [*the whinny begins to choke her, she leaves with the rest, coughing.*]

[*The girls disappear into the inner rooms, the fathers remain with* MACRO.

PYRALLIS *comes with* ERIA.]

PYRALLIS: My lord captain! My lord captain!

MACRO: And what are they after here?

ERIA: My respects to you, uncle senators!

THE SENATORS: It's the limit ...! What impudence! Throw them out!

MACRO: The girl is not on my list!

THALLUS: Don't you know the selection is only from virgins with a clean record?

PYRALLIS: My daughter is as much of a virgin as some young Roman ladies! What's more, she's young blood, not quite broken in yet! I've got her on a running rein. [*Takes out a little whip.*] A trot, my daughter, a short gallop, parade-step! Allee-hup! Or watch this, my lords, – this fiery full gallop! Charge – chaaarge! Well, dear lords?! Well?!

[ERIA *has been running on the spot, or round in small circles, following her mother's orders. The senators gaze at her with growing enthusiasm, drawing closer.*]

THE SENATORS: Clever little filly.... Lovely little filly.... Docile filly ...

MACRO: But now clear out of here!

THE SENATORS: Out of here! Out.... The emperor.... My daughter ...

ERIA: Why is it, mother, that nowadays when these lords honour me in my little room, they all insist on behaving like little horses?

THE SENATORS and MACRO: Hush! Hush!

ERIA: Yes, yes, all of them, both the dear uncle senators, and dear Uncle Macro too...! It's really all so tiresome ...!

MACRO: Beat it! If the emperor sees you here ...!

PYRALLIS: Oh the emperor, such a dear! I used to know him very well as a boy!

MACRO and THE SENATORS: Off! Off with you!

PYRALLIS: Let's go, my daughter! [*Cracking her whip.* Come on, rear! Leave the arena on two feet – just like a human being! [ERIA *and* PYRALLIS *exit.*]

[*The door opens and the three girls come out sobbing. They march off quickly, with their fathers following and casting reproachful, threatening glances in* MACRO's *direction.*]

SUFFENUS [*slinks back*]: Noble Macro! Perhaps a bridegroom could be found for my daughter among his lordship's relatives? Must be with two pairs of legs, of course!

It's easy enough to find suitors with one! After all, I've got my position to worry about ... [*Exits.*]

    [FUFICIUS, VALERIA *and* AMEANA *come.*]

FUFICIUS: Hurry up! Hurry up! The time it takes for two women to get away from the house ...!

MACRO: Well, high time!

AMEANA [*hopefully*]: Mother, all my girl friends have gone off in tears! Perhaps we girls aren't really what the lord consul wants?

VALERIA: I forbid you to think like that. Greet the lord captain, as I've told you to.

    [AMEANA *paws the ground and tosses her head, but cannot bring herself to whinny.*]

VALERIA: W-ell! It'll just do.

    [*The doors spring open: in dashes* CALIGULA, *followed by* LOLLIA, SELANUS *and* EGNATIUS.]

CALIGULA: I'll have all women in Rome killed! Let not a single Roman female survive this day! It's getting dark, and there still hasn't been an acceptable bride! My consul's person is divine! I can't have him married just to anyone! Bring for him a princess from Cappadocia! From Paphlagonia! From Judaea!

LOLLIA: Pooh, dear god, the lord consul is a thoroughbred stud-horse: you can only give him a pedigreed Roman woman to marry!

CALIGULA: Quite! I'll have the Cappadocian, Paphlagonian and Judaean princesses beheaded! But show me then a Roman girl who ...

FUFICIUS [*steps forward hastily*]: Most divine deity, and on the other hand, most divine deity!

CALIGULA: Sensible start. Who are you?

FUFICIUS: I am Fuficius, your banker, who grovels in the filthiest dust in front of you.

CALIGULA: Aha!

FUFICIUS: And this hero ,,

VALERIA: ... is his wife, Valeria, and here is ...

FUFICIUS and VALERIA [*together*]: ... our daughter, Ameana, who ...

CALIGULA [*forgets to take his eyes off* AMEANA; *with surprised admiration*]: Aha! A-ha! [*Sternly*] Set her before me! [FUFICIUS *leads* AMEANA *before the* EMPEROR.]

CALIGULA: Her teeth ...! [FUFICIUS *employs* VALERIA's *help to show* AMEANA's *teeth the way horses' teeth are shown at a market.*]

CALIGULA: Well, at last! What do the experts say ...?

SELANUS [*quickly*]: I move that we bring a princess from Mesopotamia!

EGNATIUS: Seconded ...

MACRO: A flawless, Roman thoroughbred.... I propose her! [*Stealthily indicates to* LOLLIA *that he got most money from this source.*] And what does my sweetheart Lollia say?

LOLLIA [*yawns*]: My dear little godling, the others would have done fine by me ...

SELANUS: My lord, a princess from India ...!

CALIGULA: Banker! You may collect the dowry, and pay it into the imperial privy purse! Your daughter shall be the lord consul's wife!

AMEANA [*suddenly*]: No.

VALERIA: Shut up!

AMEANA: No! No, no and no! I won't be married to a beast!

VALERIA: My lord, don't pay any attention to her!

FUFICIUS: My darling, his lordship's person is divine.

AMEANA: Divine or brute, it's all the same! I only know it's not human! Forgive my sin: I love a man! A man! [*Falls on her knees.*] Have pity, emperor! It's a man I love!

CALIGULA: Fiery little lassie! Look what a lovely curve her neck makes! Snip-snip!

SELANUS: My lord, my lord! Bring a princess for his lordship! A princess from China! A queen from Fairy-land . . . !

LOLLIA [*in a whisper to* SELANUS]: You've got your eyes on her, handsome country lad! Just a moment! [*Aloud*] This girl will either be the horse's wife, or else snip-snip!

AMEANA [*passionately*]: Then let there be snip-snip!

EGNATIUS: Let us not be over-hasty . . .

SELANUS [*suddenly strikes his forehead, cries out*]: Quite! But we haven't even consulted the bridegroom! Your divine majesty! I beg leave to introduce the engaged young pair to each other tonight, in the nightingale orchard. After all, you may take a horse to the water, but you can't make it drink.

CALIGULA: Wise words! You may take a horse to the water, but you can't make it drink. Lord Chief Equerry! It's my divine command that you introduce the young pair to each other in the nightingale orchard, tonight!

SELANUS [*helps* AMEANA *on her feet*]: Young lady, in the nightingale orchard, tonight . . .

[*All exit.*]


SCENE FOUR

*In the nightingale orchard. Night. Nightingales warbling.*

SELANUS [*enters alone*]: What a strange city Rome is! People in the country wouldn't believe me. I've learnt all I could about it, but I still don't understand it. Here no one dares to appear satisfied, since that might make him suspect. And no one dares to look disgruntled, because that might make him equally suspect. People are scared not to be afraid: nothing's more suspect than self-assurance! If a man is popular: could he be recruiting accomplices against the emperor? Suspicious! If he with-draws and shuns popularity: what's he concocting in his

solitude? Suspicious! A man is good-humoured: he's got
a secret tucked away! Down in the mouth? He's depressed
by the course of public affairs! Suspicious! Suspicious!
A man is rich: perhaps he's filching money from under the
emperor's nose? He is poor? No one is more dangerous
than a man with nothing to lose! It's impossible for a man
to have a single quality which won't make him suspect in
the emperor's eyes. It is a crime to occupy high office, it is
a crime to ask to be discharged from high office. But the
greatest crime of all crimes is to be without crime! Are
you virtuous, with high principles? You may be Brutus,
whetting your dagger for Caesar! Suspicious, suspicious,
suspicious! .... Shh! The other day in Rome someone
died a natural death. The people all flocked to gape at
him. Died in bed? Suspicious! Phew, suspicious! And
how suspicious! Suspicious, suspicious, suspicious!

[AMEANA *comes*.]

AMEANA: Is there someone here?

SELANUS: Beautiful young lady ...!

AMEANA: Oh dear, did someone call me? Who is it?

SELANUS: It's me ...

AMEANA: It's you, I know! I know very well, it's you ...!
But who that you is, I don't know ...

SELANUS [*rushes to her*]: It's me, the one who ... [*checks
himself*] ... who came to introduce your bridegroom to
you: the horse.

AMEANA [*screaming*]: You too are a monster among
monsters ...!

SELANUS [*falls on his knees in front of her*]: Ameana! Ameana!
Ameana!

AMEANA [*holds out her hand, but dares not touch him*]: Selanus!
Selanus! Selanus!

SELANUS: Ameana, marry the horse, will you, please?

AMEANA: No ... no ...

SELANUS: I, I beg you ...!

AMEANA: How can you beg me such a thing? I'd die on the spot if he came near me.

SELANUS: He won't come near.

AMEANA: And am I then to wither away untouched ...?

SELANUS: Lovely Ameana.... I know what I am talking about! In the great moment of love, we male creatures often become quite transformed. One you believed to be a man, turns into a beast. One you saw as a beast ...

AMEANA: Turns into a man ...?

SELANUS: The emperor has decreed that the lord consul's person is divine. Divine beings can take on any form they like. Jupiter ravished Europa in the shape of a bull ...

AMEANA: I don't want a bull either ...

SELANUS: He seduced Danae in a shower of gold ...

AMEANA: I don't want gold.

SELANUS: He conquered Leda in the shape of a swan ...

AMEANA: Swans disgust me.

SELANUS: But what if the lord consul visited your marriage-bed every night in the form of a youth ...?

AMEANA: And what sort of a youth?

SELANUS: Well ... some sort like me.... Ameana ...

AMEANA: I don't think I'd mind that.... Selanus ...

SELANUS [springs up]: My bride, where are your eyes? Do you really take me for Selanus? No, my love, I am Incitatus, ihaha, ihaha, I've only assumed the shape of Selanus.... In this shape I swear eternal love to you ... iha, iha ... till death do us part.... You don't mind, do you, that I'm a horse?

AMEANA: I don't mind anything.... [She falls into his arms; after a long kiss, shouts at the top of her voice] Emperor! God! World! This is the horse I want! This is the horse I want!

CURTAIN

# ACT THREE

## SCENE ONE

*In the consul's palace.*

CLODIA, TULLIA *and* JULIA *have come to visit* AMEANA, *bringing presents. Now, too,* AMEANA *is wearing a pony-tail. Both the girls and the young men who come later, paw with their feet, whinny curtly and play at horses with mechanical ease and in a conventional, almost completely symbolic, fashion.*

TULLIA: Ameana, my dear ...!

AMEANA: Girls, my dear friends ...!

CLODIA: Are you happy?

AMEANA: I am happy!

JULIA: Perfectly?

AMEANA: Perfectly!

CLODIA: You love your husband?

AMEANA: Beyond bounds!

TULLIA: Your husband loves you?

AMEANA: Beyond words!

TULLIA: Ameana! We too are going to get married soon. ... Reveal to us, what it felt like ...

CLODIA: Of course, we know there's that difference, but all the same ...

JULIA: Tell us ...

AMEANA [*almost panicking*]: No ...!

CLODIA: We never had any secrets before ...

TULLIA: We've promised to tell each other from start to finish about our wedding nights.

CLODIA: You haven't forgotten?

AMEANA: Don't ask me!

JULIA: I'm dying to hear ...

TULLIA: Whisper it in our ears!

AMEANA [*seriously*]: No, girls, anything else but not that! I am very fond of you, you are my friends, but never a word on that subject.... I took an oath! I had to. It's a secret and secret it will remain for ever!

[*Enter* LENTULUS, FABULLUS, VERANIUS.]

THE YOUNG MEN: Ihaha, lady consul! Our fiancées, iha, iha!

VERANIUS: His excellency the consul received our morning salutation most graciously.

LENTULUS: Oh, what a great feeling: the divine lord consul was gracious to us!

FABULLUS: He made distinct, one might almost say friendly, noises.

VERANIUS: This'll be something to boast about to my grandchildren! Iha.

[*They put down their presents.*]

LENTULUS: Our deepest respects to the consul's consort!

VERANIUS: We wish her health and much joy ...

FABULLUS: And an abundant blessing of children!

TULLIA [*cries out softly*]: Oh, I'd never thought of that ...

CLODIA: Quite! If a child comes.... What sort will it be? What ... what will it be?

LENTULUS [*wisely*]: What should it be? A centaur!

VERANIUS: A divinely bestowed, dear little centaur.

LENTULUS: A little horse behind, a manikin in front!

JULIA [*ardently*]: Mother of centaurs, oh!

TULLIA: I envy you, Ameana! Only you will bear centaurs ...!

FABULLUS: Yes, lots of little creatures, lined up like organ pipes!

CLODIA: Bless their darling little hearts! You will let us play with them, won't you ...?

TULLIA: When it begins kicking in there with its tiny hooves ...

LENTULUS: I wish with all my heart that the first one – may be a little boy.... I mean ... what is it ... a little stallion ... well, I mean ... in a word ... that he will proudly uphold his distinguished pedigree ...

FABULLUS: His noble pedigree, distinguished on both sides ...

VERANIUS: Three whinnies to the lord consul and his family!

ALL: I-ha! I-ha! I-ha!

AMEANA [*greatly embarrassed*]: Yes ... quite ... thank you, and come again.... And remember me.... Girls ... friends.... [*Paws once.*] Oh dear me.... [*Quickly goes out.*]

FABULLUS [*in a whisper*]: Do you know what I've heard? The consul's marriage is not altogether a bed of roses!

CLODIA: No, really! You frighten me!

VERANIUS: They say the lord consul is keeping up his former love affairs.

TULLIA: He keeps mistresses?

VERANIUS: A number of them every day. And what's worse: they're horses!

JULIA: Fie, consul!

CLODIA [*to* LENTULUS]: Nothing like this must happen with us!

LENTULUS: I swear to you!

JULIA: Poor Ameana!

TULLIA: This is the price she pays for being the consul's wife!

JULIA: No, I must say I feel sorry for her! [*All exit.*]
   [*Enter* SELANUS *from one side,* LOLLIA *from the other.*]

LOLLIA: Well, handsome country lad?

SELANUS: More orders from your ladyship? Another sackful of nightingales? Another ten sackfuls?

LOLLIA: No use. The imperial garden stays hushed. Nightingales can't bear the stink of incense. They either keep silent, drop dead, or escape.

SELANUS: Or one finds out that they weren't nightingales after all. So, what's your ladyship's command?

LOLLIA: I command you to come to your senss ... handsome country lad!

SELANUS: I haven't left my senses yet, beautiful Roman lady!

LOLLIA: Still buzzing around the horse's wife?

SELANUS: I serve the horse.

LOLLIA: The first woman of Rome could be yours.

SELANUS: The first woman of Rome belongs to the god.

LOLLIA: And is sharing with a god not to your taste? You'd rather share with a beast? Queer taste, I must say! That kind of thing is much more up my little godling's street; just you leave it to him too!

SELANUS: What's that?

LOLLIA: Hahaha! Have I brought you news? You can't imagine, ever since he made the banker's daughter the dapplegrey's wife, our emperor's been simply wild about that Roman cow whom the divinely bestowed horse has honoured. I tell you, if I didn't keep him back ...

SELANUS: But you must keep him back ...! I beg you ...! For the love of all the gods, I beg you ...!

LOLLIA: Beg me for your own love!

SELANUS: I call down all the blessings of Olympus, or else all the curses of Orcus!

LOLLIA: Olympus or Orcus, whatever the emperor takes a fancy to, he'll take away.

SELANUS: Stop the emperor, or dreadful things will follow!

LOLLIA: Really, do you care all that much whether the horse's lady cheated on his lordship or not?

SELANUS: There's nothing in the world I care for more!

LOLLIA: Really! And why?

SELANUS [*sobering*]: Why? ... Because my Incitatus would in his grief lose the next chariot-race. ... That's why.

LOLLIA: Haha! Such wild passion joins them?

SELANUS: The sight no night has never seen greater!

LOLLIA: Well then, country boy, bid all your fancies farewell! Ameana will become imperial mistress, and then
snip-snip!

SELANUS: Woman! Don't you dare ...!

LOLLIA: Tut, tut! No tantrums! So far the emperor's been
racking his brain, in what shape he should suddenly
appear before the horse's wife, to kindle her to irresistible
passion. Should he come with the two heads of Castor and
Pollux, should he glitter in the seven colours of the rain-
bow, or fall into her lap, as a ripe pear? ... Yes, nowadays the emperor likes to make quite a song and dance
over such things. But I know what I'll suggest to him,
handsome country lad! Tonight the god will pay his
respects to the horse's wife!

SELANUS: At night?

LOLLIA: Tonight.

SELANUS: At night will I stand in his way!

   [LOLLIA *exits*.]

SELANUS: At night will I stand in his way. ... At night love
sweeps away everything.... At night our marriage is
joyful and unassailable. ... But by day ...? Who am I by
day...? Whom does she love from dawn till dusk...?
Would she love me, if she knew in the light of day I was
the same she loved by moonlight? And what will happen ... if the emperor really were to come tonight...!?
The god...?! He who's a million times stronger than
me...?! Oh Rome, Rome! You can make it tough for a
country boy ...!

   [*The* TAVERNER *enters*.]

TAVERNER: My lord, lord Selanus ...

SELANUS [*startled*]: Who is it? What d'you want?

TAVERNER: It's only me, my lord, from whose modest
tavern your shining career was launched. I am your
admirer, but what's my admiration compared to the
ardent admiration of my aged she-ass for your stallion...!

Ever since she heard his first whinny...! Perhaps you
may remember ...

SELANUS [*absent-mindedly*]: Perhaps ... perhaps ...

TAVERNER: Well, that's why I thought, perhaps if I asked
you nicely.... A mighty lord, most mighty is his excellency, lord Incitatus the consul, but we taverners know
what sort of gentlemen these stallions are ... married or
single – they look at quantity, not quality.... And an
experienced, good old she-ass, believe me sir, slipped in
with the rest, might even do some good ...

SELANUS [*his mind is elsewhere*]: What's that ... yes ... is
that all? ... Good, good, I see.... I'll drop him a
message ...

TAVERNER: But now seems to be the time for it, my
lord.... Perhaps you could talk with the lord consul ...

SELANUS: I'll mention it, I'll certainly mention it ... of
course ...

TAVERNER: Let me give you some frank advice, my lord,
to show my gratitude, but strictly between us.... Keep a
close eye on the lord consul! ... There's a lot of them in
the Senate grudge him his office.... And he's got Teuton
bodyguards. And, my lord, a Teuton is the kind of
watch-dog who is likely to bite his master, particularly if a
bone's the reward. They'll want to exploit the first major
riot that occurs in the city.... Beware, my lord, look out
for your horse's life.... Milonia. Milonia is the name of
my good old donkey. Light up, my lord, light up the dusk
of her diligent years.... My lord! Milonia yearningly
awaits lord Incitatus' message of love ...

[TAVERNER *exits*.]

SELANUS [*aloud*]: Milonia yearningly awaits ... what was I
told about some Milonia just now ...? Where was I just
going? Yes ... the oat granary ... [*Exits*.]

[AMEANA *enters from another direction*.]

AMEANA [*alone*]. Could it be true? Could the gods do that

77

to me? . . . But at night I am embraced by human arms.
. . . Human lips kiss my lips. . . . Human words tease me.
. . . But the daytime! . . . These comfortless, ceaseless
days, the four-footed bleakness of the day. . . . Centaurs . . .? No, that can't be. . . . For what sin should I
give birth to monsters? . . . Who can tell me what the
truth of this is? My mother? Oh, no . . .! My father? Poor
man. . .! There's only one man in whom I have bound-
less confidence, in whom both body and soul I believe . . .
and he – he isn't human. . . . But really, on whom am I to
call, if I'm worried, or in trouble? My love, my husband,
my life, help me! [*Calls*] Incitatus. . .! Incitatus . . .!
[SELANUS *rushes in.*]

SELANUS [*with open arms*]: Ameana . . .!

AMEANA [*sees him, wants to fly towards him*]: Incita. . . . [*She
freezes.*] Young lord Selanus . . .

SELANUS [*calms down*]: What's your ladyship's wish . . .?

AMEANA: How's my gracious husband?

SELANUS: Would it please your ladyship to attend the fod-
dering? The hay's ready; his excellency's already water-
ing at the mouth.

AMEANA: No, I beg my gracious husband kindly to excuse
me . . .

SELANUS: Perhaps attend the scrubbing? The harnessing?
Maybe your excellencies might one day – like to have a
ride out together?

AMEANA: Selanus, sir . . . just between us two. . . . Oh, my
dear, Selanus, you don't know . . . you can't even
imagine . . . what inexpressible gratitude we owe you . . .
my husband and I . . . dear, dear Selanus. . . . But what
am I babbling about? This doesn't even concern you . . .

SELANUS: No that doesn't concern me . . .

AMEANA: Perhaps it'd be better. . . . Master Selanus . . . for
reasons which don't concern you either . . . perhaps it'd
be better, if my husband didn't send during the day. . . .

I mean with you ... love messages. ... No, that's not true! Bring me his passionate confessions, more often still! Bring a hundred from dawn till dusk! A thousand! What does he say now, what did he say to me an hour ago, what will he say in a quarter of an hour? Say! Say! Say!

SELANUS [*very near to her*]: He told me to say that he is aflame with love of you, body and soul; from dawn till dusk he's here around you ... and he lives not a minute from you ...

AMEANA: That he's happy?

SELANUS: That he's happy ...

AMEANA: That he's faithful to me ...?

SELANUS: For ever faithful ...!

AMEANA: That our joy will never end?

SELANUS [*loses control*]: No, no, it will never end, and come a thousand tyrants, our happiness, our love must conquer ... will conquer. ... That's what he said!

AMEANA [*loses control*]: And I send back word, that for him my body will bear even centaurs...! What do I care! I await his embrace ...

SELANUS: He sends you word that he'd sooner murder, sooner die for you, he'd sooner take you on his back and gallop away with you to the ends of the earth, but he won't let you down. ... His message is ... [*passionately*] ihaha ...

AMEANA: And mine is ... [*almost breathing it*] ihaha ...
[*Both exit quickly in different directions.*]


SCENE TWO

*The nightingale orchard. Moonlit night. Nightingales warbling.*
[SELANUS *comes with* EGNATIUS.]

EGNATIUS: My son, this is an amazing secret you've just told me. So that's the way you live your life? You see what has become of our Rome...! The more beautiful and human a thing, the more truthful and innocent it is, the more it must be camouflaged as something base before the tyrant will tolerate it.

SELANUS: Advice, uncle, give me advice!

EGNATIUS: Your fate is – Rome's fate, your happiness is – Rome's happiness, you will only laugh – when Rome will laugh ...

SELANUS: Shhh! Who comes there?

[CALIGULA *enters with* LOLLIA *and* MACRO. CALIGULA *is already partly dressed up as a dapplegrey horse; the remaining parts of his costume are carried by* MACRO *and* LOLLIA. MACRO *has a lyre,* LOLLIA *a flute. They keep their voices low.* EGNATIUS *and* SELANUS *draw into cover to observe.*]

MACRO: Here we are. Those are the windows there: Ameana's bedroom ...

LOLLIA: Her lamp is burning; she's waiting for her husband: the horse.

CALIGULA: That's me! Get me dressed! My divine command is that you make a complete horse of me!

LOLLIA: Keep your sacred head still, godling.

[*They dress him up.*]

CALIGULA: Careful, my head will be hardest to fit in. It's too big: It's all that expanse of intellect ...

LOLLIA: We know, we know. Stop blabbering and fidgeting so! Any decent stallion would be more dignified.

SELANUS [*half aloud to* EGNATIUS]: Uncle, whatever are these up to?

EGNATIUS [*quietly*]: Watch!

CALIGULA: Jupiter, that bungler, assumed the image of Amphitryon to steal into Mrs Amphitryon's bed. Behold, the four-footed Amphitryon!

MACRO: You are two up on Jupiter once again, gracious god!

LOLLIA: Keep your mouths shut, will you?

CALIGULA: Ulysses built a huge wooden horse to smuggle himself into Troy. Behold the one-man Trojan horse!

LOLLIA: Ready!

MACRO: Split image of Incitatus!

CALIGULA: Ho! Ho! Stop! We've left my arms out!

MACRO: Credit them to your divine person's account, my lord!

LOLLIA: Hide them! Hide them! Like that!

CALIGULA: Comb my mane a bit.... That's it, and now my tail too. I can't turn up before my love scruffy.

LOLLIA: All right, now walk up and down a bit.... That's it, bear the head more proudly! Let's have more assurance in the swing of the rump! Swell that chest! Place your hooves more delicately!

MACRO: Divine! Perfect beast! Whoopee!

CALIGULA: Ihahaha!

LOLLIA: More base! More virile!

CALIGULA: Am I irresistible?

LOLLIA: Absolutely, absolutely!

MACRO [*whispering to* LOLLIA]: What's all this for, woman? Can anyone fail to recognize him?

LOLLIA [*the same*]: Can anyone dare to recognize him?

MACRO: What's the point then?

LOLLIA: So that all Rome will laugh at that yokel Selanus and the horse's wife!

CALIGULA [*suddenly bursting into a stormy whinny*]: Ihahaha-hahahaha, Iha-iha...!

LOLLIA: Splendid, little godling! Absolutely splendid! A super-Incitatus!

SELANUS: Uncle, I am beginning to understand them!

EGNATIUS: I fear I do too.

[LOLLIA *and* MACRO *get out their musical instruments, and stand round for a serenade. They sing, accompanying themselves on the lyre;* CALIGULA *whinnies now and then.*]

81

CALIGULA, LOLLIA, MACRO: Be for ever constant to your
husband's trust,
plim-plim-plim-plim tululu,
oh, Ameana, oh, Ameana!
Be ever constant to your husband's trust!
Iha! Iha! Iha!
Open the door, blow out the light,
your faithful horse is here at last,
plim-plim-plim-plim tululu,
oh, Ameana, oh, Ameana!
Ihaha! Ihaha! Ihaha!
Tululu, tululu, plim-plim, Ameana!
Ihaha! Ihaha! Ihaha!
Iha-ihahahahaha!
Plim-plim!

SELANUS: Uncle! Now do what I tell you!

EGNATIUS: What are you planning to do?

SELANUS: Leave it to me! Send your fastest slave with a
message . . .

EGNATIUS: Where to?

SELANUS: [*whispers*]

EGNATIUS: What is he to say?

SELANUS: [*whispers*]

EGNATIUS: I don't understand, but I'll do it.

SELANUS: Hurry!

    [EGNATIUS *steals away.*]

CALIGULA, LOLLIA, MACRO:
Four hooves of mine
tread your silken bed,
plim-plim-plim-plim, tululu,
Ameana! Iha! Iha! Iha!
My dapplegrey haunch quakes the marriage couch!
Oh, Ameana, oh, Ameana!
Tululu, tululu, plim-plim, Ameana!
Beauteous Ameana! Ihaha, Ameana!

Constant to a constant horse, iha, Ameana!
Never has such a love, such burning love,
such ihaha love been seen
since the world was! [CALIGULA *dances*.]
Plim-plim-plim, tululu,
tululu, ihaha, tululu,
ihaha, tululu, Ameana,
ihaha, Ameana, ihaha, Ameana,
Ihahahahahaha ...
Ihahahahahaha ...
Ihaha, ihaha, ihaha...! [LOLLIA *and* MACRO *gradually withdraw*].

SELANUS [*steps forward*]: Who's this I hear whinnying? Your excellency, the lord consul?

CALIGULA: Ihaha!

SELANUS: I am your excellency's most obedient servant. Accept my respects.

CALIGULA [*condescendingly*]: Iha.

SELANUS: Has it pleased your excellent lordship to escape from the stable? Oh dear, oh dear! Perhaps it will please your lordship kindly to retrace your steps?

CALIGULA [*shaking his head*]. Ihaha

SELANUS: Whoever heard of such a thing: a four-footed consular excellency straying like that! How lucky I'd recognize my Incitatus among ten thousand horses! His whinny ...

CALIGULA: Ihaha ...

SELANUS: The clatter of his hooves ..
    [CALIGULA *clatters them*.]

SELANUS: The sway of his rump ...
    [CALIGULA *sways it*.]

SELANUS: The flick of his tail ...

CALIGULA [*flicking it*]: Ihahaha ...

SELANUS: This is my true Incitatus! Here, eat this, your excellency, gingercake ...

[CALIGULA *backing*.]

SELANUS: What's up? Do you refuse to eat from my hand, you beast? I haven't known you to do that since you were a colt! Not like you at all!

CALIGULA [*approaches hurriedly, eats from* SELANUS' *hand, thanks him with a neigh*]: Ihihihihi ...

SELANUS: That's better! You're yourself, old friend! [*Pats him.*] Pity, his divinity, our lord the emperor has commanded me to make sausages out of you ...

[CALIGULA *rears up in fright.*]

SELANUS: Now-now! Come! We can't do such a thing to a newly-wed.

CALIGULA [*pacified*]: Iha ...

SELANUS: But why is his consular excellency straying loose in the moonlight, to the warbling of nightingales, when he ought to be conducted to his loving wife?

CALIGULA: Iha, iha ... [*Prances.*]

SELANUS: Now I get it! A little infidelity, a little jaunt, eh what?

CALIGULA [*shakes his head*]: Ih, ih, ihaha!

SELANUS: All right, I am a good friend, you can trust me. – Do you hear that?

[*Approaching noise.*]

CALIGULA: Iha?

SELANUS: They're bringing your secret lover now! [*Calls*] Milonia! Milonia!

[*Long emotional braying.*]

CALIGULA [*pricks up his ears in terror*]: Iha-iha?

SELANUS [*patting and scratching him*]: Milonia! The taverner's good old she-ass: Milonia!

[TAVERNER *enters with halter in hand, followed by the* DRUNK SAILOR *and many others from the tavern, armed with whips, clubs, and cudgels.*]

TAVERNER: Here we are, my lord! Many thanks for remembering so soon my aged and lovesick donkey!

SELANUS: Have you brought enough people to help? Because sometimes his excellency can be very wilful! Have you got a halter? Sticks, clubs, whips – have you? At times you have to bring his excellency round to do it.

DRUNK SAILOR: Let's s … start, your excellency!

CALIGULA [*tries to escape in panic*]: Ih-ih-ihaha!

SELANUS: Stop being so fussy! You know very well how a mule is made! Throw a halter round his neck!

[*The* TAVERNER *throws the halter round* CALIGULA*'s neck. Inviting braying from within.*]

TAVERNER: D'you hear, your excellency, this is for you!

DRUNK SAILOR: O … off we go!

[*Braying within.*]

CALIGULA: Ihaha! [*Fearing the halter, tries to free himself, rears, prances. kicks.*]

SELANUS: Obstinate brute! Whip him!

[*They beat him.*]

CROWD [*yelling*]: Don't spare him! Clout his head!

CALIGULA: Ouch! Ouch! Ihaha! Ihaha!

TAVERNER: What? Isn't my Milonia good enough for you? [*Kicks him.*] Tyranny, violence, taxes, pinching money from people's pockets, all that – yes! [*Kicks him.*] But making a poor man a mule – no?

DRUNK SAILOR [*with blows and kicks*]: M … making wars, shedding blood, will you? M … making love to Mi … Milonia, won't you?

[AMEANA*'s window opens.*]

AMEANA: What's this noise? … What's happening…? Oh, I am frightened! What's keeping you, Incitatus…!

SELANUS: Keep calm, Ameana, my love!

CALIGULA: Ameana, my love! Ameana! Iha!

TAVERNER [*thrashing him*]: Milonia, my love, Milonia! I-ha!

CROWD: Come on! Beat him! Don't spare the rod!

[*They beat and buffet him: Milonia brays.* CALIGULA

*mixes human yells with neighing. The crowd shouts.*
SELANUS *splits his sides with laughter.* AMEANA *slams her
window with a scream. Suddenly, in extreme desperation,*
CALIGULA *violently tugs the halter and, freeing himself with
a bursting whinny, escapes.*]

TAVERNER: After him! Catch him!

DRUNK SAILOR: A ... a ... after him!

CROWD: Catch Incitatus!

[*The crowd dashes off after the Pseudo-Incitatus.* EGNATIUS
*steps forward from darkness. Enter the three* SENATORS.]

THE SENATORS: What's happened? Has the consul got
away?

SUFFENUS: Here's our chance! Put an end to him now!

COMINIUS: Hey, Teutons!

[*The* TEUTONS *march in. The senators whisper briefly with
their leader, and then run after the crowd.*]

THE SENATORS: After him! After him!

FIRST TEUTON: Schwulenbubenkuppelmutter!

TEUTONS: Eins, zwei, drei! [*The Teuton leader divides his
men; three steal away in a different direction, the rest run after the
chasers.*]

[*Enter* VALERIA *and* FUFICIUS.]

VALERIA: Has my horse-in-law escaped? Has my horse-in-
law escaped? After him!

FUFICIUS: After him! After him! After him! [*They rush off.*]

[ERIA *and* PYRALLIS *come.*]

ERIA: Mummy, who's got away?

PYRALLIS: A male! After him!

[*They rush off. The young men come.*]

VERANIUS: Haho! The lord consul has escaped!

FABULLUS: What with? The state treasury?

LENTULUS: Catch the consul!

YOUNG MEN: After him! After him!

[*They run after him.*

CALIGULA, *trying to slip away, half limping, and half*

*trotting, with broken whinnies, once more runs across the stage, and stops for a moment.*]

CALIGULA [*to the audience*]: Save me! Hide me! What wrong have I done? Am I not what an emperor should be like? [*To his pursuers, still in the distance*] You're to blame! Everybody gets the kind of emperor they deserve. [*To the audience*] You think you'd make a better emperor? Or you a better empress? [*To his pursuers*] But just you wait, you wait! Let me sit on my throne again ...! [*Approaching noise of the chase.*] Ihahahaha! [*He runs off, the rest yelling in hot pursuit.*]

EGNATIUS: I don't know, my son, what all this will come to, but old Egnatius has had a good laugh for the first time in years!

SELANUS [*laughing*]: So much for that – good night, uncle, Ameana is waiting for me now ...

[*The* DRUNK SAILOR *rushes in.*]

DRUNK SAILOR: M ... men of Rome! They've k ... killed the emperor!

SELANUS: What on earth?

EGNATIUS: Already?

[*TAVERNER dashes in.*]

TAVERNER: You drunken ox! Not the emperor! It's the other horse they've killed, the real one!

SELANUS [*roaring*]: Incitatus!?

TAVERNER: Yes ... Teutons ... on the sly, in his stable ...

[*Mournful, sobbing braying heard.*]

SELANUS [*beside himself*]: Murderers! Was that poor beast to blame ...?!

[*They all rush off.*]


SCENE THREE

*In the emperor's palace.*

CALIGULA *comes in groaning, beaten black and blue, with*

*bandages on his head and limbs.* MACRO *and* LOLLIA *support him up to his throne, prop him up with cushions.*

[*Enter the* SENATORS *with* EGNATIUS.]

CALIGULA: I, Caius, the divine Caesar ... ouch ... who am also called Caligula.... Stop! Trumpets!

MACRO: Trumpets!

[*Flourish of trumpets.*]

CALIGULA: Ouch ... who am also called Caligula, pronounce my latest and most ancient divine decree ...

SENATORS: We await the decree, divine god!

CALIGULA: Firstly: I, Caligula, the divine god ... oh! ... have fought a decisive battle against the despicable rebels, Jupiter ... ouch ... and his associates. Here are the wounds received in this heroic struggle ... oh.... I've won, I've won and on the other hand, I've won!

SENATORS: Long live the emperor, long live the god!

CALIGULA: I have made the Jupiter clique my servants, from now on they worship me, day in day out.

LOLLIA: Clever, good lord, clever.

CALIGULA: Secondly: this triumph of mine is joyfully appreciated by every one of my subject races, except ... who was it?

MACRO: Except the Jews, who didn't worship Jupiter anyway.

CALIGULA: Therefore I will have the Jews exterminated ...

SENATORS: Down with them!

CALIGULA: ... and from their money I will have a statue made of me.

COMINIUS: Thank you!

SENATORS: We thank you!

CALIGULA: Thirdly: since the nightingales stubbornly refuse to warble in my incense-scented garden, I divest Rome's nightingales of their rank of nightingales!

SENATORS: Down with them!

CALIGULA: And I promote in their stead the sparrows

abounding in my garden – to be imperial nightingales!

THALLUS: Long life to Rome's new nightingales!

SENATORS: Long may they live!

CALIGULA: Fourthly: his excellency the consul has passed away. I don't feel like experimenting with a new consul. I appoint Egnatius, sometime owner of nightingales, temporary consul.

EGNATIUS: My lord, I've grown used to the life of a tight-rope walker. I undertake it for the time being for the sake of order, and sooner or later something is bound to come up.

SUFFENUS: Long live the temporary consul.

SENATORS: Long live the temporary!

CALIGULA: Fifthly and lastly: bring in the prisoner.

[*Teuton music. The Teuton bodyguards march in* SELANUS.]

FIRST TEUTON [*presenting himself*]: Runkelrubenwurzelputzer!

THE TEUTONS: Eins! Zwei! Drei!

LOLLIA [*in a low voice to* SELANUS]: Well, handsome country lad, who has won?

CALIGULA: Selanus, son of Marcus, the late consul no longer protects you from my divine wrath. You didn't look after the lord consul's life properly. My divine wrath will descend upon you!

SENATORS: Down with him!

EGNATIUS: My lord, why do you punish one who was simply careless? Why not him who has murdered?

CALIGULA [*at first can find no answer, then replies smartly*]: Because I am the god!

[VALERIA *and* FUFICIUS *enter with* AMEANA *in mourning.*]

VALERIA: My lord, my emperor, my god! Help us, the injured party!

FUFICIUS: Our daughter has become widowed. She's the horse's widow ...

CALIGULA: Aha, aha ... ouch. ... I remember ...

VALERIA: Who will marry her now? After a horse ...

AMEANA: My lord, don't listen to my parents complaining!
... Allow me to wear my widow's weeds to the grave and
never to embrace a man again! With undying passion I
love the deceased and will love him for all eternity ...!

SELANUS [*steps forward*]: My lord, the death of my dear
horse touches me with greater grief than anyone else.
Although that wise woman did foretell even before his
birth that he won't have a long life, still. ... Allow
me, my lord, to make amends for my negligence.

CALIGULA: How?

SELANUS: Condemn me to marry Incitatus's widow!

AMEANA [*passionately*]: No! Anyone else but not him! Him
least of all! Never! This constant, painful memory...!
It's him and yet it's not him ...

SELANUS: It's him and yet it is him ...!

AMEANA: What do you mean?

SELANUS: I'll whisper it in your ear, my lovely widow ...

AMEANA: No, you mustn't – Whisper it!

SELANUS: [*whispers*]

AMEANA [*screaming*]: It's not true! You liar! You cheat! It
wasn't you!

SELANUS: Shall I prove it? Do you remember, lovely
Ameana, when ... [*Whispers.*]

AMEANA [*hiding her face*]: No! No! How dare you ...? –
Yes!

SELANUS: And do you remember, when ... [*Whispers.*]

AMEANA [*scarcely audibly*]: How can one forget it?!
[*Vividly*] And do you remember that time when ...
[*Whispers.*]

SELANUS: I do ... [*Whispers.*]

AMEANA [*with ticklish laughter*]: Pig! Sweet lord, what a foul
pig!

LOLLIA: Enough of all this! Snip-snip!

CALIGULA: Selanus, on the one hand child of Marcus, but on the other hand, child of doom ... !

SENATORS: Snip-snip!

CALIGULA: Now, that I am left the one and only god in the running, I recognize no power beside me ... except that of dice. You have the luckiest hand I've ever met. I don't dare to condemn you. But I will challenge you to one last throw. If you lose, you lose your head. If you win, your life and the widow are yours.

SELANUS: And you will fulfil any one other request of mine!

CALIGULA: And I shall fulfil any one other request of yours. Well?

[*General excitement and interest.*]

AMEANA: My lord, have pity! If he's lucky in love ...

SELANUS: Don't you worry on my behalf, Ameana my love! Give me the dice!

[CALIGULA *himself takes out the dice and the box: he always has them with him.* CALIGULA *shakes and throws. They look at it; all eyes are fixed on* SELANUS.]

SELANUS [*for a second stands lost in thought, then sighs deeply*]: Incitatus, help me!

[*A beauteous and beneficent, celestial whinny is heard from the clouds.* SELANUS *shakes, all hold their breaths.* SELANUS *throws.*]

CALIGULA: You've won! The widow is yours, your head likewise. Fuficius! Pay the price of the wedding present into the imperial privy purse! You may go!

SELANUS: Stop! I haven't had my any one request yet!

CALIGULA: True — let my divine ears hear the any one request.

[*Confused tension.*]

LOLLIA [*suddenly beseeching*]: Don't take vengeance! Handsome country lad, don't take vengeance!

MACRO: We beseech you! Be magnanimous!

SENATORS: Have mercy on us!

TEUTONS [*beating their chests*]: Mitterschandervatermorder, eins, zwei, drei ...!

> [*They all fall at* SELANUS' *feet. He ignores them all, takes* AMEANA *by the arm and steps before* CALIGULA.]

SELANUS: It is my wish that in place of the one Incitatus I may breed for Rome generations of Incitatuses.

CALIGULA: What's the meaning of that?

SELANUS: I want to go to the country – as director of a stud-farm.

CALIGULA: I grant it.

SELANUS: And I want to take Ameana there with me.

CALIGULA: Take her, I don't care if I never see her again ... ouch.... Fuficius, pay the money for parting drinks into the imperial privy purse!

ALL: Hurrah! Hurrah!

> [*Music. The* TAVERNER *enters with all the remaining characters of the play not already present. They bring in a huge silver plate under cover.*]

TAVERNER: My lord, the last homage of remembrance: from the dear body of his late excellency Incitatus the lord consul – here are the sausages!

> [*He rolls out a long string of sausages from the plate and begins distributing them.*]

CALIGULA [*with sausage in hand, deeply moved*]: He was a great horse ...

MACRO: His memory shall live for ever.

TAVERNER: May I add a pinch of horse-radish?

CALIGULA: What for? Can't you see we are crying already ...!

ALL [*weeping*]: Ihahahaha ...!

CURTAIN

# TANGO

*Slawomir Mrozek*

TRANSLATED BY NICHOLAS BETHELL
AND TOM STOPPARD

All inquiries concerning performing rights in Great Britain and the Commonwealth, professional or amateur, should be directed to Hope Leresche & Steele, 11 Jubilee Place, London, SW3.

# CHARACTERS

ARTHUR
STOMIL *Arthur's father*
ELEONORA *Arthur's mother*
EDDIE
EUGENIA *Arthur's grandmother*
EUGENE *Arthur's great-uncle*
ALA *Arthur's cousin*

# ACT ONE

NOTE: *The setting is the interior of a large, high-ceilinged room. The right-hand wall cannot be seen. (All references to 'right' and 'left', both here and elsewhere, should be considered as viewed from the audience.) The area on the right is cut off by the end of the stage, i.e. part of the room lies beyond it. The left-hand wall does not come down to the footlights. It breaks off a few yards upstage, and turns a right angle, running further on to the left, parallel to the footlights. In this flat surface, which faces the audience and lies between the corner and the left wing, there is a door into another room. It is as if there was a corridor disappearing into the left wing and leading from it into the main room.*

*In the wall opposite, the middle wall, there are two doors, one on the left and one on the right. All the doors are identical. They are double-doors, tall, dark-coloured and ornamental in the style of old, solid apartments. Between the doors in the central wall there is a recess, covered by a curtain.*

*In the room are the following pieces of furniture. An eight-seat table, complete with chairs. Armchairs. A large wall mirror on the left wall. A sofa. Some little tables. The furniture is laid out completely asymmetrically, as if it had just been moved in, or was about to be moved out. Everything is topsy-turvy. Also the stage is got up with a mass of draperies so that the material, half hanging, half lying and half coiled up, gives an impression of blur and lack of contour in the room. In one place the material makes a sort of raised platform, like a bed. An old-fashioned black perambulator with high narrow wheels. A wedding dress covered in dust. A bowler-hat.*

*A velvet table-cloth is rumpled halfway up the table to leave half of it bare. Round the bare part of the table three people are sitting. The one they call 'Grandmother' is old, but alert and healthy-looking. Only occasionally does she show signs of senile decay. She*

97

*wears a dress which trails on the ground, very brightly coloured and with enormous flowers on it, a jockey cap and sloppy plimsolls. She is short-sighted. The older of the two men is white-haired, with excellent manners, and wears glasses with narrow gold frames. But his clothes are unexceptional, dusty and unkempt-looking. A swallow-tail coat, a high stiff collar, white but dirty, a wide cravat with a pearl tie-pin. Knee-length khaki shorts. Long Scottish socks, cracked patent-leather shoes. Bare knees.*

*The third person is the most shady and suspicious-looking of them all. He wears an ugly check shirt, open too wide at the front, hanging outside his trousers and with rolled-up sleeves. Light grey trousers, wide, dirty and creased. Bright yellow shoes and very loud socks. Every now and again he scratches his fat thigh. Long greasy hair which he likes to take care of with a comb that he keeps in his hip pocket. A small, square moustache. Unshaven. On his arm is a watch with a 'gold' bracelet. All three are playing cards, fiercely, completely absorbed in the game.*

*On the other side of the table, which is laid for eating, there are plates, cups, wine carafes, artificial flowers, the remains of food, and also a number of objects with little apparent connexion between them, such as a large empty birdcage without a bottom, a woman's shoe, a pair of riding breeches. This table, even more than the rest of the interior, gives an impression of confusion, haphazardness and slovenliness. Every plate, every object comes from a different set, a different age and a different style.*

*Enter from the right a young man, twenty-five at the most, mature, good-looking and with regular features. He wears a good ordinary dark suit that fits him to good effect, a white shirt and a tie. The suit is clean and well pressed. He is carrying some books and papers under his arm, since he has just returned from a university lecture. He stops and observes the scene. The rest are engrossed in their game and do not see him. The table is situated a little to the left, so it is quite a long way from the entrance on the right. The person they call 'Grandmother' is sitting with her back to him, and her side to the audience. Opposite her sits the older man, and the third person is at the end of the table, with his back to the audience and his side to the man who has just come in.*

EUGENIA [*with an exaggerated flourish, throws a card on to the table*]: There's my trumper, stick it up your jumper!

EDDIE [*playing a card*]: Flickerty-flick – and that's my trick! [*He takes a swig from a bottle of beer he keeps on the floor by his chair.*]

EUGENE [*clears his throat timidly, speaks with an obvious effort*]: Ah ... yes ... that's – snap!
    [*A disapproving silence.*]

EUGENIA: Snap what?

EUGENE [*stammering helplessly*]: Snap ... *snap*.

EDDIE: The old git's off his game again. Have another bash. [*Takes a swig.*]

EUGENIA: Eugene, if you're going to play with us, you'll have to play properly. I repeat – snap what?

EUGENE: What's wrong with just snap?

EUGENIA: Oh God, he's blushing again.

EUGENE: Can I say – snap-clap?

EUGENIA: Never heard such rubbish. Eddie, will you tell him, please.

EDDIE: Certainly. 'Course, it's a dodgy one to rhyme ... I'd say – Follow suit or I put in the boot.

EUGENE: Very well. ... What does it mean? – put in the boot?

EDDIE: It's just an expression.

EUGENIA: Stop pulling faces. Eddie knows what he's doing.

EUGENE [*throws the same card down*]: Follow suit or I put in the boot.

EUGENIA: There you are – you can do it if you try.

EDDIE: He's a bit shy.

EUGENIA: Bless you, Eddie. I don't know what we'd do without you.

EDDIE: Any time. [*He notices the young man and quickly hides the bottle under the table.*] Hello-ello-ello – time I was on me way.

EUGENIA: What do you mean? – we're in the middle of a round.

ARTHUR: Good morning.

EUGENIA [*turns round, greatly displeased*]: Oh, it's you.

ARTHUR: Yes, me. What's going on?

EUGENIA: We're playing cards.

ARTHUR: Who with? – that's the point.

EUGENIA: What do you mean, who with? Don't you remember Uncle Eugene?

ARTHUR: I wasn't referring to Uncle Eugene – we'll get round to him in a minute. [*Points at* EDDIE.] Who's that?

EDDIE [*standing up*]: Yes, well I'll see you, then. Au revoir, duchess, and many thanks.

EUGENIA: Don't go, Eddie.

ARTHUR: Get out!

EDDIE [*to* EUGENIA, *accusingly*]: What did I tell ya? – we shouldn't have played today.

EUGENE [*pointing at* EUGENIA]: It's all her fault! – I didn't want to.

ARTHUR [*advancing*]: I said, get out!

EDDIE: All right – I'm going.

[*He walks towards the exit. On the way he stops behind* ARTHUR, *takes one of the books from under his arm and opens it.*]

ARTHUR [*running towards the table*]: How many times have I begged you not to – ?

[*Goes round the table chasing* EUGENIA. *She runs away from him.*]

EUGENIA: No – please – no!

ARTHUR: Yes! – and now.

EDDIE [*looking at book*]: Cor ... get a load of this ...

EUGENIA: What do you want?!

ARTHUR: You know damn well what I want. [*Chasing her.*]

EUGENE: Arthur, have pity on her, she is your grand-mother.

ARTHUR: So you've got something to say, have you?

EUGENE: I have nothing to say, I was merely observing that just because Geenie forgot herself –

ARTHUR: Well, I'm reminding her! And I'll remind you too. Who are you to talk about pity? Which of you pities me? Does any one of you understand me? And she's not the only one. Why aren't you working? You're supposed to be writing your memoirs.

EUGENE: I wrote a bit this morning, Arthur, but then they came to get me –

EUGENIA: Traitor!

EUGENE [*hysterically*]: Will you all leave me alone!

ARTHUR: All right, but you've still got to take your punishment. [*Puts the bottomless birdcage over* EUGENE'S *head.*] Sit down till I let you go.

EUGENIA: Serves him right.

ARTHUR: And don't think you're getting away with it.
[*He uncovers the recess in which there lies a catafalque covered by an old black cloth, with thick candles standing around it.*]
Catafalque, Grandma!

EDDIE [*thumbing through book, his interest increasing*]: Fantastic . . .! [*Sits down on one side.*]

EUGENIA: Please, Arthur – not again – oh, please!

ARTHUR: Shut up!
[EUGENIA *obediently walks up to the catafalque;* EUGENE *offers her his hand.*]

EUGENIA [*icily*]: Thank you, Judas.

EUGENE: Well, you had a rotten hand anyway.

EUGENIA: Clown!

ARTHUR: That's what you get for trying to be funny. [*Hits his hands against his pockets.*] Matches, who's got some matches?

EUGENIA [*laying herself out on the catafalque*]: Arthur, please –
not the candles ...

ARTHUR: Quiet! or it'll be the worse for you.

[EDDIE, *without taking his eyes off the book, produces a box of matches*.]

EDDIE: Here.

[ARTHUR *takes the matches and lights the candles.* EUGENE *takes the artificial flowers off the table and puts them next to* EUGENIA. *He walks back a few paces to observe the effect, then adjusts them.*]

[*An approving whistle.*]

First-class pictures ...

EUGENIA [*lifting her head*]: What's he got there?

ARTHUR: Down!

EUGENE [*walks up to* EDDIE *and peers over his shoulder*]:
'Handbook of Applied Anatomy'. University Edition.

EUGENIA: Hasn't he got anything better to do?

EDDIE: So the young master is going to be a medical man,
is he?

EUGENE: Arthur is studying three subjects, including
philosophy.

EDDIE: Do you get this sort of stuff in philosophy?

EUGENE: Don't be silly – philosophy is never illustrated.

EDDIE: Pity ... I wouldn't mind having a look.

EUGENIA [*rising*]: Let me have a look.

ARTHUR: Down!

EUGENIA: What is the younger generation coming to! Why
don't you go into a monastery?

ARTHUR: Why don't you try to understand me?

EUGENE: Exactly – why don't you try to understand him?

ARTHUR: How can I live in this world!

[ELEONORA *enters from left facing audience. She is a woman in the flower of middle age.*]

ELEONORA: Which world? What's going on?

ARTHUR: Good morning, Mother.

ELEONORA: Granny on the catafalque again?

EUGENIA: Good job you came – you see what he gets up to.

ARTHUR: What *I* get up to? – She asks for it.

EUGENIA: He's teaching me a lesson.

ARTHUR: She went too far this time.

ELEONORA: How far?

ARTHUR: Ask her.

ELEONORA: But why the catafalque?

ARTHUR: So that she can lie there and contemplate eternity.

ELEONORA [*noticing* EDDIE]: Ah, Eddie ...

EDDIE: Wotcher.

ARTHUR: You two know each other?

EUGENE [*to himself*]: Here we go.

ELEONORA: Everyone knows Eddie.... Any objections?

ARTHUR: I think I'm going mad. I come home and find the place cluttered up with a lot of deadbeats – it's impossible to tell where anyone stands – and now it looks as if my own mother – no – I refuse to believe it. Where's it all leading, that's what I want to know.

ELEONORA: Do you want something to eat?

ARTHUR: No, I don't – I want to get the situation under control.

ELEONORA: Eddie sleeps with me now and again. That's right, isn't it, Eddie?

EDDIE [*absent-mindedly*]: That's right. [*Opens out one of the plates.*] Gaw, get this – in colour!

ARTHUR: He what?

ELEONORA: I'll go and get you a snack.

[*She exits through door on left facing audience.* ARTHUR *sits down and looks blank.*]

EUGENE [*to himself*]: Well, you can't say she beats around the bush.... [*To* ARTHUR] Can I take it off now? [*Pause.*] Arthur?

ARTHUR: Yes, take it off. What does it matter now?

EUGENE [*freeing his head from the cage*]: Thank you, Arthur.

[*Sits down next to* ARTHUR.] Arthur ... don't be depressed ...

EUGENIA: This thing is not exactly comfortable.

EUGENE: I can understand how this business about your mother must affect you. ... I really understand – I'm not one of your modernists – you know. ... But Eddie isn't so bad, really. He's got a kind heart, even if he doesn't look very bright. [*More quietly*] Between ourselves, he's a cretin ... [*Louder*] Anyway, we must take life as we find it, don't you think? [*Softer*] Or don't you? [*Louder*] Come on, Arthur – chin up! Eddie's got his points, goodness me, and it isn't like it *used* to be with your mother. [*Softer*] You should have seen her when she was young, before you were born, of course, before she met Stomil, even ... [*Ponders for a moment, then edges himself and his chair up to* ARTHUR. *He talks very softly.*] What are you going to do about Eddie? I agree with you – he's a fat disgusting slob – slurps his food, cheats at cards and carries on as if he owned the place; and his finger-nails are filthy! If it wasn't for Geenie I wouldn't shake hands with the man. Do you know what he did yesterday? – I said to Geenie – Listen, I said, if Eddie doesn't want to clean his teeth that's his business, but if he's going to use my toothbrush, does he have to use it on his shoes? But Eddie said, there was nothing wrong with his teeth, it was his shoes that were dirty. And then he threw me out the door. ... Listen, far be it from me to put ideas into your head, but if I were you I'd fix him. How about chucking him down the stairs?

ARTHUR: That doesn't solve anything.

EUGENE: Or punching him on the nose.

ARTHUR: It's not just a matter of punching a man on the nose.

EUGENE: It wouldn't do him any harm, though, would it? If you like, I'll tell him to get ready.

[*Meanwhile* EUGENIA *has been sitting up on the catafalque, listening in.* EUGENE *realizes this, moves away from* ARTHUR *and raises his voice.*]

Eddie is a simple honest man. In all my life I've never met anyone so simple.

EUGENIA: What's wrong with him?

EUGENE: I don't know. He doesn't react to anything.

EUGENIA: What were you whispering?

EUGENE: Nothing. We were discussing the life of the bee.

ELEONORA [*entering with a tray on which is a cup and some tea biscuits*]: Breakfast ready.

ARTHUR [*awakening from his thoughts, mechanically*]: Thank you, Mummy.

[ARTHUR *sits down at the table.* ELEONORA *puts the tray in front of him, casually pushing everything else aside.* ARTHUR *puts the teaspoon into his cup. The tray is lying crooked.* ARTHUR *pulls a shoe out from under the tray and throws it angrily into a corner.*]

EDDIE: Can I borrow this till Tuesday?

ARTHUR: No. I've got an exam on Monday.

EDDIE: Pity. There's some good bits in here.

ELEONORA: You can get down now, Mother. You look like something out of Edgar Allan Poe.

EUGENIA: What?

ELEONORA: On that catafalque, I mean. And *so* old-fashioned.

EUGENIA [*pointing at* ARTHUR]: What about him?

ELEONORA: He's eating now. He won't interfere.

EUGENIA: Can I get down, Arthur?

ARTHUR: Do what you like. [*Drinks.*] Sugar.

ELEONORA: There isn't any. Eugene ate it.

EUGENE: Excuse me, I only ate the jam. Eddie ate the sugar.

[EUGENIA *comes down off the catafalque.*]

ELEONORA: And put the candles out, Mother. We're

economizing. [*Looks at cards lying on the table.*] Who's winning?

EUGENIA: Eddie.

EUGENE: Edward was born under a lucky star.

ELEONORA: Did you cheat, Eddie?

EDDIE: Me? Never.

ELEONORA: Oh dear, you promised to lose today. I need the money for housekeeping.

EDDIE [*spreading his hands*]: Can't help you.

[*Enter* STOMIL, ARTHUR'*s father and* ELEONORA'*s husband. He has overslept and is in his pyjamas, yawning and scratching himself. He is tall and well built, with an enormous white mane of hair.*]

STOMIL: I thought I smelt coffee. [*Notices* EDDIE.] Hello, Eddie.

[ARTHUR *pushes aside the tray and carefully observes the scene.*]

ELEONORA: You're supposed to sleep till lunch-time. The bed is occupied this afternoon.

STOMIL: I can't sleep – I've had one of my ideas. Who's got the coffee? – Oh, it's you, Arthur. [*Walks up to the table.*]

ARTHUR [*in disgust*]: I wish you'd do up your flies.

STOMIL: Why?

ARTHUR: What do you mean why?

STOMIL: Why? The simplest of questions, and you're stuck for an answer.

ARTHUR: Because – because it's simply not done.

STOMIL [*drinks* ARTHUR'*s coffee*]: There you are – meaningless. A typically conventional reply which fails to survive intellectual analysis.

ARTHUR: Isn't that enough?

STOMIL: Too superficial. If we're going to discuss it we'll have to dig deeper.

ARTHUR: For God's sake, Father, can't you do your flies up and *then* discuss it!

STOMIL: That would be a reversal of the rational process – the act before the thought. Man must live rationally, not mechanically.

ARTHUR: So you're not going to do yourself up.

STOMIL: No. Anyway, I can't. The buttons are missing.

[*Takes another gulp of coffee. Puts the cup back on the table.* EDDIE *stands unnoticed behind* ARTHUR'*s back.*]

ARTHUR: I might have known.

STOMIL: You were wrong, you see – it's a case of mind over matter.

[EDDIE *slips his hand under the arm of* ARTHUR, *who is immersed in conversation, and drinks a mouthful of coffee.*]

ARTHUR: That's just what I've got to talk to you about, Father.

STOMIL: Not now, my boy, not now.

[*Takes a mouthful of coffee from the cup* EDDIE *has just put down. Looks at catafalque.*]

When is someone going to get rid of that box?

ELEONORA: Why?

STOMIL: I don't object to it in principle. One might even say that it enriches our experience and inspires the imagination. But I need room for my experiments.

ELEONORA: You've got quite enough as it is.

EUGENIA: I wish you'd take it away, too. Then Arthur couldn't torment me with it.

ARTHUR [*beats his fist on the table*]: That's just what I'm on about! – This house is a bedlam of anarchy and chaos! Grandfather has been dead ten years. And no one has thought of taking away that catafalque. It's unbelievable. It's a wonder they took *Grandfather* away.

EUGENE: Grandfather was becoming impossible to live with.

ARTHUR: I'm not interested in the details – it's the principle of the thing.

STOMIL [*drinking coffee, bored*]: Oh yes ...?

ARTHUR [*jumps up and runs round the stage: kicks his pram*]: And what's my pram doing in here? — It's twenty-five years since I was in it! Why isn't it in the attic? And look at this — Mother's wedding dress — There should be a cupboard for that kind of thing! — And Uncle Eugene's jodhpurs — his last horse died without issue forty years ago, and his breeches are still lying around the living-room! Left-overs — cast-offs — it's just a load of junk! And furthermore there's no humility around here and no initiative either. It's impossible to breathe, walk or live in this place.

[*Profiting from the confusion,* EDDIE *drains the coffee cup in one gulp.*]

ELEONORA [*aside to* EDDIE]: Why Eddie, you're a *beautiful* drinker.

STOMIL: My dear boy, I find this outburst a tiny bit ridiculous — you're going on as if I were some kind of traditionalist. Surely you can see that we attach no importance to these mementoes of our past — they're just lying where they happened to fall; the strata of our cultural heritage. [*Looking into his cup*] What happened to my coffee?

ARTHUR: No, you've got me wrong, Father — that isn't the point at all.

STOMIL: Be a little more specific. [*To* ELEONORA] Is there any coffee?

ELEONORA: The day after tomorrow.

STOMIL: Why not till then?

ELEONORA: No idea.

STOMIL: Oh, all right. The day after tomorrow.

ARTHUR: Listen — I've got nothing against tradition. But in this house there's no tradition and there's no order, there's nothing but dust and debris. Dead objects. You destroy, and you've gone on destroying for so long that you've lost sight of the point where it all started from.

ELEONORA: There's something in that. Stomil, can you remember the first time we broke with tradition? You made love to me in front of my mother and father, in the front row of the stalls during the première of *Tannhäuser*. ... It was a gesture of protest. There was a terrible scandal. Ah, those were the days! – a thing like that, it made an impression. After that you asked for my hand in marriage.

STOMIL: As far as I remember it was in the National Gallery during the Modern Art exhibition. We got rave notices.

ELEONORA: No, no, it was at the opera. At the exhibition either it wasn't you or it wasn't me. You're so forgetful about everything.

STOMIL: Maybe you're right. [*Becoming excited*] Ah yes! – the old days – Revolution! – with one jump into the modern age! Free at last from the old art and the old life! – Man goes forward, on his own two feet, topples the old gods and climbs up on the pedestal – the chains broken, the fetters smashed! – Revolution and expansion – they're our watchwords! Down with the old forms, crack convention wide open and long live the new life – dynamic, creative, free! – beyond form! – oh yes – beyond form!

ELEONORA: Why, Stomil, that's just how I remember you!

STOMIL: Yes, we were young once.

ELEONORA: But we haven't grown old, we've never betrayed those ideals. It's just as it always was – onward we go, onward!

STOMIL [*without enthusiasm*]: Yes, I suppose so.

ELEONORA: We're not held back by prejudice or convention. Don't we still wage war against the old times? Aren't we free?

STOMIL: What old times?

ELEONORA: Those old times. You know. What we were

just saying – all those knots and handcuffs and – you know – the chains of religion and morality – society ... art – specially art, Stomil ... art!

STOMIL: Oh yes – yes, yes.... When *was* all that?

ELEONORA: Ah ... hang on, I'll have to count up – Er, we were married in nineteen hundred and – no – just a second, don't stop me – Arthur was born in thirty – was it – no – in forty –

STOMIL: Oh, *those* old times.... [*Goes to mirror and wipes his hand across his face.*]

ELEONORA: Don't interrupt, you're muddling me. [*Starts counting in a whisper, completely absorbed*] ... Nineteen fourteen ... eighteen ... nineteen ... twenty-two ...

STOMIL [*in front of mirror*]: We're still young. Eternally young.

ARTHUR: You're right, Father – it's all over.

[ELEONORA *walks about, absorbed in calculations.*]

STOMIL: What is?

ARTHUR: All those chains and shackles – they've all gone. More's the pity.

STOMIL: What do you mean, more's the pity? You don't know what you're talking about. If you'd been alive back in the old days you'd know what we've done for you. You've no idea what it was like – It was an act of courage just to dance the tango! And the number of fallen women was pitiful. And the arts! – naturalism! – and the bourgeois theatre! Muck! And you couldn't eat with your elbows on the table – oh, I remember the student demonstrations, way back in nineteen – whenever it was – yes, the really heroic ones refused to give up their seats to elderly passengers. We fought for those rights, and now you can do what you like to your grandmother – For your tomorrow we gave up our today! And now you sneer at this freedom which we fought to create.

ARTHUR: This is all you created – this brothel where anything goes and nothing works! – where there aren't any rules.

STOMIL: There's only one rule: do as you please. We've all got the right to our own kind of happiness.

ELEONORA: I've got it! – It was nineteen twenty-eight!

STOMIL: What was?

ELEONORA [*confounded*]: There you have me.

ARTHUR: Your freedom has corrupted this generation from top to bottom. Look at her [EUGENIA] – she's completely off her head. Don't you care?

EUGENIA: I knew he'd get back to me.

STOMIL: There's nothing wrong with her – what are you talking about?

ARTHUR: That's it, isn't it? – she's senile and degenerate, and you don't turn a hair. But there was a time when she was an honoured, respectable grandmother – And what's it all come down to? – playing poker with Eddie!

EDDIE: And bridge – beggin' your pardon, squire – we play bridge sometimes.

ARTHUR: I'm not talking to you – you peasant.

STOMIL: Everyone is free to do what they like with whoever they like. Even the old.

ARTHUR: But with you freedom is compulsory! – immorality is a moral obligation.

STOMIL: Honestly, you amaze me – you're so decadent. When we were your age we'd have rather died than conform. To rebel! – that was the only thing of any value.

ARTHUR: What value?

STOMIL: The value of dynamic force – bang on target in its very aimlessness – You don't think we were just blundering about like blinded anarchists, do you? We were a march into the future, a movement, a historical process. Progress begins with rebellion, and revolution is the rock on which progress builds her church. The greater the revolution the greater the reconstruction – and believe me, we cleared a lot of ground.

ARTHUR: Then ... what's gone wrong? If you're all in favour of construction why can't you all work together?

STOMIL: Work together?! The very idea! – my dear boy, I was merely giving you the historical view – the outsider looking back. That's quite a separate matter from what we're actually *doing*. We have always gone our own way. And in opposition to everything past we're paving the way for the future.

ARTHUR: What future?

STOMIL: That's not my affair. I'm concerned with getting rid of form.

ARTHUR: So we're on different sides after all.

STOMIL: Well, what if we are? The main thing is to stop you worrying your head about rules.

ELEONORA: It's quite extraordinary – you're the youngest and you keep wanting to lay down rules. It always used to be the other way round.

ARTHUR: Because I'm at the beginning of my life and I don't know what sort of life I'm supposed to be beginning – I have to create it so that I can move into it.

STOMIL: But you want to be up to date, don't you? At *your* age.

ARTHUR: Ah, now that's what hurts, isn't it? In your brave new cock-eyed world, Granny has grown old; in the midst of modernism, obsolescence creeps over her. And all of you – here you are in the new life, growing older and older and older.

EUGENE: But – if I may interrupt for a moment – there are certain achievements; for instance, the right to wear shorts ...

ARTHUR: Now you shouldn't have said that, Uncle. Don't you see that now everything is allowed nothing is possible? All right, so you put on a pair of shorts and you think you're defying convention – but there aren't any conventions left to defy! You emerge without a stain on your character – you and your avuncular defiance – you've missed the bus!

STOMIL: So what do you want? Tradition?

ARTHUR: World order!

STOMIL: Oh, is that all?

ARTHUR: That and the right to rebel.

STOMIL: But you've got it! – I keep telling you rebel!

ARTHUR: Can't you see that you've destroyed any chance I ever had? You've been kicking over the totems for so long that there's nothing left for me to kick against – nothing! Abnormality is the new norm, and all I've got to rebel against is you and your muck.

STOMIL: Well, go ahead – I'm not stopping you.

EUGENE: Yes, go on, Arthur – show them.

ELEONORA: Perhaps it'll get it out of your system. You've been so irritable lately.

[EUGENIA *makes a sign to* EDDIE. *They go behind* ARTHUR's *back and start shuffling the cards.*]

ARTHUR [*his nerve gives way*]: I can't!

ELEONORA: Why not?

EUGENE: We want you to.

ARTHUR: Rebel against you? How the hell can I fight a blob? – Nothing is integrated so how can it disintegrate? Your world has no shape, no structure and no substance – it's indestructible.

STOMIL: You mean we're no help?

ARTHUR: No help at all – you're all so tolerant.

STOMIL: Yes ... It's a difficult situation. But I wouldn't want you to think that your own family won't stand by you.

ELEONORA [*standing behind* ARTHUR, *strokes his head*]: Poor Arthur. Don't think that your mother has a heart of stone.

EUGENE: We all like you, Arthur. We want to help you.

EUGENIA [*to* EDDIE]: No bid.

ARTHUR: There's nothing you can do. You've set your-selves up as anti-conformists and now you spend your time trying to make me conform to *that*. The trouble is, I can't conform all my life – I'm grown up now. All my friends are laughing at me.

STOMIL: What about art, Arthur – think of art!

ELEONORA: Exactly! – took the words out of my mouth.

ARTHUR: What art?

STOMIL: Art in general. All my life I've devoted myself to art – it's a revolution in itself. Why not give it a try?

EDDIE: Shoot, baby!

EUGENIA: Wuba – do – duba – do – bach!

ARTHUR: You shouldn't turn my head, Father. I want to be a doctor.

ELEONORA: A doctor! The family would never live it down! Oh, and I dreamt of him being an artist. While I still carried him in my womb I used to run naked through the woods, singing Bach cantatas. . . . I might as well have stayed at home.

ARTHUR: Obviously you were off key.

STOMIL: Don't give up hope, boy – you're not giving art its due. For example, I've just had an idea for a new experiment – I'll show you.

ELEONORA [*clapping her hands*]: Listen everybody! – Stomil has come up with something new!

EUGENIA: What, again?

STOMIL: Yes. It flashed into my mind this morning. Some-thing completely original.

ELEONORA: He's going to demonstrate it now, aren't you, dear?

STOMIL: Ready!

EUGENE: Oh God.

ELEONORA: Eugene, move that table out of the way.

[EUGENE *starts moving the table, crashing and banging.* EUGENIA *and* EDDIE *take the cards and move to one side. Amongst a pile of material which looks like a low couch with rumpled bedclothes, something begins to move. The head of cousin* ALA *appears.*]

ALA [*A mature eighteen-year-old, long straight hair. Blinks and yawns*]: Where am I? – What's all the noise? – What's the time?

ARTHUR: Ala!

ELEONORA: I forgot to tell you. Ala arrived here at six this morning.

STOMIL: Good Ala, you're invited to my première. [*To* EUGENE] That'll do. Now the catafalque.

ARTHUR: Why didn't you speak up? – If I'd known I would have kept them quiet. [*Notices* EDDIE *is approaching* ALA *with some interest.*] Eddie, go and stand in the corner. [EDDIE *obediently goes and stands with his face to the wall.*] Did you sleep well?

ALA: Not too bad.

ARTHUR: How long are you staying?

ALA: I don't know. I told my ma maybe I'd never be back.

ARTHUR: Really? What did she say?

ALA: Nothing. She wasn't in.

ARTHUR: What? – How did you tell her then?

ALA: I forget now. Maybe I didn't.

ARTHUR: Can't you remember?

ALA: It was a long time ago.

ARTHUR: Do you want any breakfast – oh, no, sorry – the coffee's finished. Well, do you mind if I sit next to you?

ALA: Help yourself.

[ARTHUR *brings up a chair and sits down near the bed.*]

ARTHUR: You look nice. [ALA *laughs very loudly.*] What's so funny?

ALA: How do you mean?

ARTHUR: Well, you were laughing.

ALA: Who, me? You're joking.

ARTHUR: No, you were laughing.

ALA: Don't argue.

ARTHUR: I've been thinking about you, Ala.

ALA [*vulgarly*]: Tell me more.

ARTHUR: I've often imagined us – meeting.

ALA: Yes, more!

ARTHUR: ... and sitting close ...

ALA: More, more!

ARTHUR: ... and talking ...

ALA: ... and more! –

ARTHUR: ... about certain matters –

ALA: – more, I tell you, more, more!

ARTHUR [*raising his voice*]: ... about various matters –

ALA: More, more, more!

[*With all his force,* ARTHUR *throws a book at her – the one* EDDIE *left near by.* ALA *avoids the blow and hides under the blanket.*]

ARTHUR: Get out!

ALA [*sticking her head out from under the blanket*]: What's up with you? [ARTHUR *says nothing.*] Why did you say that? [ARTHUR *says nothing.*] What are you after?

ARTHUR: Everyone asks me that.

ALA: Good. In that case I won't.

STOMIL: Take your seats please, take your seats.

[*The stage is now ready for* STOMIL's *experiment. The table is moved to one side. Near the front of the stage are four chairs in a row with their backs to the audience.* EUGENIA, ELEONORA *and* EUGENE *occupy three from left to right.* EDDIE *takes an unfinished bottle of beer and on tiptoe surreptitiously tries to escape into the wings.* EUGENE *notices him and points him out to* ELEONORA.]

ELEONORA: Where are you going, Eddie?

EDDIE: Shan't be a minute – I just –

ELEONORA: Come back here at once!

[EDDIE, *resigned to his fate, comes back and takes the chair on the far right next to* EUGENE. *At the first opportunity he gives* EUGENE *a hard painful kick on the leg.* STOMIL *goes out through the door by the left wing, in the corridor.*]

[*To* ARTHUR *and* ALA] What are you doing, you two? Come and join us.

ALA: What's going on?

ARTHUR: Theatrical experiment. It's my father's mania.

[*Gives her his hand.* ALA *jumps off the bed. She is wearing a full length nightdress – producers who are quick to jump to conclusions please note – it is quite opaque, full of pleats and flounces and looks more like a dress than a nightdress. They stand next to the chairs on the right.* EDDIE, *without standing up, stretches out an arm and puts it round* ALA's *waist.* ARTHUR *changes places with her.*

STOMIL *has meanwhile returned carrying a large box, and gone behind the catafalque. At the moment only his head is visible.*]

STOMIL: Ladies and gentlemen, your attention, please. It gives me great pleasure to introduce the heroes of our play. [*With great emphasis like a circus ringmaster introducing an act*] Adam and Eve in Paradise!

EUGENE: We've already had that.

STOMIL [*worried*]: When?

EUGENE: At the creation of the world.

STOMIL: That was the original. I've done an adaptation.

EDDIE: Wha' about the snake, then?

ELEONORA [*silences him with a whisper*]: Sssssh!

STOMIL: We'll have to imagine the serpent. We all know the plot. Now then – pay attention. [*In a rough deep voice*] So here we are in Paradise,
and I am Adam, as you might have known
– it's a situation that could lead to anything.
And it's starting now! – Created from my bone,
Eve appears. What change does she bring?
Oh Fate, in you the answer lies!

[*In a higher pitched voice*]
Adam came first, as you all know,
but he was nothing till I came by.
He walks around with his head held high –
can't he see, though he seems all-seeing,
that the only perfection is in non-being.
When the sun comes out, where does the darkness go?
Oh Fate –

[*A very loud bang and the lights go out.*]

ELEONORA [*unseen*]: Stomil, what's happened – are you alive?

EUGENE: Get the fire brigade!

[*A match flares, lit by* ARTHUR, *who lights the candles.* STOMIL *can be seen with a revolver, a large six-shooter, in his hand.*]

STOMIL: Aha! Well? Did you like it?

ELEONORA: You scared the life out of us.

STOMIL: An experiment must astound – that's my first rule.

EUGENE: Well, if that was all you were after, you certainly succeeded. It's given me palpitations.

ELEONORA: Darling, how did you do it?

STOMIL: I fused the lights, at the same time firing my revolver.

ELEONORA: *Most* unusual.

EUGENE: What's unusual about it?

STOMIL: Weren't you with it?

EUGENE: Far from it.

ELEONORA: Take no notice of him – he always was the stupid one.

STOMIL: What about you, Gennie?

EUGENIA: Uh?

STOMIL [*louder*]: I said, did you understand the experiment?

EUGENIA [*as loud as she can*]: What?

ELEONORA: The experiment's deafened her.

EUGENE: I'm not surprised.

118

STOMIL: Let me explain. By a direct act we have achieved unity in a moment of action and perception. All right?

EUGENE: Yes, all right. Go on.

STOMIL: What do you mean?

EUGENE: What's that got to do with Adam and Eve?

ELEONORA: Concentrate, Eugene.

STOMIL: It's got something to do with theatrical phenomena. The dynamic of the sensual fact. Didn't you feel yourself respond to it?

EUGENE: To tell you the truth, not very much.

STOMIL [*throwing the revolver on to the catafalque*]: God give me strength!

ELEONORA: Don't lose heart, Stomil. If you don't experiment, who will?

[*Everybody stands up and starts moving back their chairs.*]

EUGENE: Gentlemen, a failure!

EDDIE: Give me the pictures, every time.

ELEONORA: What are we going to do now?

ARTHUR: All right! – I want you all out of here!

STOMIL: What, again?

ARTHUR: Out! – Get out of my sight, the lot of you!

STOMIL: That's a fine way to treat your father.

ARTHUR: I've *got* no father. As of now, I'm finished with him. I'm going to create my father from scratch!

STOMIL: Create me?

ARTHUR: You and all the rest of them. And to begin with I want this room cleared.

STOMIL: He's getting too big for his boots.

ELEONORA: Calm down, darling – we're broadminded, don't forget.

STOMIL: You think I ought to go?

ELEONORA: Yes, come on. What do you care about all that? – you've got your experiments.

STOMIL: Yes! – art. The avant-garde! Give me God himself and I'll make an experiment out of him!

ELEONORA: There, there ...

[*They walk out through door opposite, left.*]

EDDIE [*to* EUGENIA]: Are we off, then, Gran?

EUGENIA: Take the cards.

[EDDIE *takes the cards. He and* EUGENIA *walk out.*]

EDDIE [*turning round*]: Mr Arthur, sir, should you require anything ...

ARTHUR [*stamping his foot*]: Get lost!

EDDIE [*conciliatory*]: All right, all right ...

[*Exit left with* EUGENIA.]

EUGENE [*after making certain that the others have all left*]: I do agree with you, dear boy. Strictly between ourselves, they're a bunch of lunatics.

ARTHUR: You, too, Uncle.

EUGENE: My dear boy, of course, of course – I'm going. All I have to say is: you can count on me.

ARTHUR: What exactly do you have in mind?

EUGENE: In mind? – Nothing, nothing at all – you do as you think best. But remember: I could be very useful to you. I haven't lost my reason like them. [*Lowering his voice*] I am behind the times.

ARTHUR: Very well, Uncle. Now would you please leave us alone.

[EUGENE *goes out into the corridor on the left. Before he leaves the stage he turns round and repeats with emphasis:*]

EUGENE: Behind the times! [*Exit.*]

ALA: Well, now what?

ARTHUR: I am about to explain.

BLACKOUT

# ACT TWO

*The same. Night. One small standard lamp.*

    [ARTHUR *is sitting in the armchair. Someone enters.*]

ARTHUR: Who's there?

PERSON: Me.

ARTHUR: Who's me?

PERSON: Uncle Eugene.

ARTHUR: Password?

EUGENE: Rebirth. Countersign?

ARTHUR: Renaissance. All right, Uncle, you can come
forward.

    [EUGENE *walks in towards the light. He sits down opposite*
    ARTHUR.]

EUGENE: I'm exhausted.

ARTHUR: Is everything ready?

EUGENE: I've got all the stuff down from the attic. You've
never seen so many moths. Well, what do you think –
will we succeed?

ARTHUR: We've got to.

EUGENE: What worries me is that they're beyond redemp-
tion. Just think – their whole lives spent in this brothel –
er – I do beg your pardon – in this mess then. You see,
I'm being corrupted too.

ARTHUR: Never mind that. What's my father doing?

EUGENE: He's in his room, working on a new production.
I suppose he should be pitied – he really believes in that
art of his.

ARTHUR: In that case why aren't you more sympathetic?

EUGENE: Pure perversity. I like annoying him. Besides,
I'm an honest man and his experiments leave me cold.
What do you think of them?

ARTHUR: I've got other things to think about. What's my mother doing?

[EUGENE *gets up, walks over to the door in the wall opposite, on the left, and peers through the keyhole.*]

EUGENE: Can't see a thing. Either she's got no light in there or she's blocked up the keyhole.

ARTHUR: And Granny?

EUGENE: Probably making up her face.

ARTHUR: All right. You can go. I've got an important meeting in here in a minute.

EUGENE [*getting up*]: Any new orders?

ARTHUR: Mouth shut, eyes open, alert, be prepared.

EUGENE: Yessir! [*Leaving.*] May the good Lord watch over you, Arthur. The good times may yet return.

[*Exits firmly to the right, the same side from which he came in. Through the left wing, the corridor side,* ALA *comes, wearing the same nightdress.*]

ALA [*yawning*]: Did you want something?

ARTHUR: Ssssh! – Hush!

ALA: Why?

ARTHUR: I don't want us to be disturbed.

ALA: Do you think they care *what* we do?

[*She sits down, which makes her squirm around in pain.*]

ARTHUR: What's the matter?

ALA: Stomil pinched me. Twice.

ARTHUR: The pig!

ALA: He's your father!

ARTHUR [*charmingly kisses her hand*]: I'm obliged to you for drawing that fact to my attention.

ALA: You're so square – nowadays people don't talk about their fathers like that.

ARTHUR: How do they talk about them, then?

ALA: They don't talk about them at all.

ARTHUR: So I got it wrong.

ALA: One's relatives are a private affair. Anyway, Stomil's rather nice.

ARTHUR [*contemptuous*]: He's an artist!

ALA: What's the matter with artists?

ARTHUR: They're a plague upon the earth – they were the first to undermine the age.

ALA [*becoming bored*]: What of it? Well, what do you want? It's cold and I'm almost naked. [*Pause.*] Have you noticed?

ARTHUR: Listen, about what I was telling you this morning – have you thought about it? Are you with me?

ALA: Do you mean about marrying you? I told you. I don't see the point.

ARTHUR: You mean you won't?

ALA: Honestly, I don't know why you're making such a fuss. If it's so important to you we can get married to-morrow. After all, we're already cousins.

ARTHUR: For God's sake, stop being so casual about whether you're going to marry me or not marry me. You've got to realize it's important.

ALA: What's important about it? Either it happens or it doesn't, and then either I have a baby or I don't, and if I do it'll be yours and not the priest's. So what?

ARTHUR: All right. Then we'll make it important.

ALA: Why?

ARTHUR: Nothing's important seen on its own – every-thing's neutral. If we don't give things character our-selves then we just submit to their nothingness. We have to create meanings where they don't exist.

ALA: What for?

ARTHUR: ... Let's say for our own pleasure and profit.

ALA: What pleasure?

ARTHUR: Pleasure derives from profit, and we profit by achieving something which is worth more than other things – something exceptional, or more difficult, or more worthwhile. In other words, we have to establish a set of values.

ALA: I find philosophy rather boring. I think I prefer Stomil. [*Stretching one leg out from under the nightdress.*]

ARTHUR: You only think you do. Kindly put away that leg.

ALA: Don't you like it?

ARTHUR: It's not what we're talking about.

ALA [*persisting*]: Don't you like it?

ARTHUR [*turning his eyes away from the leg with some difficulty*]: All right, so stick your leg out as far as you like – it just shows how right I am.

ALA: My leg? [*Looking at it with new interest.*]

ARTHUR: That's right. You can't understand why I don't leap at you like my artistic father and whoever else, so you hang out your leg. You're worried. I surprised you this morning, when we were alone. You thought you knew what I wanted.

ALA: That's not true.

ARTHUR: Isn't it? Do you think I didn't notice how embarrassed you were when I asked you to marry me instead of dragging you straight to the nearest bed?

ALA: I had a headache –

ARTHUR: You don't know what to make of it. Your charms don't seem to work on me, and you're worried. What you want me to do is what my father did this morning - that would reassure you at once, though of course, you'd get your own back by running away.

ALA [*with dignity, standing up*]: I'm running away now.

ARTHUR [*seizes her by the arm and replaces her in the armchair*]: I haven't finished. All you can think about is how attractive you are. You're so primitive – it's the only thing you're good for, and to top it off you don't know anything about anything.

ALA [*tries to stand again*]: You think I'm retarded?

ARTHUR [*not letting her stand*]: Siddown! – You're bearing

out what I said: I didn't behave to pattern, and you were intrigued. It was exceptional and that gave it value. And so I gave meaning to our meaningless encounter – I did it.

ALA: Well you can do it without me if you think you're so marvellous. You're on your own!

ARTHUR: Don't lose your temper, Ala.

ALA: We'll see how you make out. Go and do it with your Uncle Eugene.

[*She firmly pulls down her nightdress and buttons it up at the neck. She also pulls a blanket over herself, rams the black bowler over her head, right over her eyes.*]

ARTHUR [*sheepishly*]: Don't be cross.

ALA: I've got every right.

ARTHUR: Aren't you a bit warm ... in that blanket ...

ALA: No.

ARTHUR: That's Uncle Eugene's hat. It's not at all you.

ALA: I don't care.

ARTHUR: Please yourself. Now, where were we? Yes ... set of values ... [*Draws his chair up to* ALA.] ... So, generally speaking, the creation of a set of values is essential to the proper functioning of the individual and of society no less ... [*Takes her by the hand.*] Without suitable standards we can never succeed in establishing a harmonious whole, or even an essential balance of those elements normally defined as good or bad – I speak in the broad sense, of course, not merely from the moral standpoint. Having said this, let me at once say, to begin with, that is, that we must restore a practical significance to these concepts, and – secondly – we must establish codes of behaviour which –

[*He throws himself upon* ALA *and tries to kiss her. She tears herself away by force. An ugly struggle ensues. Enter* EDDIE, *a towel round his neck, and wearing a hairnet.*]

EDDIE: Oh – ex-cuse me!

[ARTHUR *lets* ALA *go, pretending that nothing has*

*happened.* ALA *puts her hat straight and exaggeratedly rubs her arm.*]

ARTHUR: What are you doing here?

EDDIE: I was just going to the kitchen for some water. – Sorry, I didn't know you were having a 'tête-à-tête'.

ARTHUR: Water? – what water?

EDDIE [*with dignity*]: Terrible thirst, Mr Arthur.

ARTHUR: Now? In the middle of the night?

EDDIE [*offended*]: I'll do without if you like.

ARTHUR [*fiercely*]: Have your drink and get out!

EDDIE: Certainly, Mr Arthur. [*Walks majestically towards the door in the centre wall on the left.*]

ARTHUR: Just a minute!

EDDIE: Yes?

ARTHUR: The kitchen's on the right.

EDDIE: Impossible!

ARTHUR: It's my house – I ought to know where the kitchen is.

EDDIE: You can't be sure of anything nowadays. [*Changes direction and walks out through right-hand door.*]

ARTHUR: Moron! I'll have to straighten him out.

ALA [*icily*]: Have you finished straightening me out?

ARTHUR: It's all his fault.

ALA: His fault that you nearly twisted my arm off?

ARTHUR: Does it hurt?

ALA: Fat lot you care.

    [*She gives an artificial cry of pain.* ARTHUR, *disturbed, wants to inspect her arm.*]

ARTHUR: Where? Show me. [*Touches her arm, without any of his former intentions.*]

ALA [*uncovers her arm*]: Here . . .

ARTHUR: I'm really very sorry –

ALA [*raises one leg*]: . . . and here . . .

ARTHUR: Honestly, I didn't mean to . . .

ALA [*bares her shoulders*]: . . . and here . . .

ARTHUR: I don't know what to say –

ALA [*points to one of her ribs*]: ... and there ...

ARTHUR: Please forgive me.

ALA: You've given yourself away. You're as brutal as all the rest. First a bit of the chat, then a bit of the other. [*Falls tragically into an armchair.*] Ah, the tragic fate of womankind! What have we done to deserve our bodies? If only we could leave them somewhere like a cloakroom, then we'd be safe from the assaults of so-called cousins. All I can say is I didn't expect it of you – I thought you were supposed to be an intellectual.

ARTHUR [*completely confused*]: All I did was ...

ALA: Don't try and get out of it. It may surprise you to know that I occasionally feel like having a serious discussion about important matters – quietly, though, without wondering whether some philosopher's going to grab me by the leg. Now – what were we talking about? – You were just getting to the interesting part.

[*Noise of flowing water and gurgling from the other side of the door* EDDIE *has just walked through.*]

ARTHUR: Do you really think I tried to rape you?

ALA [*becoming worried*]: Why, didn't you?

ARTHUR: Certainly not. That was a demonstration.

ALA: Thanks very much, but I know how.

ARTHUR: One-track mind. So why did you resist?

ALA: You're disgusting.

ARTHUR: Science knows no shame. Why did you resist?

ALA: Why did you attack me?

ARTHUR: I sacrificed myself.

ALA: You what?

ARTHUR: Yes, sacrificed myself – I had to demonstrate something to you. It was an exercise in sexual pragmatism.

ALA: You beast! You rotten scientific beast! And what's pragmatism may I ask? – some new kind of perversion?

ARTHUR: There's nothing new about it. Come on – we can be allies. And women will join my crusade.

ALA: What women?

ARTHUR: All women! – the women of the world will follow me. The first thing women have got to do is stand up for their rights. As soon as they realize that, men will have to take it or leave it.

ALA: What women? – that's what I should like to know. Anyway, I don't care what you do with them – it's nothing to do with me.

ARTHUR: Listen – the history of the world is the history of man's brutal suppression of women, children and artists.

ALA: You don't like artists.

ARTHUR: That's by the way. Men don't like artists because artists are not men – that's what has always brought them closer to women, unfortunately. Artists don't understand ideas of honour or logic or progress or anything invented by men. It is only in the recent past, and with great difficulty, that the male sex have begun to suspect the existence of ambiguity, relativity and transience: all of which contradict the doctrine of unity, self and consequence which man originally produced out of his thick bruiser's skull and inscribed upon his banner and tried to shove down the throats of women, children and artists. He thought up the world in his own image. In his cave, or farm, or business, he discovered logic. But he saw himself as all-powerful in the world and in his pride insisted that his views on life should be shared by everyone. So, giving way to his aggressive nature, he announced that his ideas were unique, universal and compulsory and by brute force tried to impose them on the weak. And when it turned out that women thought differently, he lost his temper and called them stupid, or illogical, which in the male vocabulary means the same thing.

ALA: What about you? You're a man.

ARTHUR: I rise above myself. I'm objective. I have to be, to carry out my plan.

ALA: How do I know if I can trust you?

ARTHUR: ... In his attempt to find a dogma to suit his lack of imagination, man thought up the idea of honour. He also thought up the negative idea of effeminacy. Both these ideas serve to protect the male community from desertion – any man who has his doubts is kept firmly in the ranks for fear of being despised. Now, as a natural reaction to all this, on the opposite side, a community of women, children and artists was formed – as an act of self-defence. Generally speaking, men do not bring up their children – the most they do is pay a monthly sum of money for this purpose. So it's not surprising that ultimately mass murder strikes them as being a commendable, pleasant and even profitable activity. Excuse me –

[*All this time the gurgles from the kitchen have continued.* ARTHUR *interrupts his speech and walks up to the kitchen door.*]

What's he doing in there?

ALA: Maybe he's having a wash.

ARTHUR: Eddie? Not on your life. [*Goes back.*] Where were we?

ALA: I'm not taken in. I know your game.

ARTHUR: My game is simply to make you understand what lies behind your position as a woman in society. I want you to open your eyes.

ALA: And take my clothes off.

ARTHUR: Don't be boring. You'll see that our interests are the same in this – we'll be partners. Now what is man's secret dream? It's to do away with all the etiquette involved in seduction. He is merely irritated by all the business between the desire and the fulfilment.

ALA: That's true – they hurl themselves at you like animals – I've just had proof of that.

ARTHUR: I admit that as an individual I am subject to natural impulses, but on the whole I have a higher purpose. Men – exploiting the laxity of the times – have done everything they can to remove the remaining taboos in the field of sex. But I do not believe that women find this entirely to their liking – and it's on this that I base my plan.

ALA: Personally, I like things just as they are.

ARTHUR: You can't do. You're lying.

ALA: I do. I like it. I can do what I want. Everything's free. For instance, suppose I take all my clothes off, what would you do then? [*Throws away the blanket and takes off the bowler hat.*]

ARTHUR: Please – this is serious.

ALA [*undoes the ribbons on her nightdress*]: Why? Who's going to stop me? You? Or my mother? Or God Almighty? Go on – who? [*Takes nightdress off her shoulders.*]

ARTHUR: Stop it! – For God's sake put it on properly. [*Desperately turns his eyes away.*]

ALA: I wouldn't dream of such a thing. It's my nightdress. [EDDIE'*s head appears in the kitchen doorway. He has been attracted by raised voices.*] Ah, Eddie! – do come in.

ARTHUR [*pushing* EDDIE *back*]: Get back or I'll kill you! Undressing in front of that – moron. Aren't you ashamed?

ALA: He may be uneducated. But he has nice eyes.

ARTHUR: He's got the eyes of a pig.

ALA: I like them.

ARTHUR: I'll kill him.

ALA [*sweetly*]: You're jealous.

ARTHUR: I'm not jealous.

ALA: First violent, then jealous. Better and better!

ARTHUR [*extremely angry, stands in front of* ALA]: All right

then, strip! Go on, then – I'm not stopping you. Take it
off!

ALA: I don't feel like it now.

ARTHUR: Oh, come on – don't be shy.

ALA [*hesitantly*]: I've changed my mind.

ARTHUR: You don't want to? Why not, then? – tell me
why not.

ALA: My God, he's some kind of maniac.

ARTHUR [*grabs her arm*]: Why?

ALA: I don't know.

ARTHUR: Why!

ALA: What do you want me to say? I don't know, that's all.
Let go of me.

ARTHUR [*releasing her*]: You know damn well. It's because
you don't really like all this degenerate anarchy – you're
only pretending to like it.

ALA: Am I?

ARTHUR: Of course. You don't like it because it doesn't
suit you. It takes away your choice and limits your scope.
All you've got left is getting in and out of your clothes.

ALA: That's not true!

ARTHUR: Why did you resist, then?
  [*Pause.*]

ALA: You're being logical, and just now you said that logic
was bunk. Get out of that.

ARTHUR: I said that?

ALA: Yes, you did. I heard you.

ARTHUR [*dissatisfied*]: You must have misheard.

ALA: Misheard, nothing. I heard perfectly well.

ARTHUR: Well, let's get back to the point – I still think
you're pretending. What it boils down to is that this
conventional Bohemianism doesn't really appeal to you.
You didn't choose it.

ALA: Who did, then?

ARTHUR: We did. You fall in with it and pretend to like it

because there's nothing else you can do. No one likes to admit they're dominated.

ALA: So why do I admit it, if I don't like it?

ARTHUR: From fear of not being liked. It's always the same with fashion.

ALA: No. I'm not owning up to anything.

ARTHUR: So there *is* something to own up to, isn't there? Why go on denying it? – I promise you, this is much more important. You see, I don't believe that you want to sleep with every single man in the world – All right, so you might fancy the top hundred – two hundred, ten thousand – a million! – but not every single one, surely? You'd like them all to fancy *you*, of course – that's a different thing, that just gives you the choice. But what choice have women got if you do away with all the conventions? You tell me.

ALA: I'm perfectly independent. I know what I want.

ARTHUR: But you're weak by nature. What chance have you got if you find yourself alone with a strange man who's stronger than you and doesn't give a damn for etiquette? Look what happened a minute ago – if Eddie hadn't come into the room you would have been at my mercy.

ALA: I can take judo lessons.

ARTHUR: I'm being hypothetical! Why can't women grasp a simple generalization?

ALA: Lots of women take judo lessons. I'd like to have you on your knees, begging for mercy.

ARTHUR: That's it! – but you don't need judo for that. All you need is a well thought-out code of conventions. With that, you'd *have* me on my knees – here in front of you – with a bunch of flowers in my hand, and I'd be begging you to have pity on me and grant me hope. And you, without raising a finger or getting a hair out of place – which is more than you can say for a wrestling match –

you could wallow in the power you have over me. Now isn't that better than judo?

ALA: You mean you really would kneel?

ARTHUR: Of course I would.

ALA: Go on then.

ARTHUR: What?

ALA: On your knees!

ARTHUR: I'm afraid that's impossible.

ALA [*disappointed*]: Why?

ARTHUR: Because those conventions don't exist. You see the position we're in?

ALA: Can't we do anything?

ARTHUR: Yes, we can!

ALA: What?

ARTHUR: We can either establish new conventions or bring back the old ones. And I'll do it if you'll help me. Everything's ready – all I need is your help.

ALA: Super! – And then you'll kneel?

ARTHUR: Cross my heart.

ALA: What do I have to do?

ARTHUR: Marry me. For a start. No casual liaison – no taking the easy way out. It's got to be marriage, and I don't mean any old marriage, I don't mean changing your name in the coffee break. I mean a real marriage, with an organ, bridesmaids, all the trappings. And above all, a wedding procession. It must take them by surprise, they must have no chance to collect themselves and organize resistance and break up what I've started. We shall strike immediately and at the heart, so fast that once the formalities have taken hold of them they won't be able to escape. I shall drag them to that wedding, and they'll have to play it my way. I'll make *them* into a wedding procession, and at last my father will have to do his buttons up. What do you think?

ALA: Will I be in white?

ARTHUR: White as snow. Everything traditional. You'll be striking a blow for every woman in the world. The current standards will be overturned and women will get back their freedom. What happens now when a man meets a woman? His seductive patter consists of a few animal grunts on the way to the bedroom. But what used to happen? Conversation. Semi-articulate noises were made. He had to say something. And as he spoke you would sit modestly silent, recognizing your enemy. The more you made him speak the more he showed his hand. And you would listen calmly and plan your campaign. You noted his technique and controlled the game accordingly. You could study the position, and make your move. You could reflect before committing yourself – you had time, all the time in the world without worrying whether he was going to knock you about, even if he was secretly grinding his teeth and cursing you. You could create an aura of uncertainty – mystery – diffidence – whatever suited your purpose. And behind this mask you could either put on his favourite dress, which would clinch the matter, or alternatively beat a retreat with everything intact. You risk nothing, and you leave him frustrated and half out of his mind. Right up to the end you remain free, safe and victorious. Even if you get engaged it commits you to nothing, and guarantees you everything. Especially conversation. Nowadays a man doesn't even feel he has to introduce himself, and surely the least you want to know is who he is, and what he does.

[EDDIE *is carefully and quietly creeping out of the kitchen towards the left-hand door in the opposite wall.* ARTHUR *notices him at the last minute, just when he is vanishing through the other door. He goes after him.*]

ALA: Who was that?

ARTHUR [*goes back to where he was*]: No one.

ALA: I thought someone came in.

ARTHUR: We have to pack this up now. I take it you're with me?

ALA: I don't know.

ARTHUR: You mean I still haven't convinced you?

ALA: Yes.

ARTHUR: I *have* convinced you?

ALA: No ...

ARTHUR: Which?

ALA: I need time to think.

ARTHUR: What is there to think about? It couldn't be simpler. I have to rebuild the world and for that I've got to have a wedding. It seems perfectly obvious to me. What don't you understand?

ALA: All of it, I'm afraid. Wait till I –

ARTHUR: Look, I can't wait any longer. We're wasting time. Go and do your thinking and then come back and give me your answer. I'm sure you'll say yes – I've explained the whole thing.

ALA: Didn't you leave something out?

ARTHUR: Go on – off you go. See you in a bit.

ALA: You're getting rid of me?

ARTHUR: No. But I've got a personal matter to attend to.

ALA: Can't I stay and watch?

ARTHUR: No. It's family business.

ALA: All right, but just you wait – I'll have secrets of my own – one day.

ARTHUR [*becoming angry*]: For God's sake, on your way! – And remember, we meet again soon. Same place.

[*Exit* ALA *right. At once* ARTHUR *goes and listens at the door opposite and to the left. And then he goes over to the door in the corridor and knocks quietly.*]

VOICE OF STOMIL: Who is it?

ARTHUR [*not too loud*]: It's me – Arthur.

STOMIL: What do you want?

ARTHUR: I want to talk to you.

STOMIL: At this time of night? I'm busy – come back in the morning.

ARTHUR: It's urgent.

STOMIL: We can discuss it tomorrow.

[ARTHUR *tries the handle, checks that the door is locked, then flings his shoulder against it.* STOMIL *opens the door and comes out in his perpetual pyjamas.*]

Have you gone raving mad? What the hell are you doing?

ARTHUR [*in an urgent whisper*]: There's no need to shout, Father.

STOMIL [*automatically lowering his voice*]: Why aren't you asleep?

ARTHUR: I can't sleep. It's time for action.

STOMIL: Well, good night. [*Tries to go back into his room, but* ARTHUR *does not let him.*]

ARTHUR: Tell me, doesn't it make you furious?

STOMIL: What?

ARTHUR: Eddie.

STOMIL: He's all right.

ARTHUR: You think so?

STOMIL: He's quite amusing.

ARTHUR: He's disgusting.

STOMIL: Oh, you're going a bit far. Eddie's a very interesting person. Very contemporary, in some ways. He's authentic, you see.

ARTHUR: Anything else?

STOMIL: My dear boy, our trouble is we've been polluted by too much knowledge – the cursed inheritance of our age-old culture. Of course, we've done our best to get rid of it, but we're still a long way from nature. Eddie is a child of happiness. He was born the sort of person we should all like to become. What we have to attain through art, with great effort, he has received as a gift of nature. Therefore, he interests me as an artist. He is to me what a beautiful view was to a landscape painter.

ARTHUR: Some landscape.

STOMIL: Morality and aesthetics have had their day. You
keep making me repeat the obvious, Arthur. If there are
times when Eddie annoys me, it's because I've been
contaminated by too much useless knowledge. Yes. I
occasionally entertain guilty thoughts about him, but I
take a grip on myself.

ARTHUR: Otherwise everything's okay, is it?

STOMIL: I've been completely frank with you.

ARTHUR: All right. I'll start from the beginning. Why do
you tolerate him in your house?

STOMIL: Why not? He provides a bit of local colour, enrich-
es our household with a welcome breath of authenticity.
In fact he even helps me by arousing my imagination.
We artists need a touch of the exotic.

ARTHUR: Don't you know what's been going on?

STOMIL: No. No, I don't.

ARTHUR: You know very well.

STOMIL: I assure you I don't know about it and I don't
wish to know.

ARTHUR: He's sleeping with Mother.

[STOMIL *walks up and down the room.*]

Any comment?

STOMIL: My dear boy, let us suppose you're right. Sexual
liberty is one of the basic conditions of man's freedom.
So what's your answer to that?

ARTHUR: But it's true! She's sleeping with him!

STOMIL: Well, even assuming that she is, there's nothing
we can do about it.

ARTHUR: You're going on as if it was all an abstract play
of words, a sort of intellectual concept.

STOMIL: Well, why not? I'm not one of your stupid ana-
chronisms. On a purely intellectual level I am quite
prepared to discuss the most delicate and personal
matters. Otherwise we'd never get anywhere, and that

goes for the human race. So you needn't be embarrassed in front of me, we can discuss this without prudery. Now then, what's your opinion about it?

ARTHUR: I haven't got any opinion and I certainly don't intend to discuss it. This isn't a game of intellectual ping-pong – this is life. Do you understand? – You're a cuckold! Your horns reach from here to the ceiling. You can't get away from *that*.

STOMIL: Horns, horns … that's a ridiculous figure of speech, it has no validity in rational dialectic. [*Becoming angry*] We must not lower our standards!

ARTHUR: Cuckold!

STOMIL: Shut up! How dare you talk to me like that?

ARTHUR: Cuckold!

STOMIL: Anyway, I don't believe it.

ARTHUR: Aha! That's what I was waiting for. You want proof? You can have it. Just open that door. [*Points to door facing the audience on the left.*]

STOMIL: No!

ARTHUR: Scared? Oh yes, when it comes to theoretical experiments you're a giant, aren't you? You're all right on theory. But in life you're a pathetic, dominated, impotent old pigmy!

STOMIL: Old? *Me*? I'll show you! – I'll show them all! Where are they? – I'll show them. [*Runs to the door, stops.*] Yes … I think I'll show them all, tomorrow. [*Starts to walk back.*]

ARTHUR [*stands in his way*]: No. Now.

STOMIL: Tomorrow. Yes, perhaps I'll write him a letter. What do you think?

ARTHUR: You cardboard dummy!

STOMIL: How dare you – [ARTHUR *puts two fingers on his head, making them look like horns.*] All right – if that's the way you want it.

ARTHUR [*holding him back*]: Wait –

138

STOMIL [*belligerently*]: Let me get at them!

ARTHUR: Just one thing – take this with you.

[*He takes the revolver which* STOMIL *had thrown on to the catafalque during the first act and hands it to* STOMIL.]

STOMIL: What's this?

ARTHUR: You don't want to go in there empty-handed ...
[*Pause.*]

STOMIL [*quietly*]: So that's it.

ARTHUR [*pushing him towards the door*]: Quick – there's no time to waste – Get in there.

STOMIL [*freeing himself*]: I see your game. It's tragedy you want.

ARTHUR: Tragedy? – Now look, Father ...

STOMIL: You miserable little swine – you adolescent worm –

ARTHUR: What's the – ?

STOMIL [*throws the revolver on to the table*]: You want me to shoot him, do you? And then her and then myself, I suppose?

ARTHUR: No, of course not – I was only kidding – On the other hand, if Eddie were to – you know ... I mean, he's capable of anything.

STOMIL: That would suit you down to the ground. The betrayed husband washes away his shame in blood. From what romantic novel did you get hold of that?

ARTHUR: That's not fair –

STOMIL: I know young people value ideas more than human life, but I didn't know my own son would sacrifice his father for them. Siddown! [ARTHUR *sits obediently.*] Now let's talk sense. You want to bring the world back to normal – don't ask me why, that's your business and I've had my fill of it. I have never interfered before but this time you've gone too far. Oh yes – what a splendid idea! – a tragic resolution – that's just what you needed. Up to now tragedy has always been the final throw of societies based on rigid ideas. So you thought you'd push me into a tragic act. That would save a lot of messing about, wouldn't it? – no need for laborious reconstruction – you'd have got it made. And if someone happens to die in the process, or your father goes to gaol, if not worse, that's of no concern as long as you gain your end. A tragedy would suit you fine, wouldn't it? You know what you are? – you're just a dirty little formalist. You don't give a damn about me, or your mother. They can all drop dead so long as the form is preserved. And worst of all you don't even care about yourself. You're a fanatic!

ARTHUR: What makes you so sure that form is the only thing I'm after?

STOMIL: Why? – you don't like Eddie?

ARTHUR: I hate him.

STOMIL: What for? Eddie is simplicity and truth – he is the basic essential which we've been seeking for so long in all the wrong places because we didn't know what we were looking for. I'm afraid Eddie is a fact, and you can't hate something which is elemental. You should love it.

ARTHUR: So I should give him a kiss? Thanks, I'll make my own essentials.

STOMIL: Oh dear – you will keep talking like a sulky child – 'Don't like it! Don't like it!' Well if that's all there is to it, the answer's obvious – you've got an Oedipus complex!

ARTHUR: No. I admit Mother's a bit of all right but I don't *fancy* her.

STOMIL: Pity. I mean, that would have been a theory. And it's better than being a lunatic. Anyway, you're certainly a formalist.

ARTHUR: I'm not.

STOMIL: Yes you are. A pathetic and dangerous one.

ARTHUR: Maybe that's the way it looks, but it's simply that I can't go on. I can't live the way you do.

STOMIL: Tell you what – let's suppose. Let's suppose you're an egoist.

ARTHUR: Call me what you like. I have to do it.

STOMIL: So what do you get out of sacrificing me?

ARTHUR: Something would be achieved. Tragically, it's true. You're right there, Father, and I'm sorry. Nevertheless, tragedy is a great and powerful convention, reality would be trapped within it.

STOMIL: You fool – is that what you think? Don't you see that nowadays tragedy isn't possible any more? Reality is stronger than any convention, even tragedy. Do you know what you'd have got if I'd shot him?

ARTHUR: Something irrevocable, something on the scale of the old masters.

STOMIL: Not at all. A farce, that's what. Today farce is the only thing possible. A corpse is no help at all. Why not accept this? – Farce can still be fine art.

ARTHUR: Not for me.

STOMIL: You're stubborn.

ARTHUR: I can't help that. I have to find a way.

STOMIL: Despite reality?

ARTHUR: At any price.

STOMIL: Tricky business. I'd like to help you but I don't see how I can.

ARTHUR: Why don't we try it anyway?

STOMIL: Try what?

ARTHUR [*points to door in opposite wall, left*]: That.

STOMIL: Still on about the need for action?

ARTHUR: Well even if it's true about farce . . . [*Resuming his old aggressiveness*] it's because you're all cowards. You're all griping about being trapped by farce, because no one's got the guts to do anything about it. You don't like it? – so why don't you free yourselves by force? You've explained it all so pat – analytically, logically, abstractly

and I don't know what else, and you think that's the end
of it. We can all go home and nothing has changed.
You've gone a long way, Father, but how? By sitting
around nattering. Action is what you need! Tragedy
doesn't exist because you don't believe in it – and that's
because of your damned everlasting compromises.

STOMIL: Well, why should I believe in it anyway? So
Eleonora's sleeping with Eddie. What's wrong with that?

ARTHUR: You don't know?

STOMIL: I promise you. When I give it my serious consideration I find that I simply don't know. You tell me.

ARTHUR: Me? I've never been in that situation.

STOMIL: Try and imagine it.

ARTHUR: How can I . . .? Give me a minute.

STOMIL: Go on, think. I'd be so glad if you could convince
me.

ARTHUR: Would you?

STOMIL: Because quite frankly I don't like it any more than
you do. I dislike it intensely. The trouble is, rationally
speaking, I don't know why.

ARTHUR: So if I was able to convince you . . .

STOMIL: I'd be extremely grateful.

ARTHUR: Then I suggest . . .

STOMIL: You suggest that I go and give them a shock
they'll remember for the rest of their lives. Fine. If only
there was one logical reason why I should.

ARTHUR: You'd do it? You mean deep inside you you
really want to?

STOMIL: I'd love to – nothing would give me greater
pleasure. I've had my eye on that so-and-so for some
time. I'd be delighted to finish him off. Just give me a
logical reason.

ARTHUR: Father! Embrace me! [*They embrace.*] To hell
with reason!

STOMIL: That's all very well but what can I do when

reason won't let me act? You mentioned compromise – that's all on account of reason.

ARTHUR: Why not go ahead anyway? There's no risk. The worst that can happen is you'll shoot him.

STOMIL: You think so? I'm not so sure ...

ARTHUR: Confidence will come later – the important thing is to make the decision.

STOMIL: Maybe you're right.

ARTHUR: Of course I'm right. You'll see – we'll have our tragedy!

STOMIL: You're giving me fresh hope – The enthusiasm of youth – ah, youth, youth ...

ARTHUR: Ready?

STOMIL: Ready! Being with you puts new spirit into me. [*They get up.*]

ARTHUR: One more thing. Please, Father, lay off those experiments of yours, they only add to the chaos.

STOMIL: What else have I got? When tragedy's impossible and farce is a bore, the only thing left is experiment.

ARTHUR: But they just make it worse. Will you give them up?

STOMIL: Oh, I don't know about that ...

ARTHUR: Promise me, please.

STOMIL: Not now – it's time we got moving.

[*Once again* ARTHUR *hands* STOMIL *the revolver.*]

ARTHUR: I'll wait outside the door. If you need help, shout.

STOMIL: Don't worry, he's the one who'll be doing the shouting.

ARTHUR: I always knew I could count on you!

STOMIL: And you were right. I was the best shot in the regiment. Farewell.

[*He walks towards the door in the wall opposite on the right.*]

ARTHUR: No, not in there. That's the kitchen.

STOMIL [*undecided*]: I'm thirsty.

ARTHUR: Later – when it's all over. No time for that now.

STOMIL: Very well. I'll shoot him with a dry throat.

[*Walks across to the door on the left and puts his hand on the handle.*]

The lout! – He's going to pay for this!

[*Walks carefully into room, closing the door quietly behind him.* ARTHUR *waits in tense anticipation. Unbroken silence.* ARTHUR *walks up and down nervously. As the waiting continues,* ARTHUR *looks at his watch and walks faster and faster. Finally he decides. He dashes in and flings both wings of the door wide open, so that the whole interior of the room can be seen. The following picture presents itself: under a low-hung lamp which is throwing a strong light on the round table, sit* ELEONORA, EDDIE, EUGENIA *and* STOMIL, *playing cards.* STOMIL *is in the process of playing a card.*]

ARTHUR: Eddie! What the hell are you doing? You're supposed to be ...

STOMIL: Ssssh! Just a second, my boy!

ELEONORA: Arthur! Why aren't you asleep?

EUGENIA: I told you he'd be on to us – you can't hide anything from him.

ARTHUR: Father ... you're ... with them ...

STOMIL: I'm frightfully sorry, it was just the way things turned out. It wasn't my fault.

ELEONORA: Stomil turned up just in time. We needed a fourth.

ARTHUR: How could you?

STOMIL: I told you it would end in farce.

EDDIE: Your go, Mr Stomil – sir.

STOMIL [*to* ARTHUR]: It's a harmless enough game. You can see what happened.

ARTHUR: You promised.

STOMIL: I promised nothing. We must bide our time.

ELEONORA: Stomil, concentrate.

ARTHUR: I've never been so humiliated.

EUGENIA [*throwing down her cards*]: I will not play under

these conditions. Will someone take that young pup out of this room?

EDDIE: Don't pay him any mind, Gran.

ELEONORA: You ought to be ashamed, upsetting your granny like that.

EUGENIA: I said we should have kept the door locked. He always wants to make a scene – I suppose it's back on the catafalque for me now.

ELEONORA: Certainly not. Not till we've finished.

ARTHUR [*banging his fist on the table*]: That's enough!

ELEONORA: We've only just begun.

EDDIE: Your mum's right, Mr Arthur. The score cards haven't been touched.

ARTHUR [*snatches away their cards*]: Now you're all going to listen to *me*! I have something to say – right now!

STOMIL: Arthur. It's a private matter, you don't have to broadcast it.

ARTHUR: With your permission or without it, the game's at an end!

ELEONORA: What on earth are you – ?

EDDIE: Very nice, I must say, v-e-ery nice! If I was your dad I'd give you a good hiding.

ARTHUR: You have the audacity to answer back? I see. [*Quietly and firmly*] Father, give me the revolver.

EDDIE: I was only kidding.

ELEONORA: Revolver? For God's sake, Stomil, don't you give him any revolver. You're his father – *you* tell *him* what to do.

STOMIL [*trying to sound strict*]: Listen to me, Arthur, you're not a child any more and I'm sorry to have to be firm with you, but for your mother's sake . . .

[ARTHUR *takes the revolver out of* STOMIL's *pyjama pocket. Everyone leaps up from the table.*]

EUGENIA: The boy's a lunatic – Stomil, I consider it highly irresponsible of you to beget him!

STOMIL: You know how things happen.

EDDIE: Mr Arthur, sir, why do you ...?

ARTHUR: Shut up! Everyone into the drawing-room!

[*The assembled company file out one by one into the middle of the stage.* ARTHUR *lets them all walk past him. To his father as he comes alongside:*]

I'll talk to you later.

STOMIL: What's the matter? I did my best.

ARTHUR: I know what that was!

[EUGENE *sits on the sofa,* ELEONORA *in the armchair.* EDDIE *stands in a corner. He takes a comb out of his hip pocket and combs his hair nervously.*]

STOMIL [*standing in front of* ELEONORA, *spreads his arms helplessly*]: I was trying to calm him down. You heard me, didn't you?

ELEONORA: You spineless lump! And you're his father. I wish I were a man.

STOMIL: Talking isn't going to turn you into one.

[EUGENE *runs in.*]

EUGENE: Are we off?

ARTHUR: Not yet. I'm still waiting for an answer.

EUGENE: I thought you had it all set up. I heard shouting so I came as fast as I could.

ARTHUR: That's all right, Uncle. I'm glad you came. Stay here and look after them. I'll be back in a second. [*Hands him the revolver.*]

EUGENE: Yes, sir.

ELEONORA: Am I dreaming?

ARTHUR [*to* EUGENE]: And see that no one moves!

EUGENE: Yes, sir.

ELEONORA: Have you both gone mad?

ARTHUR: If they try anything, shoot them through the head. Right?

EUGENE: Yes, sir.

ELEONORA: It's a conspiracy! Mummy, your brother's a gangster!

EUGENIA: Put it down this instant, Eugene. Fancy playing cowboys and Indians at your age! [*Tries to get up.*]

EUGENE: Stay where you are!

EUGENIA [*surprised*]: Eugene, it's me, your sister Eugenia.

EUGENE: I have no sisters when I'm on duty.

EUGENIA: What duty is that?

EUGENE: Ideological duty.

ARTHUR: Very good, Uncle. I see I can trust you. Shan't be a minute.

STOMIL: Speak to me, Arthur. We're friends, aren't we?

ARTHUR: All in good time.

> [*Exit* ARTHUR. EUGENE *sits down in the centre of the stage, near the wall, excitedly grasping the revolver. He aims it at each of the others in turn, not very expertly, but threateningly.*]

ELEONORA [*after a pause*]: I see. . . . So you've betrayed us, Eugene.

EUGENE: Silence! [*After a moment, defensively*] It's not true. I haven't betrayed anybody.

ARTHUR [*calling off stage*]: Ala! Ala!

ELEONORA: You've betrayed your generation.

EUGENE: It's you who are the traitors. You betrayed our glorious past. I'm the only one who's stayed true to it.

ARTHUR: Ala! Ala!

ELEONORA: You're a dogsbody to a lot of evangelical madmen. You think it'll do you any good? They'll use you then kick you out.

EUGENE: Don't be too sure who's the dogsbody.

ELEONORA: We've got your number now, you hypocrite. You've been covering up your true colours, haven't you?

EUGENE: Yes, I've been covering up. For years and years I suffered. I hated you for your dissipation and your decadence and I said nothing. You had the whip hand. But now at last the time has come when I can tell you face to face, and you just don't know what a pleasure that is.

ELEONORA: What are you going to do with us?

EUGENE: We're going to bring back some dignity to this rotten world. We'll give you back some principles.

ELEONORA: By force?

EUGENE: If we have to.

STOMIL: This is counter-reformation.

EUGENE: This is salvation.

STOMIL: Salvation? From what?

EUGENE: From your damn freedom.

ARTHUR [enters]: Uncle Eugene.

EUGENE: All present and correct, sir.

ARTHUR: I can't find her.

EUGENE: Have another look. She must be somewhere.

ARTHUR: I know. I'm waiting for her answer.

EUGENE: What? You mean she hasn't accepted yet?

ARTHUR: She'll have to accept. She can't let me down, not at the critical moment. Everything's ready.

EUGENE: Arthur, I don't want to criticize, but haven't you been a bit hasty? You should have made certain first and *then* got them together. [*Points his revolver at them.*]

ARTHUR: The time was right. I couldn't delay any longer.

EUGENE: It's always the same with revolutions. Unforeseen circumstances. We can't go back now.

ARTHUR: How was I to know? I was sure I'd convinced her. [*Shouts*] Ala! Ala! [*Angrily*] And all because of one stupid little cousin. . . . It's not possible. [*Shouts*] Ala! Ala!

EUGENE: Women have caused empires to fall . . .

ALA [enters]: My God! Aren't you asleep yet?

ARTHUR [accusingly]: At last! — I've been looking all over the house for you.

ALA: Good grief — Uncle with a gun? Is it real?

ARTHUR: Where the devil were you?

ALA: I went for a walk. Aren't I allowed to?

EUGENE: No, you're not. This is a sacred task!

ARTHUR: All right, Uncle — back to the ranks. [*To* ALA] What about it, then?

ALA: Nothing. It's a beautiful night.

ARTHUR: I'm not talking about the weather. I want to know if you accept.

ALA: I need longer to think.

ARTHUR: You've had long enough. Yes or no?

ALA: Yes.

EUGENE: Hurrah!

ARTHUR: Praise be to God. And now to business.
   [*Takes* ALA *by the hand and leads her to the sofa where* EUGENIA *is sitting.*]
   Grandmama, we ask for your blessing ...

EUGENIA [*terrified, leaps off the sofa*]: Leave me alone! I'm not doing any harm!

ARTHUR: That's all over now, Grandma. I'm going to marry Ala. You must give us your blessing and wish us a long and happy life.

EUGENE [*to the others*]: Stand up, all of you! Can't you see this is a beautiful moment?

ELEONORA: My God! Arthur's going to be married!

STOMIL: Why all the fuss?

EUGENIA: Take him away! — He's upsetting me again!

ARTHUR [*threateningly*]: Your blessing, Grandma!

STOMIL: This joke is in very bad taste. We've had quite enough of it.

EUGENE [*triumphantly*]: The joking's over! For fifty years you've been joking, Stomil, now do your buttons up! This is your son's betrothal — enough of undone buttons! Geenie, the blessing!

EUGENIA: What shall I do, Eleonora?

ELEONORA: Bless them, if that's what they want.

EUGENIA: Must I? It makes me feel so old-fash—

EUGENE: It's a betrothal – just like in the good old days! So get in there and bless or I shoot. I'll count to three. One ...

STOMIL: It's disgraceful. Can't a man dress the way he wants to in his own house ... [*Tries to adjust his pyjamas.*]

EUGENE: Twoo ...

EUGENIA [*places her hands on the heads of* ALA *and* ARTHUR]: Bless you, my children ... and now the devil take the lot of you.

EUGENE [*in great emotion*]: That's it! That's just the way it was!

ARTHUR [*stands up and kisses* EUGENIA *on the hands*]: Thank you, Grandmother.

EUGENE: And Stomil has done up his pyjamas! The new age has begun.

STOMIL: What are you crying about, Eleonora?

ELEONORA [*greatly moved, sobbing*]: I'm sorry ... but ... Arthur's betrothal ... whatever you say, he is our son ... I know I'm being old-fashioned but it's so moving ... I'm sorry!

STOMIL: Do what you like. I'm having nothing to do with it. [*Runs out and into his room, very angry.*]

EDDIE: Ladies and gentlemen! I should like to express my heartfelt congratulations on the occasion of this happy event, et cetera ... [*Offers* ARTHUR *his hand.*]

ARTHUR [*does not take his hand*]: Get into the kitchen, and stay there till I call you!

EUGENE [*imitating* ARTHUR]: Get into the kitchen!
[*He points pompously at the kitchen door.* EDDIE *walks out phlegmatically.*]

ELEONORA [*through her tears*]: When's the wedding?

ARTHUR: Tomorrow.

EUGENE: Hurrah! We've won!

CURTAIN

# ACT THREE

*Daylight. The same apartment, but not a trace of the former chaos and disorder. We see before us a classical middle-class living-room of fifty years ago. There is no more blur or lack of contour. The draperies which previously covered the stage – half hanging and half lying – looking like a set of rumpled bedclothes are now in their proper places and look like good ordinary draperies. The catafalque is there, as always, but it is covered with a cloth and a number of ornaments, like a sideboard. The recess is uncovered.*

*On stage is a group of people:* ELEONORA, STOMIL *and* EUGENE. EUGENIA *is sitting on the sofa which has been moved into the middle of the stage. She is wearing a long dark-grey or dark-brown dress, buttoned high under the neck, with lace sleeves and a lace frill. On her head is a bonnet. She is holding a pair of lorgnettes, which she makes use of frequently. On her right sits* ELEONORA, *her hair done in a chignon, wearing earrings and a long dress, taken in sharply at the waist, striped in lily-and-blue or violet-and-crimson, or something like that. Both of them sit motionless, their hands laid on their knees. Beside them stands* STOMIL, *his hair sleeked down and parted in the middle, his head pointing stiffly upwards, his eyes looking into the undefined distance. There is in fact no other way he could hold his head, since there is a fantastically high wing-collar holding his chin up.* STOMIL *is wearing a sandy-brown suit that is obviously very tight, and a pair of white spats. One arm rests on a round table, on which is a vase of flowers; the other arm is on his hip. One leg is straight while the other is bent at the knee with the tip of the shoe resting nonchalantly on the floor. In front of them, right at the front of the stage, there is a large box-camera on a stand covered with a piece of black velvet. Near the camera stands* EUGENE. *He is wearing a swallow-tail coat as before, but instead of khaki shorts a pair of check trousers. A red carnation is in his buttonhole. On the floor are his top hat, white gloves and a silver-knobbed stick.* EUGENE *is fiddling around with the apparatus while the rest pose intently. After a moment's silence, a loud crescendo: 'Aaaa . . . aaa . . .' comes from* EUGENIA, *followed by an enormous sneeze.*

EUGENE: Don't move!

EUGENIA: I'm sorry, I can't do anything about it. Mothballs.

EUGENE: Now pay attention!
  [STOMIL *takes his hand off his hip and starts scratching his chest.*]
  Your hand, Stomil!

STOMIL: I've got the most frightful itch.

ELEONORA: What itch?

STOMIL: Moths.

ELEONORA: There's one! [*Jumps up and runs to and fro about the stage chasing unseen moths and clapping her hands.*]

EUGENE: Come on, we'll never get a photograph if we go on like this. Sit down, Eleonora!

ELEONORA [*complainingly*]: Mother's got moths.

EUGENIA: It's not me, it's the clothes.

EUGENE: Stop arguing. The moths came down from the attic.
  [EDDIE *enters dressed as a butler. A bright red-striped waistcoat and black trousers.*]

EDDIE: Did you call, Madam?

ELEONORA [*stops clapping*]: What's that? No . . . or rather, yes. Would you bring me the salts, Edward.

EDDIE: I beg your pardon, Madam . . . the salts?

ELEONORA: Yes, the salts . . . you know . . .

EDDIE: Very good, Madam. [*Exits.*]

STOMIL [*watching him walk out*]: It's good to see that man in his proper place.

EUGENE: Do you think so? Well hang on because there's more to come. You won't regret it. Things are going to get better and better.

STOMIL [*trying to loosen his collar*]: If only this collar wasn't so tight.

EUGENE: But Eddie waits at your table now. You can't have everything.

STOMIL: What's going to happen about my experiments?

EUGENE: I don't know. Arthur hasn't issued any instructions yet.

STOMIL: You did mention the matter to him?

EUGENE: I didn't have a chance. He went out at the crack of dawn.

STOMIL: You will put in a word for me, won't you, Uncle?

EUGENE [*protectively*]: I'll get round to it.

STOMIL: I suggest once a week. You must understand, it's not easy to adapt oneself to all this after so many years.

EUGENE: It depends on how you behave.

STOMIL: I'm on your side, you know. I've co-operated all along the line. I'm even wearing this damn collar. [*Tries again to loosen his collar.*]

EUGENE: I can't promise anything.

[*Enter* EDDIE *carrying a tray on which is an unmistakable bottle of vodka.*]

What's that?

EDDIE: The salts for Madam, sir.

EUGENE [*threateningly*]: Eleonora, what's the meaning of this?

ELEONORA: I don't know. [*To* EDDIE] I asked for my *salts*.

EDDIE: You will not be requiring the drinks, Madam?

ELEONORA: Take it away at once!

EUGENIA: Why should he when he's brought it all this way.... I feel a little faint myself ...

EDDIE: Very good, Madam.

[*Exit. On his way out, unnoticed by anyone except* EUGENIA, *who is following him with a long yearning look, he takes a swig from the bottle.*]

EUGENE: I hope there'll be no repetition of that.

EUGENIA: Oh my God, how boring!

EUGENE: Back to your places!

[ELEONORA, STOMIL *and* EUGENIA *resume the stiff positions they held at the beginning of the scene.* EUGENE *goes under the velvet cover and we hear the hiss of the delayed action shutter release.* EUGENE *quickly picks up his top hat, stick and gloves and sits down on the sofa next to* EUGENIA, *posing exactly like the others. The hiss stops. Everyone relaxes with relief.*]

STOMIL: Can I loosen it now – just for a minute?

EUGENE: Out of the question. The wedding isn't till twelve o'clock.

STOMIL: I must have put on weight. . . . I haven't worn this suit for forty years.

EUGENE: Your experiments have fattened you up, Stomil – the avant-garde is pretty lucrative nowadays.

STOMIL: That's no fault of mine.

ELEONORA: When will the photograph be ready? I think I blinked – I'm sure I won't come out.

EUGENE: Not to worry – the camera doesn't work. It hasn't worked for years.

ELEONORA: What! What was the point of all that, then?

EUGENE: It's the custom. It's traditional.

STOMIL: You criticize me for my harmless little experiments, but what makes you think your broken-down old camera's any better? That sums up the whole fiasco of your counter-revolution. You destroy what I have achieved and you've got nothing to put in its place.

EUGENE: Watch what you say.

STOMIL: I'll say it as often as I like; even though you've got me in your power.

ELEONORA: What do you say to that?

EUGENIA: We must look a fine sight, I must say. And this is only the beginning.

EUGENE: Too bad. Right now we have to concentrate on form. Content comes later.

STOMIL: I've got a feeling, Eugene, that you've made a mess of the whole thing. Formalism won't free us from chaos. We'd do better to come to terms with the spirit of the times.

EUGENE: That'll do! – No defeatism!

STOMIL: All right, suit yourself. I take it I'm allowed to have my private opinions.

EUGENE: By all means. Provided that they're the same as ours of course.

ELEONORA: Listen!

[*Sound of far-off bells.*]

STOMIL: Bells ...

EUGENE: Wedding bells ...

[*Enter* ALA *in a wedding dress and veil.* STOMIL *kisses her hand charmingly.*]

STOMIL: Aha ... and here's our little one.

ELEONORA: Oh, your dress is so beautiful ...

EUGENIA: Welcome, my child.

ALA: Isn't Arthur back yet?

EUGENE: We're expecting him any moment. He's gone to settle all the last-minute formalities.

ALA: He's got formalities on the brain.

EUGENE: Genius can't go round naked – it must be clothed and presented right. Didn't Arthur talk to you about that?

ALA: Non-stop.

EUGENE: And he was right. One day you'll understand and be grateful.

ALA: Do stop being idiotic, Uncle.

ELEONORA: Ala, you mustn't be so rude. This is your wedding day, and we don't want to spoil it with family squabbles. Time enough for that later.

EUGENE: That's quite all right, I don't mind. I'm an understanding man.

ALA: So old and yet so stupid. With Arthur it's not so surprising, but you, Uncle ...

ELEONORA: Ala!

STOMIL: You've got trouble, Uncle.

ELEONORA: Forgive her, Eugene, she's upset. She doesn't know what she's saying. Whichever way you look at it, it's an unsettling experience for her. I remember when I had to marry Stomil ...

EUGENE: I think perhaps I shall leave the room. Only don't think you're making a fool of me, I know why you're all smirking. But childish insults won't change a thing. Stomil, you come with me. I have a proposition to make to you.

STOMIL: All right, so long as you don't preach at me. And bear in mind that I've got the vote.

[*They leave.*]

ELEONORA: You might as well go too, Mother.

EUGENIA: Suits me. This place bores me to death. [*Exit.*]

ELEONORA: Now we can talk. What's the matter, Ala?

ALA: Nothing.

ELEONORA: I can see something's worrying you.

ALA: Nothing's worrying me. I don't like this veil, I want to take it off. Will you help me, please?

ELEONORA: Of course. . . . But you don't have to take that attitude with me, Ala – I'm not like them – they're silly.

[ALA *sits in front of the mirror. Bells still ringing.*]

ALA: Why do you all despise each other?

ELEONORA: I don't know. Perhaps because there's nothing to respect.

ALA: Do you mean in yourself or the others?

ELEONORA: What's the difference ...? Shall I do your hair for you?

ALA: It'll all have to be re-done.

[*Takes off her veil.* ELEONORA *does* ALA's *hair.*]
Are you happy ...?

ELEONORA: What do you mean?

ALA: Are you happy? Don't look so surprised.

ELEONORA: It's a rather indiscreet question.

ALA: Why? Should you be ashamed of being happy?

ELEONORA: No, I don't think so, it's not that.

ALA: Oh – you mean you're not happy. That's what you're ashamed of ... everyone's ashamed of not being happy. It's like not doing your job or having spots.

ELEONORA: To be happy is the right and duty of all free people in this new enlightened age. Stomil taught me that.

ALA: No wonder everyone feels so ashamed. What do you really think?

ELEONORA: I did my bit.

ALA: For him?

ELEONORA: For myself. I did what he told me to do.

ALA: You mean for his sake?

ELEONORA: Of course. If you'd known him when he was young ...

ALA: Can you do the other side, now, please. [*Pause.*] Does he know about it?

ELEONORA: About what?

ALA: Oh, come on – I'm a big girl now. About Eddie.

ELEONORA: Of course he knows.

ALA: So what does he do about it?

ELEONORA: Unfortunately, nothing. He pretends he doesn't notice.

ALA: Fatal.

[*Enter* EDDIE *with a white table-cloth.*]

EDDIE: May I lay the table, Madam?

ELEONORA: Do what you like, Eddie. [*Corrects herself.*] Er, yes, Edward, lay the table.

EDDIE: Very good, Madam. [*Covers the table with the table-cloth and walks out, taking the camera with him.*]

ALA: What do you see in him?

ELEONORA: Oh, but Eddie's so basic ... like life itself. He's a savage, that's what I like about him. He hasn't got any complexes – he's such a relief. His desires are so real – beautiful to watch. When he eats or drinks, his stomach becomes a symphony of nature. I like watching him eat – honestly I do. It gives me a luxurious feeling of rapport with everything that's elemental. Have you ever seen him adjust his trousers – the charming way he does it – there's something almost regal about it. I appreciate the authentic just as Stomil does.

ALA: Obviously. I must say it doesn't fascinate me.

ELEONORA: Because you're too young. You haven't discovered the richness of true simplicity. But you will. It's a question of experience.

ALA: Well, I'll try. Tell me . . . do you think I'm doing the right thing, marrying Arthur?

ELEONORA: Oh, Arthur's quite different. Arthur has principles.

ALA: Stomil has principles too. You said so yourself – about our right and duty to be happy.

ELEONORA: No, those were opinions. Stomil has always been against principles. That's why Arthur's are so strong.

ALA: Yes, like a brick wall.

ELEONORA: Why, Ala, what's the matter? Arthur's the first man to have principles for fifty years. Isn't that marvellous? That's what makes him unique. And he looks the part, too.

ALA: Do you think I should settle for principles?

ELEONORA: They're a bit old-fashioned, I agree. But that's why they're so remarkable.

ALA: I want Arthur even with his principles, if I can't have him without them. But I don't want principles without Arthur.

ELEONORA: Didn't he propose to you? He's going to marry you, isn't he?

ALA: That's not him, that's just his iron principles.

ELEONORA: Then why did you accept?

ALA: Because I live in hope.

ELEONORA: Fatal.

[*Enter* EDDIE *carrying a pile of plates.*]

EDDIE: May I carry on, Madam?

ALA: Please yourself, Eddie. [*Corrects herself.*] Er, yes, Edward, get on with it – that is, carry on.

ELEONORA: Eddie, you aren't upset, are you, about the changes? It was their idea.

EDDIE: Ech, what difference does it make?

ELEONORA: Didn't I tell you? That's Eddie – free and natural as a butterfly. Eddie, you lay the table beautifully.

EDDIE: Thank you, Madam.

ALA: Eddie, come here a minute.

EDDIE: Yes, miss? [*Approaches her. Bells gradually fall silent.*]

ALA: Tell me, Eddie, do you have principles?

EDDIE: I might have.

ALA: What are they?

EDDIE: I've got some of the best principles going.

ALA: Will you tell us?

EDDIE: What's in it for me?

ALA: Will you or won't you?

EDDIE: All right then. [*Puts the pile of plates on the ground and takes a small notebook out of his pocket.*] I've got them written down. [*Turns over the pages.*] Here we are. [*Reads*] 'My love is dead to the world.'

ALA: What else?

EDDIE: No comment.

ALA: Stop messing about – read.

EDDIE: I *was* reading – that's a principle.

ALA: Oh. Go on, then. [EDDIE *giggles.*] What's so funny?

EDDIE: There's one here ...

ALA: Well, read it out.

EDDIE: Oh, I couldn't do that in front of a lady, miss – it's too saucy for that.

ALA: And those are your principles?

EDDIE: Oh no, miss, I copied them down from a friend who works in the cinema, well, he works in *a* cinema.

ALA: You didn't think up any of them by yourself?

EDDIE [*proudly*]: Not one of them.

ALA: Why not?

EDDIE: There are some things a man *knows*.

ELEONORA: Yes, Eddie, and you know them!

[*Enter* STOMIL, *followed by* EUGENE *who is carrying a laced corset.* EDDIE *goes back to laying the table.*]

STOMIL: No, I won't. This is too much!

EUGENE: You'll get used to it – you have my word.

ELEONORA: What are you up to now?

STOMIL [*escaping from* EUGENE]: He wants me to put that on.

ELEONORA: What is it?

EUGENE: Great-grandpa's corsets. Absolutely essential. It laces up at the waist and ensures a perfect figure for every occasion.

STOMIL: To hell with it! I'm already loaded with spats and this damn collar. Are you trying to kill me?

EUGENE: You might as well go the whole hog.

STOMIL: You might as well go to hell – I want to live!

EUGENE: Ancient prejudices! Come on now, Stomil, stop fooling around. You said yourself you're getting fat.

STOMIL: I want to be fat! Life according to nature!

EUGENE: You mean life according to convenience. You'd better come quietly, there's no way out.

STOMIL: Nora, protect me!

ELEONORA: Maybe it *would* improve your figure.

STOMIL: So what? I'm an artist – fat and free.

[*Runs off into his room.* EUGENE *follows him. The door closes behind them.*]

ELEONORA: Never a dull moment. So you live in hope, do you?

ALA: Yes.

ELEONORA: And suppose you're wrong?

ALA: What difference does it make?

ELEONORA [*trying to embrace her*]: My poor dear ...

ALA [*freeing herself*]: Don't start feeling sorry for me, please. It's my own decision.

ELEONORA: What's going to happen if it doesn't work out?

ALA: I'm not telling.

ELEONORA: You won't even tell me?

ALA: It's a surprise.

VOICE OF STOMIL: Help! Help!

ELEONORA: That's Stomil.

ALA: Uncle Eugene's been getting bossier and bossier. Do you think he has any influence over Arthur?

VOICE OF STOMIL: Let me go!

ELEONORA: I don't think so. More like the other way round.

ALA: Pity. I thought it might be *his* doing.

VOICE OF STOMIL: Get away!

ELEONORA: I'd better go and see what's going on – I don't like the sound of it.

ALA: Nor me.

VOICE OF STOMIL: Stop it! – You're killing me!

ELEONORA: Dear God, whatever next ...

VOICE OF STOMIL: No – I'm splitting open! Help!

ELEONORA: Really, Eugene does overdo it. And you watch your step too, Ala.

ALA: Why?

ELEONORA: Because you could be going too far. Like Uncle Eugene. [*She goes out into Stomil's room.*]

ALA: Eddie, the veil!

[EDDIE *gives her the veil and stands behind her. From Stomil's room we can hear loud unarticulated cries and the sound of a struggle. Enter* ARTHUR. ALA *and* EDDIE *do*

*not notice him because the mirror is so placed that the reflections
of people entering from the right wing cannot be seen. He is
wearing an overcoat open at the front and rather faded. His
movements are soft and unnaturally slow — bearing witness to
the great effort that is being put into them. He carefully takes
off his coat and throws it away somewhere. He sits down in the
armchair, stretching his legs out in front of him.*]

VOICE OF STOMIL: Damn you!

ARTHUR [*in a quiet weary voice*]: What's going on in there?

[ALA *turns round.* EDDIE *obediently picks up* ARTHUR's
*coat and leaves the room.*]

ALA [*in a tone of authority*]: You're late!

[ARTHUR *gets up and opens the door to Stomil's room.*]

ARTHUR: Let him go.

[*Enter* STOMIL, EUGENE, *and* ELEONORA *at the back.*]

EUGENE: Why? That was our finest hour.

ARTHUR: I said let him go.

STOMIL: Thank you, Arthur. You still have a spark of
humanity.

EUGENE: I protest.

[ARTHUR *grabs him by the tie and pushes him forward.*]

ELEONORA: Arthur, what's wrong with you? — He's so
pale.

ARTHUR: You whited sepulchre ...

EUGENE: Arthur, it's me — your Uncle Eugene. Don't you
recognize me? It's you and me — together into the new
life, redeeming the world — don't you remember? You're
strangling me — it's me — it's you and me — you're
strangling —

ARTHUR [*pushing him back step by step*]: You bulging bag of
hot air, you set of synthetic tripes, you rotten pair of
false teeth ...

ELEONORA: Do something! — He's throttling him!

ARTHUR: You swindler ...

[*Suddenly Mendelssohn's 'Wedding March' blares out loud*

*and triumphant, played by a full orchestra.* ARTHUR *lets* EUGENE *go, takes the carafe from the table and throws it into the wings, where the carafe shatters with a loud crash. The march breaks off in mid-beat.* ARTHUR *falls into the armchair, exhausted.*]

EDDIE [*enters*]: Do you want me to change the record?

ELEONORA: Who told you to put that on?

EDDIE: Mister Eugene. He said to put it on as soon as Mister Arthur arrived.

EUGENE [*getting his breath back*]: That's right ... I instructed him to ...

ELEONORA: No music for the moment, Edward.

EDDIE: Very good, madam. [*Exit.*]

ARTHUR: It's a swindle. It's all a swindle ... [*Falls into deep contemplation.*]

STOMIL [*leaning over him*]: He's completely drunk.

EUGENE: Say that again, you impudent liar! This young man knows where his duty lies.

ELEONORA: I don't believe it either. Arthur never drinks.

STOMIL: I'm not so sure.

ELEONORA: But why today?

STOMIL: He's had a bachelor party.

[ALA *pours some water into a glass and gives it to* ARTHUR.]

EUGENE: There's some misunderstanding, we mustn't jump to premature conclusions. Everything will explain itself.

STOMIL: No doubt – give him a minute and Arthur will explain everything. It looks like he's starting now.

ELEONORA: Quiet! – he's waking up.

[ARTHUR *raises his head and points at* STOMIL.]

ARTHUR: What is that?

ELEONORA: Oh dear, he doesn't recognize his own father. [*Weeps.*]

ARTHUR: Quiet, woman! I'm not talking about my pedigree. What's all the fancy dress?

STOMIL [*looking at his legs*]: These? They're spats.

ARTHUR: Yes, of course ... spats. [*Falls into contemplation.*]

EUGENE: Arthur's a little tired at the moment, but soon we shall be back to normal. Everyone to their proper places! No change in the programme! [*To* ARTHUR, *ingratiatingly*] Ha ha ha – Arthur, you were having us on, you can see we're all keen and ready to go, all done up to the last button, once and for all! Stomil even insisted on a pair of corsets! Chin up, Arthur – have a little rest and then on to the wedding!

STOMIL: You never change, do you, you old has-been? Can't you see he's tight as a tick? God give me patience.

EUGENE: Be quiet! That's not true! Come on, Arthur, let's get on with it. Everything's ready – only the final step to take.

ARTHUR [*falling down on his knees in front of* STOMIL]: Father – forgive me!

STOMIL: What's this – his latest trick?

ARTHUR [*going after him on his knees*]: I was mad! There's no going back, there's no present, there's no future, there's nothing!

STOMIL: Now he's a nihilist!

ALA [*throwing off her veil*]: What about me? Is there no me either?

ARTHUR [*changing direction and walking on his knees towards* ALA]: And you too, you must forgive me.

ALA: You baby! You gutless coward!

ARTHUR: No, no, you mustn't say that, you mustn't ... I'm not afraid, I've just lost my faith, I'd give anything, I'd give my life, but there's no going back. The old conventions won't bring back reality. I was wrong.

ALA: What are you talking about?

ARTHUR: About redeeming the world!

ALA: But what about me? Who's going to talk about me?

EUGENE: Traitor!

ARTHUR [*changing direction again and moving on his knees towards* EUGENE]: ... And you must forgive me, too, Uncle. I gave you hope, but you've got to believe me, it's impossible ...

EUGENE: Don't give me all that! – Get a grip on yourself. Get up! Get married! Start a family, clean your teeth, eat with a knife and fork! I want the world stood up straight with its shoulders back. We shall succeed! Don't throw away our last chance!

ARTHUR: It wasn't a chance. We were wrong. It was hopeless.

ELEONORA: Stomil's right. You are drunk. You don't know what you're saying.

ARTHUR: Yes, I'm drunk. Because when I was sober I was wrong. I got drunk to purge myself of folly. Have a drink, Uncle.

EUGENE: Me? I never drink! ... Well, just a small one ... [*Pours himself a glass of vodka and drinks it in one gulp.*]

ARTHUR: I was sober when I got drunk. I got drunk knowingly.

STOMIL: Oh, don't give us that. You got drunk through despair.

ARTHUR: Yes. Despair too. Despair that order will not bring the world to rights.

EUGENE: What are we to do now?

ARTHUR [*gets up off his knees, ceremonially*]: An idea!

EUGENE: What?

ARTHUR: How should I know? But convention must start from an idea. You were right, Father, I'm just a pathetic formalist.

STOMIL: Don't worry, my boy, I don't mind. You know what I've suffered through all those ideas of yours, but now, fortunately, it's all over and done with. [*Taking off his tail coat.*] Where are my pyjamas?

ARTHUR [*throwing himself upon him and stopping him taking off his coat*]: Stop it! There's no going back to pyjamas either!

STOMIL: Why not? You're not still trying to save us, are you? I thought you'd given up.

ARTHUR [*aggressively, in the way a drunk switches to an entirely different attitude, triumphantly*]: You didn't think I'd give in as easily as that!

STOMIL: For a moment there you were a human being. And now by God you want to be a saint again.

ARTHUR [*letting* STOMIL *go; emphatically*]: I decked you out with all the phony gold braid of pretentious dignity, and now with this same hand I'm going to strip it off you. If it's obeisance you want, here I am on my knees. Reason was my sin – and abstraction, reason's lecherous daughter. Now I have drowned reason in drink. I did not get drunk commonly, I got drunk rationally, though I wanted to get drunk mystically. I have passed through the fire of drunkenness and stand before you purified – so you've all got to forgive me. I stripped you of your garments because they were shrouds. But, even though you cursed me, I shall not leave you standing naked in the slipstream of history. Eddie! [*Enter* EDDIE.] Close all the doors!

ELEONORA: Yes, close the doors, Eddie. There's a draught.

ARTHUR: Quick – before anyone escapes!

EDDIE: Right, Mr Arthur, consider it done.

STOMIL: You're violating our civil rights!

ARTHUR: Oh – so it's freedom you want, is it? Well you can't get free of life; life is absolute – insoluble. And if you lot had your way you'd go on trying to break it down till you were dead. It's lucky for you I'm here.

EUGENE: Arthur, don't think that I'm siding with Stomil, but aren't you going a bit far? I must warn you, I put freedom of the individual above all else.

ARTHUR: And now all we need is the idea.

STOMIL: ⎫ How dare you talk to me like that?

EUGENE: ⎬ I'm washing my hands of the whole thing.

ELEONORA: ⎭ Now lie down, Arthur, I'm going to make you a hot compress.

ARTHUR: No one leaves this room till we find the idea. Don't let anyone out, Eddie.

EDDIE: Aye, aye, sir!

ELEONORA: For God's sake, find him something so that we can all have some peace. I can't stay, my cakes are burning.

EUGENE: We'd better not resist. There are two of them.

ARTHUR: Got any ideas, Uncle?

EUGENE: How should I know? . . . What about God?

ARTHUR: Too late, that's been done.

EUGENE: You're right. God wasn't much good even in my day. I was brought up in the age of enlightenment and exact science. I merely suggested God for the tradition's sake.

ARTHUR: No more tradition if you don't mind. We want a living idea.

EUGENE: How about . . . sport, then? I was once quite a horseman.

ARTHUR: Everyone does exercises nowadays. All quite useless.

EUGENE: Well, I can't think of anything else. Maybe Stomil has an idea.

STOMIL: Experiment – like I always said.

ARTHUR: Let's be serious, shall we?

STOMIL: I am being serious. We have to break the trail – man is pushing back the frontiers all the time and that comes from experiment. Continual trial and error towards the new life.

ARTHUR: The new life! I don't know what to do with the old one and you talk to me about the new life.

STOMIL: Please yourself, but we're only in the experimental stage so far.

EUGENE: Eleonora, maybe you've got an idea?

ARTHUR: It's no good asking a woman.

ELEONORA: I did have one but it's gone. There's so much to worry about. Ask Eddie. He's got common sense – you can believe what he says.

STOMIL: Oh yes, Eddie's collective wisdom.

ARTHUR: Well, Eddie?

EDDIE: Progress, sir.

ARTHUR: And what does that mean?

EDDIE: Progress.... General progress ...

ARTHUR: But what progress?

EDDIE: Progress. Ahead.

ARTHUR: You mean ... forward?

EDDIE: That's it. Forward.... The front.

ARTHUR: What about the back?

EDDIE: The back forward too.

ARTHUR: Then the front will be at the back.

EDDIE: Depends how you look at it. If you look at it from the back, the front will be at the front, though from the back view.

ARTHUR: It all sounds a bit woolly to me.

EDDIE: But very progressive.

[*Enter* EUGENIA, *leaning on a stick.*]

EUGENIA [*timidly*]: I have something to tell you all.

ELEONORA: Not now, Mother. Can't you see the men are talking politics?

EUGENIA: This won't take a minute ...

ARTHUR: No, I don't go for it. I must have an idea that gives me a form. Progress just begs the question. It's formless.

EUGENIA: Will you please listen to me, my dears ...

STOMIL: What is it?

ELEONORA: I don't know. There's something wrong with Mother.

STOMIL: Later. We're busy just now. [*To* ARTHUR] I still say we should go back to experiment. The idea will come later.

[EUGENIA *takes the napkins and ornaments off the catafalque.*]

ELEONORA: What are you doing, Mother?

EUGENIA [*matter-of-fact*]: I'm going to die.

ELEONORA: Are you joking?

[EUGENIA *does not reply but goes on tidying up the catafalque, wiping the dust off with her sleeve and such.*]

Quiet, everyone – Mother says she's dying.

EUGENE: What do you mean, dying? We're discussing important business.

ELEONORA: Hear that, Mother?

EUGENIA: Help me, please.

[ELEONORA *automatically gives her her hand.* EUGENIA *climbs up on to the catafalque.*]

ELEONORA: Stop playing the fool, Mother. Today's the wedding day. Do you want to die and spoil it all?

STOMIL: What's this about death? I never thought of death ...

ARTHUR [*to himself*]: Death ... that's not a bad idea.

EUGENE: This is madness, Geenie. Be sensible, who ever heard of anyone dying?

ALA: It's unnatural, Granny.

EUGENIA: I can't understand you. You're so clever, and as soon as someone does something ordinary like dying, you're all amazed. What a lot you are! [*Lies down on her back. Lays her hands on her breast.*]

ELEONORA: Just look at her! Well, do something somebody – maybe she really is going to ...

EUGENE: Geenie, you're going too far. We've never had anything like this in our family.

STOMIL: Quite right – it really is the height of hypocrisy.

ARTHUR: Death . . . what a magnificent form.

EUGENIA: I have left the key to my room on the table. The cards are in the drawer. They're all marked.

ARTHUR: It's superb . . .

STOMIL: But it's not exactly a living idea.

ARTHUR: Why not? If someone else's . . . [*Strikes himself on the forehead with inspiration.*] Granny, I've got it!

ELEONORA: You should all be ashamed of yourselves!

EUGENE: Well try and lie straight, Granny, not all slumped. Elbows at your sides. Or better still, get up. You can't behave like this, it's unscientific. You're insulting all these modernists here.

STOMIL: No sarcasm, if you don't mind. Anyway as far as experiment's concerned, death's useless. Experiment entails repetition. If Mother were rehearsing, of course, that would be different. As it is, death must be discarded.

ALA: Stop it! – pay attention to her!

EUGENIA: Come to me, my children.

[*They all walk towards her except* EDDIE.]
And you, Eddie. [EDDIE *joins them.*] Who are you?

EUGENE: We're us.

[EUGENIA *giggles, quietly at first, then louder and louder.*]
She's laughing at me. Did I say something funny?

STOMIL: I still don't feel terribly well. I think I've got a headache.

[STOMIL *walks to one side. Takes his pulse. Takes a mirror out of his pocket and looks at his tongue.*]

ARTHUR: Thank you, Granny, you've given me an idea which I think I can use.

STOMIL [*putting the mirror away*]: It's all nonsense. The only important thing is to wear comfortable clothes.

[EUGENIA *dies*.]

ELEONORA: Keep going, Mother.

ARTHUR: She's dead. How strange. She was so insignificant.

ALA: No – it's not true ...

EUGENE: I don't get it.

STOMIL: I'm not having anything to do with it.

ELEONORA: I had no idea ... Stomil, why didn't you warn me?

STOMIL: Oh yes, it's all my fault as usual. Anyway, I can't see that anything's changed. I'm sorry, but my collar is pinching me again.

ARTHUR [*drawing the curtain in front of the catafalque*]: Eddie, come here! [EDDIE *walks up to* ARTHUR *and stands to attention.* ARTHUR *tests his biceps.*] Have you got a good punch?

EDDIE: Not bad, sir.

ARTHUR: And if it came to the point, you'd know how to ... [*Draws his finger across his throat.*]

EDDIE [*phlegmatically after a pause*]: Was that a question, Mr Arthur? I'm not sure if I'm quite with you ...

[*Pause.* ARTHUR *laughs uncertainly as though practising and waits for a second.* EDDIE *replies ' Hee Hee' in the same way.* ARTHUR *in turn says 'Hee Hee' a little more certainly and loudly, after which* EDDIE's *'Hee Hee' grows louder and louder.* ARTHUR *claps him on the shoulder.*]

ARTHUR: I like you, Eddie, I've always liked you.

EDDIE: I had an idea we'd get together in the end, sir.

ARTHUR: Do you see what I'm getting at ...?

EDDIE: I've been around, sir.

STOMIL: I'm going. This business has exhausted me, I've got to lie down.

ARTHUR: Stay where you are.

STOMIL: Stop telling me what to do, you young brat! I'm tired. [*Goes off in the direction of his room.*]

ARTHUR: Eddie! [EDDIE *stands in* STOMIL's *way.*]

STOMIL: What's the meaning of this? [*Turns savagely upon* ELEONORA, *pointing at* EDDIE.] Have you been fornicating with this servant?

ELEONORA: My God, not now. Not in front of Mother!
[EDDIE *pushes* STOMIL *into an armchair.*]

ARTHUR: Ladies and gentlemen! Settle down! Everything's clear now. I shall lead you to a happy future.

EUGENE [*sits down resignedly*]: I can't go on. . . . It's my age. We're not as young as we were, are we, Stomil?

STOMIL: Speak for yourself. You're nearly as decrepit as Eugenia was, you sanctimonious old fool. Personally, I feel in tremendous shape . . . just tremendous . . . [*Beseechingly*] Eleonora, where are you?

ELEONORA: Here I am, darling, I'm at your side.

STOMIL: Come to me.

ELEONORA [*laying her hand on his forehead*]: How are you feeling?

STOMIL: I feel . . . a bit weak . . .

ARTHUR: All doubts are resolved. Our road is bright and clear. There will be one law and one flock.

STOMIL: What's he on about – oh, my head . . .

EUGENE: Something about law, and shepherding.

ARTHUR: Have you got it yet? Some hope – you hunks of meat, worrying about your glands and your immortality. But I understand what we've arrived at. I am your redeemer, you vacant cattle. I shall raise you above this world. I shall embrace you all, because I have a mind independent of stomachs and digestions. I have a mind!

EUGENE: Instead of insulting us, it might help if you explained things a bit more clearly.

ARTHUR: You rotting vegetation, don't you see it yet? You're dithering about in endless circles like lost pups. You're without form or idea. And without me you would have burned up in the vacuum. You want to know what I'm going to do with you? I'm going to create a system in

which rebellion will be joined with order and nothingness
with existence. I shall destroy contradiction.

EUGENE: The best thing would be for you to leave the
room. I'm disappointed in you. It's all over between us.
[*To himself*] I think I'll go on with my memoirs.

ARTHUR: I'll put it to you as a question: if nothing exists
and even rebellion is impossible, what is it that can be
created out of nothing and given reality?

EUGENE [*takes out his watch and chain*]: It's getting late. It's
about time we had something to eat.

ARTHUR: Anyone?

STOMIL: Eleonora, what's for lunch today? I'd like something light, my stomach feels a bit off. It's time I started
worrying about it.

ELEONORA: Yes, dear, I quite agree. It's time you began
organizing your life. From now on we shall concentrate
on your health. Afternoon – a nap and a stroll. In the
morning – experiment.

STOMIL: Cooked in butter, possibly, or boiled ...

ELEONORA: Naturally. Nothing that will keep you awake.

ARTHUR: All right, if that's the way you want it. I'll give
you the answer. [*Places a chair on the table. Climbs groggily on
to the table and sits in the chair.*]

ELEONORA: Arthur, do be careful of the plates.

ARTHUR: The only possible thing is power!

EUGENE: Power? What do you mean, power? We're all in
the same family, aren't we?

STOMIL: He's raving. Don't pay any attention to him.

ARTHUR: Only power can be created out of nothing.
Power can be, where nothing ever was. Here I sit, up
high, above you, and you're all down there.

EUGENE [*sarcastically*]: Brilliant.

ELEONORA: Arthur, get down at once, you're dirtying the
table-cloth.

ARTHUR: Go on – prostrate yourselves in the dust.

EUGENE: Are we going to let him treat us like this?

STOMIL: He can say what he likes for the moment. We'll deal with him after lunch. Though really, I can't think where he got these tendencies from. What a way to behave.

ARTHUR: One only needs the will and the strength. And I've got it. Look at me – I've crowned your wildest dreams. Uncle, we shall have law and order. Father, you did nothing but rebel, and your rebellion led only to chaos, and destroyed itself. But look at me! – Isn't power rebellion? Rebellion in the form of order, the top against the bottom, the high against the low. There can be no high without a low and no low without a high – and that's what power is all about: the opposites don't cancel each other out, but define one another. I am neither compound nor component, I am the act itself. I am will, I am energy, I am power! I am above, within and around everything. You should fall on my neck – I have fulfilled your youth. It's yours! And I get something out of it too – form, any form I fancy, not one but a thousand possibilities. I can create and demolish at will, it's all within me, here! [*Strikes himself on the chest. Everybody looks at him aghast.*]

EUGENE: So where does that leave us?

STOMIL: I don't see that we have to take any notice. Just a lot of puppy games. Words, words, words. What powers has he got over us?

EUGENE: Exactly. Talk, talk, talk and not a leg to stand on. We are joined by ties of blood, not a lot of abstractions. There's nothing he can do to us.

ARTHUR: Isn't there? It's quite simple. I can kill you.

STOMIL [*getting up out of the chair and falling back again*]: No, I forbid you. There's a limit to everything.

ARTHUR: Limits are there to be overstepped. Didn't you

teach me that? Power over life and death, there's no greater power than that. It's a simple and magnificent discovery.

EUGENE: Rubbish. I'm going to live as long as it pleases me. I mean, as long as it pleases ... er, who, exactly? Stomil, do you know?

STOMIL: Well, let's say ... nature.

EUGENE: Ah yes, nature ... or fate.

ARTHUR: That's where you're wrong.

EUGENE: Are you trying to be funny?

ARTHUR: And what if I become your fate?

EUGENE: Eleonora, Stomil, what's he on about? – Do something, he's your son.

ELEONORA: There, look what you've done, Arthur, you've scared your uncle out of his wits. Lie down, Stomil, and don't move. I'll bring you a cushion.

ARTHUR: Do you think I'd have started all this without the means to carry it off? Death is inside you all, like a nightingale in a cage. All I have to do is to let it out. Come on, what do you take me for? – An idealist, a gasbag, a dreamer?

EUGENE: Ha! ha! ha! You know, Arthur, one's got to admit it, you've got a brain in your head. You can work things out. They do a good job at that University of yours. Oh yes, but here we are, my boy, and time flies. I don't mind a little philosophical discussion, especially with young people. But we've had our chat, the idea's been turned down and it's time for something a little more concrete. No more theories for now, we ought to get a bite to eat – don't you agree, Eleonora?

ELEONORA: That's just what I've been wanting to say all along if only you'd let me speak. We've had enough, Arthur. Get down from the table, or else take your shoes off.

ARTHUR: Precisely, Uncle, you hit the nail on the head.

It's time for something a little more concrete. Eddie, my dark angel of divine abstraction, are you ready?

EDDIE: Ready, chief.

ARTHUR: Then get him.

EUGENE [*backing away towards the exit*]: What do you want?

ARTHUR: We'll start by knocking off Uncle Eugene.

ELEONORA: 'Knocking off'? – What a vulgar expression.

STOMIL: And just when I've got this terrible blood pressure.

EUGENE [*as he reaches the door*]: Why me?

[EDDIE *blocks his path.*]

ARTHUR: Theories! Eddie, show him how wrong he is. What do you take me for, you scum.

[EDDIE *blocks* EUGENE's *path again.*]

EUGENE: This isn't a system. This is thuggery!

ARTHUR: Do your duty, Eddie.

EUGENE [*running away from* EDDIE *who pursues him with deliberate cat-like movements*]: What does this butler want with me?

ARTHUR: He's not a butler. He's the arm of my will. The embodiment of my word.

STOMIL [*pulling up his collar*]: Eleonora, I feel weak ... Eleonora.

ELEONORA: Your father's fainted!

EUGENE [*running away*]: Murderer! Madman!

ARTHUR [*rising from his chair and lifting one hand*]: No! – Merely a man who does not shrink from the only possibility. I'm as uncommitted as nature – I'm free!

ALA: Arthur ...

ARTHUR: Not now – can't you see I'm saving the world?

ALA: I've been unfaithful to you. With Eddie.

[EDDIE *stops chasing* EUGENE. *Both of them stand still and gaze at* ARTHUR *and* ALA. ELEONORA *is busy slapping* STOMIL's *face and suchlike.*]

ARTHUR [*slowly lowering his hand, after a pause*]: What did you say?

ALA: I didn't think you'd mind. After all, you're only marrying me for the principle of the thing.

ARTHUR [*stunned, sits down on the chair*]: When?

ALA: This morning.

ARTHUR [*to himself*]: Yes ... Yes ...

ALA: You mustn't worry about it. All I did was. ... Look, I'm all ready for the wedding. [*Puts on her veil.*] Do I look nice?

ARTHUR [*climbs down from the table, hanging on to it blindly*]: No ... wait, wait. Why ...? You ... me? ... You ... me?...

ALA [*artificially casual*]: I meant to tell you but it slipped my mind, and you were so busy. ... Shall we go now? Do you want me to put my gloves on? They're a bit tight. Do you like my hair like this?

ARTHUR [*shouts*]: *Me?*

ALA [*pretending to be surprised*]: Oh dear, are you still going on? I never thought you'd make such a fuss. We'd better change the subject.

ARTHUR [*collapses into himself. He walks around the table blindly. All his mental powers seem to have lost contact with his body, which is behaving mechanically, but without co-ordination. He speaks in a moaning monotone, a complaining sort of voice*]: How could you. ... How could you ...?

ALA: According to you you needed me as an ally – remember? Did I get it wrong? We talked about serious matters, and you were so clever, I was very impressed. Eddie couldn't have done that.

ARTHUR [*shouts*]: Eddie!

ALA: Eddie isn't like that at all.

ARTHUR [*tearfully*]: Why did you do it ...?

ALA: Oh, darling, I told you, I was sure you wouldn't mind. I'm surprised at you – such a fuss over nothing. I wish I hadn't told you now.

ARTHUR: But why ...?

ALA: Oh, you do go on. I ... had my reasons ...

ARTHUR [*shouts*]: What reasons?

ALA: ... which we'd better not go into. It might upset you.

ARTHUR: Tell me!

ALA: We just had a little ...

ARTHUR: *Tell me!*

ALA [*frightened*]: ... just a teeny-weeny little ...

ARTHUR: TELL ME!

ALA: I'm not going to tell you anything! It'll make you angry.

ARTHUR: Oh my Christ!

ALA: All right, we needn't discuss it then. Do you blame me?

[ARTHUR *walks towards* STOMIL *and* ELEONORA.]

ARTHUR: Why are you all against me? What have I done to you? Mother, I'm talking to you!

ELEONORA: Ala, I warned you.

ARTHUR [*grabbing hold of* ELEONORA]: Tell her she can't do that to me – tell me – tell her I can't. ... Why does she treat me like this? [*Weeps.*]

ELEONORA [*tearing herself away*]: Get away from me, you stupid child.

ARTHUR [*repulsed, he staggers into the centre of the stage. He speaks through his tears*]: I wanted to save you. I was nearly there, and you ruined it all. The world is rotten through and through!

ALA: Arthur ... come to me. [*Walks up to him.*] You poor darling, I'm so sorry ...

ARTHUR [*pushes her away*]: You? Sorry? You dare to pity me? I don't need your condescension! You don't know me – I'll show you all. Even now. All right, so you didn't want my ideas, so you walked all over me! [*To* ALA] You whore! I conceived the most noble idea in history and you flung dirt over it! And in your blindness you didn't even know whom you were betraying. And who did you pick? Him – that degenerate, that walking turd who stands for the world's decay. I'm going, but I'm not leaving you behind. You don't know what life's about. Where's that sweet gigolo of yours? – Where's his great rotten belly? I'll disembowel him. [*Dashes frantically around the room searching everywhere – the tables, the sofa.*] Revolver! – Give me the revolver! – Everything's so bloody tidy around here I can't find a thing. Has anyone seen the revolver – Mother?

[EDDIE *creeps up on him from behind, takes the revolver from his inside pocket, and with the butt of it hits* ARTHUR *hard on the back of the neck.* ARTHUR *falls on his knees.* EDDIE *throws away the gun, carefully pushes* ARTHUR'*s head forward. When* ARTHUR'*s unprotected head is almost on the floor,* EDDIE *interlaces the fingers of his hands, stands on tiptoe and, as if he were wielding an axe, brings down another terrible blow on to* ARTHUR'*s bare neck.* ARTHUR *goes on all fours, his forehead touching the floor.*

NOTE: *It is essential that this scene appear entirely realistic. Both blows must be executed in such a way that their theatrical fiction is not apparent. Perhaps the revolver could be made of rubber, or even of some material stuffed with feathers. Or perhaps* ARTHUR *could wear some sort of lining under his collar. But the important thing is that none of it should look theatrical.*]

ALA [*kneeling down next to* ARTHUR]: Arthur!

ELEONORA [*kneeling down on the other side of him*]: Arthur, my son!

[EDDIE *moves to one side, looks at his hands. In a tone of surprise:*]

EDDIE: He was a hard one.

ARTHUR [*slowly and quietly as if completely amazed*]: Strange ... everything's disappeared ...

ALA: I didn't mean it ... it wasn't true!

EDDIE: Do me a favour!

ARTHUR [*still with his forehead touching the floor, quietly*]: I loved you, Ala ...

ALA: Why didn't you tell me ...?

EDDIE: 'My love is dead to the world.'

[ELEONORA *runs over to* STOMIL *and shakes him.*]

ELEONORA: Wake up, your son is dying!

STOMIL [*opens his eyes*]: What now? I can't take much more of this.

[*Gets up with difficulty, and, supported by* ELEONORA, *approaches* ARTHUR. ARTHUR *is in the middle of the stage, all the time in the same position.* ELEONORA, STOMIL *and* EUGENE *stand over him.* ALA *is kneeling.* EDDIE *is to one side comfortably seated in an armchair.*]

ARTHUR [*collapses entirely on to the floor. Emphatically*]: I wanted ...! I wanted ...! [*Pause.*]

ALA [*gets up on her knees, matter-of-factly*]: He's dead.

EUGENE: A merciful release.... I thought I'd had it.

STOMIL: Forgive him. He was not happy.

EUGENE [*generously*]: I don't bear him any grudge. He can't hurt me now.

STOMIL: It was the apathy and the monotony that he couldn't take. He wanted to destroy them. He was ruled by the mind, but with too much passion. Abstraction betrayed his sentiment, and sentiment killed him.

EDDIE: He had the right ideas, only he was too nervous. Those ones never make it. [*The others turn round and face him.*]

STOMIL: Shut up, you pig, and get out of this house. And thank us for letting you off so lightly.

EDDIE: What's there to go for? I told you, he had the right ideas. I'm staying.

STOMIL: What for?

EDDIE: I'm having my go now. You're going to take your orders from me.

STOMIL: What?

EDDIE: Yeh. You saw what a punch I've got. Now don't be frightened – sit still, don't leap about, pay attention to what I say and you'll be all right. You'll see – I'm a decent bloke. I like a laugh, a bit of fun. Only I've got to have obedience.

EUGENE: Back in the soup again.

EDDIE: That's not a very polite thing to say, Mr Eugene. I think you'd better take my shoes off.

EUGENE: All right, I'll submit to brute force ... though in my heart I despise it.

EDDIE: Despise away, but first take my shoes off. Go on, jump to it, one, two!

[EUGENE *kneels down and takes* EDDIE'*s shoes off.*]

STOMIL: I always thought that we were ruled not by people but by ideas – and that violence was the animal in us taking its revenge. But now I see it's only Eddie.

ELEONORA: It may not be so bad, Stomil. He'll let you go on a diet.

EUGENE [*with the shoes in his hand*]: Shall I clean them?

EDDIE: No, you can take them away. I'm going to change. [*Gets up and pulls off the jacket from* ARTHUR'*s body. He puts it on and looks at himself in the mirror.*] A bit tight but it'll do.

STOMIL: Come on, Eleonora. We're nothing but a pair of old parents.

EDDIE: Don't go too far away. I may want you.

ELEONORA: Are you coming, Ala?

ALA: Yes, I'm coming. ... He loved me. No one can take that away from me.

STOMIL [*to himself*]: I suppose it was love ...

ALA: Did you say something?

STOMIL: No, nothing.

[ELEONORA *and* STOMIL *leave arm in arm.* ALA *follows.* EDDIE *turns to and fro in front of the mirror, making various dignified and handsome poses, thrusting forward his jaw, with arms akimbo, and so on.* EUGENE *walks across the stage with*

EDDIE's *shoes in his hand. He stands over* ARTHUR.]

EUGENE: It looks as if no one needs you any more, Arthur.
[EUGENE *stands over* ARTHUR, *meditating.* EDDIE
*leaves the stage and returns immediately, carrying a tape
recorder. He places it on the table and switches on. At once we
hear a loud and strident version of the tango 'La Cumparsita'.
This tune and no other.*]

EDDIE: Mister Eugene, shall we dance?

EUGENE: Dance? With you? well, you know ... the way
things are, I think I'll accept.
[*Puts the shoes down next to* ARTHUR *and walks into* EDDIE's
*embrace. They stand in the prescribed position, wait for the beat
and launch forth.* EDDIE *leads. They dance.* EUGENE *is
grey-haired, dignified, wearing a black jacket, check trousers and
a red carnation in his buttonhole.* EDDIE *is wearing* ARTHUR's
*jacket. It is too tight. The sleeves are too short, and through
them protrude* EDDIE's *great arms as he holds* EUGENE *round
the waist. They dance in the classic style, with all the figures
and passages of an exhibition tango. They dance right up to the
fall of the curtain, after which 'La Cumparsita' still continues
for some time; even after the lights have been turned on, it can
be heard through loudspeakers everywhere in the theatre.*]

# THE MEMORANDUM

*Václav Havel*

TRANSLATED BY VERA BLACKWELL

All inquiries concerning performing rights should be directed to Margaret Ramsay Ltd, 14a Goodwin's Court, St Martin's Lane, WC2.

# CHARACTERS

JOSEF GROSS *Managing Director*

JAN BALLAS *Deputy Director*

OTTO STROLL *Head of the Translation Centre*

ALEX SAVANT *Ptydepist*

HELENA *Chairman*

MARIA *Secretary at the Translation Centre*

HANA *Secretary to the Managing Director*

MARK LEAR *Teacher of Ptydepe*

FERDINAND PILLAR

GEORGE *Staff Watcher*

PETER THUMB *A Clerk*

MR COLUMN

THREE CLERKS

The action takes place in three office rooms within one large organization. Each office differs from the other in its particulars (placing of furniture, office equipment, etc.), but they all exude the same atmosphere and thus resemble each other. In each, there are two exits: a back door (B.D.) and a side door (S.D.).

# SCENE ONE

*The Director's office. Large office desk, small typist's desk, a fire-extinguisher on the wall, a coat-rack in the background. The stage is empty. Then* GROSS *enters by B.D., takes off his coat, hangs it on the rack, sits at his desk and begins to go through his morning mail. He skims each letter, then puts it either into waste-paper basket or into out-tray. One letter suddenly arrests his attention. He glares at it and then starts to read it aloud.*

GROSS [*reads*]: Ra ko hutu d dekotu ely trebomu emusohe, vdegar yd, stro reny er gryk kendy, alyv zvyde dezu, kvyndal fer tekynu sely. Degto yl tre entvester kyleg gh: orka epyl y bodur deptydepe emete. Grojto af xedob yd, kyzem ner osonfterte ylem kho dent de det detrym gynfer bro enomuz fechtal agni laj kys defyj rokuroch bazuk suhelen. Gakvom ch ch lopve rekto elkvestrete. Dyhap zuj bak dygalex ibem nyderix tovah gyp. Ykte juh geboj. Fyx dep butrop gh –

[GROSS *does not notice that meanwhile* BALLAS *and* PILLAR *have quietly entered by S.D.* BALLAS *coughs discreetly.*]

GROSS: Are you here?

BALLAS: Yes, we are.

GROSS: I didn't hear you come in.

BALLAS: We entered quietly.

GROSS: Have you been here long?

BALLAS: Not long.

GROSS: What is it?

BALLAS: We've come to ask your advice, Mr Gross.

GROSS: Go on.

BALLAS: Where should Mr Pillar record the incoming mail?

GROSS: Couldn't be more obvious, Mr Ballas. In the incoming-mail book.

BALLAS: It's full, isn't it, Mr P.?

[PILLAR *nods.*]

GROSS: So soon?

BALLAS: I'm afraid so.

GROSS: Good gracious! Well, he'll have to get a new one.

BALLAS: We've no funds to get a new one, have we, Mr P.?

[PILLAR *shakes his head.*]

GROSS: What do you mean no funds? As far as I recall a purchase of two incoming-mail books was budgeted for this quarter.

BALLAS: It was. But in accordance with the new economy drive all budgeted expenditures were cut by half, with the result that we were able to purchase only one incoming-mail book which is, as I've just mentioned, full. Isn't it, Mr P.?

[PILLAR *nods.*]

GROSS [*hands* PILLAR *some money*]: Here. Buy yourself a new one.

[PILLAR *pockets the money. Both bow respectfully.*]

BALLAS: We thank you, Mr Gross. Thank you very much.

[*They leave by S.D.* GROSS *picks up his letter and examines it with curiosity.* HANA *enters by B.D., wearing a coat and carrying a vast shopping bag.*]

HANA: Good morning.

GROSS [*without looking up*]: Good morning.

[HANA *hangs her coat on coat-rack, sits down at typist's desk, takes a mirror and a comb out of her bag, props mirror against typewriter and begins to comb her hair. Combing her hair will be her main occupation throughout the play. She will interrupt it only when absolutely necessary.* GROSS *watches her stealthily for a moment, then turns to her.*]

GROSS: Hana –

HANA: Yes, Mr Gross?

GROSS [*shows her the letter*]: Any idea what this is?

HANA [*skims the letter*]: This is a very important office memorandum, Mr Gross.

GROSS: It looks like a hotch-potch of entirely haphazard groups of letters.

HANA: Perhaps, at first glance. But in fact there's method in it. It's written in Ptydepe, you see.

GROSS: In what?

HANA: In Ptydepe.

GROSS: In Ptydepe? What is it?

HANA: A new office language which is being introduced into our organization. May I go and get the milk?

GROSS: There's a new language being introduced into our organization? I don't remember having been informed.

HANA: They must have forgotten to tell you. May I go and get the milk?

GROSS: Who thought it up?

HANA: It seems to be a full-scale campaign. Elsie said it's being introduced into their department, too.

GROSS: Does my deputy realize what's going on?

HANA: Mr Ballas? Of course he does. May I go and get the milk?

GROSS: Run along.

> [HANA *takes empty bottle from her shopping bag and hurries out by B.D.* GROSS *paces thoughtfully up and down. Again does not notice when* BALLAS *and* PILLAR *enter by S.D.* BALLAS *coughs.*]

GROSS: Are you here again?

BALLAS: We've come to tell you that we've just purchased a brand new incoming-mail book. It's lying on Mr Pillar's desk. Isn't it, Mr P.?

> [PILLAR *nods.*]

GROSS: Good.

BALLAS: But the Department of Authentication refuses to authenticate it.

GROSS: Why?

BALLAS: The new book hasn't been registered by the Purchasing Department on account of its not having been purchased with the department's funds. So, legally, it doesn't exist, does it, Mr P.?

[PILLAR *shakes his head.*]

GROSS: Say I ask them to authenticate it on my personal responsibility. My position's solid now, I think I can go so far.

BALLAS: Excellent! Would you mind giving it to us in writing? It'll simplify things a great deal.

GROSS: I would. I don't mind taking risks, but I'm not a gambler. A verbal order will have to do.

BALLAS: Well, then, we must try to talk them into accepting it. Mr P., let's go.

[*They turn to leave.* GROSS *stops them.*]

GROSS: Just a moment, Mr Ballas.

BALLAS: Yes, Mr Gross?

GROSS: Do you know anything about a new language?

BALLAS: I think I've heard about it. I seem to recall Mr Pillar told me about it some time ago, didn't you, Mr P.?

[PILLAR *nods.*]

GROSS: Do you also recall who ordered its introduction into our organization?

BALLAS: Who was it, Mr P., do you know?

[PILLAR *shrugs.*]

GROSS: Mr Ballas. You are my deputy, aren't you?

BALLAS: Yes.

GROSS: Well then. I didn't order it. So it could only have been you.

BALLAS: One gives so many orders every day, one can't be expected to remember them all.

GROSS: Don't you realize you ought to consult me on such matters?

BALLAS: We didn't want to bother you with trifles.

GROSS: Actually, why is it being introduced?

BALLAS: As a sort of experiment. It's supposed to make office communications more accurate and introduce precision and order into their terminology. Am I putting it correctly, Mr P.?

[PILLAR *nods*.]

GROSS: Was it ordered from above?

BALLAS: Not directly –

GROSS: To tell you the truth, I'm far from happy about it. You'll have to find some way to stop the whole thing at once. We don't want to be somebody's guinea-pig, do we?

[HANA *re-enters by B.D. with a bottle of milk.*]

HANA [*to* BALLAS]: Good morning.

[*She puts bottle on her desk, opens it, drinks, then continues combing her hair.*]

BALLAS: All right, I'll cancel my directive, and try to retrieve all the Ptydepe texts sent out so far, and have them translated back into natural language. [*To* HANA] Good morning.

GROSS: Kindly do that.

BALLAS: We don't want to be somebody's guinea-pig, do we?

GROSS: Exactly.

BALLAS: Mr P., let's go.

[*They leave by S.D.* GROSS *crosses to* HANA's *desk, reaches for her milk bottle.*]

GROSS: May I?

HANA: Yes, of course, Mr Gross.

GROSS [*drinks, returns to his desk, sits down. Pause*]: Strange relationship between those two.

HANA: I know a great many particulars about it.

GROSS: I don't want to hear them! They're both exceptionally good workers. The rest is not my business. [*Pause. Again stares at his letter. Then turns to* HANA.] Thank God,

I've nipped it in the bud. Did they seriously think anybody would want to learn this gibberish?

HANA: Special Ptydepe classes have been set up for all departments.

GROSS: Indeed! Anybody joined them?

HANA: Everybody except you, Mr Gross.

GROSS: Really?

HANA: It was an order.

GROSS: Whose order?

HANA: Mr Ballas's.

GROSS: What! He didn't tell me anything about that! [*Pause.*] Anyway, I fail to see how our staff could be expected to use this Ptydepe when most of them couldn't possibly have learnt it yet.

HANA: That's why a Ptydepe Translation Centre has been set up. But it's supposed to be only temporary, until everybody has learnt Ptydepe. Then it'll become the Ptydepe Reference Centre. May I go and get the rolls?

GROSS: Well, well! A Translation Centre! Where on earth did they find room for it all?

HANA: The Translation Centre is on the first floor, room six.

GROSS: But that's the Accounts Department!

HANA: The Accounts Department has been moved to the cellar. May I go and get the rolls?

GROSS: Also on his order?

HANA: Yes.

GROSS: That's too much!

HANA: May I go and get the rolls?

GROSS: Run along.

[HANA *pulls a string bag from her shopping bag and leaves by B.D.* GROSS *again does not notice when* BALLAS *and* PILLAR *enter by S.D.* BALLAS *coughs.*]

GROSS: Now what?

BALLAS: Mr Gross, I'm afraid you'll have to give us the order in writing, after all.

GROSS: I'll do nothing of the sort.

BALLAS: It'd be in your own interest.

GROSS: What do you mean – in my own interest?

BALLAS: If you'll give it to us in writing, you'll greatly simplify the work of our clerical staff. They won't have to fill out a special voucher to go with each incoming letter, you see. And in view of the rumours which have lately been circulating among them, it would certainly be a good tactical move on your part. Am I not right, Mr P.?

[PILLAR *nods*.]

GROSS: What rumours?

BALLAS: Oh, about that unfortunate rubber-stamp.

GROSS: Rubber-stamp? What rubber-stamp?

BALLAS: Apparently during the last inventory it transpired that you're in the habit of taking the bank endorsement stamp home for your children to play with.

GROSS: That's ridiculous. Of course I have taken that particular rubber-stamp home a few times. But not as a plaything. There are nights when I have to take my work home to get it all done.

BALLAS: You don't have to explain it to us, Mr Gross. But you know how people are!

GROSS: And you think this bit of paper you want would smooth things over?

BALLAS: I'll guarantee you that.

GROSS: All right then. As far as I'm concerned, have it typed, and I'll sign it.

BALLAS [*at once produces a typed sheet of paper, unfolds it, and places it on* GROSS's *desk*]: Here you are, Mr Gross.

[GROSS *signs.* BALLAS *snatches the document and quickly folds it.*]

Thank you, Mr Gross. We thank you very much in the name of our whole organization.

[BALLAS *and* PILLAR *are about to leave.*]

GROSS: Mr Ballas.

BALLAS: Yes, Mr Gross?

GROSS: Have you cancelled the introduction of Ptydepe?

BALLAS: Not yet.

GROSS: Why not?

BALLAS: Well, you see, we've been waiting for the right moment. There doesn't seem to be the right sort of atmosphere among the authorities for this move just now. We wouldn't like it to be used against us in any way, would we, Mr P.?

[PILLAR *shakes his head.*]

GROSS: That's just an excuse.

BALLAS: Mr Gross, you don't believe us and we're hurt.

GROSS: You've bypassed me. You've moved the Accounts Department to the cellar.

BALLAS: That's only half the truth!

GROSS: What's the other half?

BALLAS: That I've ordered a ventilator to be installed in the cellar next year. Mr P., speak up, didn't I give such an order?

[PILLAR *nods.*]

GROSS: What about the light?

BALLAS: The temporary accountant has brought a candle from her home.

GROSS: Let's hope so!

BALLAS: Mr P., speak up! She did bring a candle, didn't she?

[PILLAR *shrugs.*]

BALLAS: Mr P. doesn't seem to know about it. But she did! You can go and see for yourself.

GROSS: Be that as it may, you bypassed me. You organized Ptydepe classes, you set up a Ptydepe Translation Centre, and you made the study of Ptydepe obligatory for all staff members.

BALLAS: Outside their working hours!

GROSS: That's beside the point.

BALLAS: Mr Gross, I fully agree that I may not bypass you in things concerning the activity of our staff during their working hours. But as for anything outside those hours I believe I can do as I please.

GROSS: I don't quite know what answer to give you at this moment, but I'm sure there is a fitting one somewhere.

BALLAS: Perhaps there is, perhaps there isn't. In any case, at this point we're not concerned with anything but the good of our organization. Are we, Mr P.?

[PILLAR *nods*.]

BALLAS: Naturally, we hold the same critical attitude towards Ptydepe that you do, Mr Gross. Only we think that if, before the inevitable collapse of the whole campaign, we can manifest certain limited initiative, it'll be of great help to our whole organization. Who knows, this very initiative may become the basis on which we might be granted that snack-bar which we have been trying to get for so long. Imagine that our staff would no longer have to travel all that way in their coffee-break.

GROSS: All right. It's quite possible that in this way we might indeed get the snack-bar. This, however, in no way changes the fact that you've bypassed me a number of times and that, lately, you've been taking far too many decisions on your own authority.

BALLAS: I? I beg your pardon! Haven't we just been consulting you about such a trifle as a new incoming-mail book? You're not being fair to us, Mr Gross. You're not at all fair.

GROSS: Mr Ballas, let me make a suggestion.

BALLAS: Yes?

GROSS: Let's be quite blunt with each other for a while, shall we? It'll simplify the situation a great deal and speed up the clarification of our points of view.

BALLAS: Shall we accept, Mr P.?

[PILLAR *nods.*]

BALLAS: I accept.

GROSS: Why did you say that you hold a critical attitude towards Ptydepe and that you're only interested in the snack-bar, when in fact you believe in Ptydepe and do everything you can to get it quickly introduced?

BALLAS: Matter of tactics.

GROSS: A little shortsighted.

BALLAS: I wouldn't say so.

GROSS: It never occurred to you that sooner or later I'd see through your tactics?

BALLAS: We knew you'd create obstacles and therefore we arranged it so you wouldn't see what we were after until we were strong enough to surmount your obstacles. There's nothing you can do to stop us now. The overwhelming majority of our staff stands resolutely behind us, because they know that only Ptydepe can place their work on a truly scientific basis. Isn't that so, Mr P.?

[PILLAR *nods.*]

GROSS: You seem to forget that it is I who bear the full responsibility for our organization, I in whom the trust has been placed. Thus, it is up to me to judge what is good for our organization, and what is not. So far, it is I who am the Managing Director here.

BALLAS: We cannot ignore the stand of the masses. The whole organization is seething and waiting for your word.

GROSS: I won't be dictated to by a mob.

BALLAS: You call it a mob, we call it the masses.

GROSS: You call it the masses, but it is a mob. I'm a humanist and my concept of directing this organization derives from the idea that every single member of the staff is human and must become more and more human. If we take from him his human language, created by the centuries-old tradition of national culture, we shall have

194

prevented him from becoming fully human and plunge him straight into the jaws of self-alienation. I'm not against precision in official communications, but I'm for it only in so far as it humanizes Man. In accordance with this my innermost conviction I can never agree to the introduction of Ptydepe into our organization.

BALLAS: Are you prepared to risk an open conflict?

GROSS: I place the struggle for the victory of reason and of moral values above a peace bought by their loss.

BALLAS: What do you say to this, Mr P.?

[PILLAR *shrugs in embarrassment.*]

GROSS: I suggest to you that we all forget what has just happened between us and that we part in peace before I'm forced to take the whole matter seriously.

[*A short pause.* HANA *enters by B.D., carrying a string bag full of rolls, puts it into her shopping bag, sits down and begins to comb her hair.*]

BALLAS [*turns to* PILLAR]: It seems he's not yet ripe for realistic discussion. We've overrated him. Never mind. Let's give him – [*looks at his watch*] – what do you say, an hour?

[PILLAR *nods.*]

BALLAS: Time is on our side. An hour from now we'll no longer be handling him with kid gloves. The patience of the masses is great, but it is not infinite. He'll be sorry. Let's go.

[*They leave by S.D.*]

GROSS: Unheard of! [*Sits down, notices his memorandum, stares at it, turns to* HANA.] Hana!

HANA: Yes, Mr Gross?

GROSS: Do you know Ptydepe?

HANA: No.

GROSS: Then how did you know that this was an official memorandum?

HANA: They say that in the first stage Ptydepe was used

only for important official memoranda and that these are now being received by some of the staff.

GROSS: What are these memos about?

HANA: They are supposed to inform the recipients about decisions based on the findings of the last audit in their departments.

GROSS: Indeed? What sort of decisions?

HANA: All sorts, it seems. Very positive and very negative ones.

GROSS: Damn that rubber-stamp! Where on earth did you learn all this?

HANA: Oh, in the dairy shop this morning.

GROSS: Where did you say the Translation Centre is?

HANA: First floor, room six. To get to it one must go through the Ptydepe classroom.

GROSS: Ah yes! Former Accounts Department. Well, I'm off to lunch. [*Takes his memorandum from his desk and hurries out B.D.*]

HANA [*calls after him*]: You'll like it, Mr Gross. They have goose in the canteen today!

# SCENE TWO

*The Ptydepe classroom. Teacher's desk in the background; in the foreground five chairs.* LEAR *is standing behind his desk, lecturing to four* CLERKS *who are seated with their backs to the audience. Among them is* THUMB.

LEAR: Ptydepe, as you know, is a synthetic language, built on a strictly scientific basis. Its grammar is constructed with maximum rationality, its vocabulary is unusually broad. It is a thoroughly exact language, capable of expressing with far greater precision than any current natural tongue all the minutest nuances in the formulation of important office documents. The result of this precision is of course the exceptional complexity and difficulty of Ptydepe. There are many months of intensive study ahead of you, which can be crowned by success only if it is accompanied by diligence, perseverance, discipline, talent and a good memory. And, of course, by faith. Without a steadfast faith in Ptydepe, nobody yet has ever been able to learn Ptydepe. And now, let us turn briefly to some of the basic principles of Ptydepe. The natural languages originated, as we know, spontaneously, uncontrollably, in other words, unscientifically, and their structure is thus, in a certain sense, dilettantish. As far as official communications are concerned, the most serious deficiency of the natural languages is their utter unreliability, which results from the fact that their basic structural units – words – are highly equivocal and interchangeable. You all know that in a natural language it is often enough to exchange one letter for another (goat – boat, love – dove), or simply remove one letter (fox – ox), and the whole meaning of the word is thus changed. And then there are all the homonyms! Consider what terrible mischief can be caused in inter-office communications when two words with entirely different meanings are spelled exactly the same way. P–o–s–s–u–m. Possum – possum. The first, designating an American small arboreal or aquatic nocturnal marsupial mammal with thumbed hind-foot –

[THUMB *giggles.*]

LEAR: The second, the Latin equivalent of 'I am able'. Such a thing is quite unthinkable in Ptydepe. The significant aim of Ptydepe is to guarantee to every statement, by purposefully limiting all similarities between individual words, a degree of precision, reliability and lack of equivocation, quite unattainable in any natural language. To achieve this, Ptydepe makes use of the following postulation: if similarities between any two words are to be minimized, the words must be formed by the least probable combination of letters. This means that the creation of words must be based on such principles as would lead to the greatest possible redundancy of language. You see, a redundancy – in other words, the difference between the maximum and the real entropy, related to the maximum entropy and expressed percentually – concerns precisely that superfluity by which the expression of a particular piece of information in a given language is longer, and thus less probable (i.e. less likely to appear in this particular form), than would be the same expression in a language in which all letters have the same probability of occurrence. Briefly: the greater the redundancy of a language, the more reliable it is, because the smaller is the possibility that by an exchange of a letter, by an oversight or a typing error, the meaning of the text could be altered.

[GROSS *enters by B.D., his memorandum in hand, crosses the room and leaves by S.D.*]

LEAR: How does, in fact, Ptydepe achieve its high re-dundancy? By a consistent use of the so-called principle of a sixty per cent dissimilarity; which means that any Ptydepe word must differ by at least sixty per cent of its letters from any other Ptydepe word of the same length (and, incidentally, any part of such a word must differ in the same way from any Ptydepe word of this length, that is from any word shorter than is the one of which it is a part). Thus, for example, out of all the possible five-letter combinations of the twenty-six letters of our alphabet – and these are 11,881,376 – only 432 combinations can be found which differ from each other by three letters, i.e. by sixty per cent of the total. From these 432 combinations only seventeen fulfil the other requirements as well and thus have become Ptydepe words. Hence it is clear that in Ptydepe there often occur words which are very long indeed.

THUMB [*raising his hand*]: Sir –

LEAR: Yes?

THUMB [*gets up*]: Would you please tell us which is the longest word in Ptydepe? [*Sits down.*]

LEAR: Certainly. It is the word meaning 'a wombat', which has 319 letters. But let us proceed. Naturally, this raises the question of how Ptydepe solves the problem of manageability and pronounceability of such long words. Quite simply: inside these words the letters are inter-spersed with occasional gaps, so that a word may consist of a greater or smaller number of so-called subwords. But at the same time the length of a word – as indeed everything in Ptydepe – is not left to chance. You see, the vocabulary of Ptydepe is built according to an entirely logical principle: the more common the meaning, the shorter the word. Thus, for example, the most commonly used term so far known – that is the term 'whatever' – is rendered in Ptydepe by the word 'gh'. As you can see, it is a word consisting of only two letters. There exists, however, an even shorter word – that is 'f' – but this word does not yet carry any meaning. I wonder if any of you can tell me why. Well? [*Only* THUMB *raises his hand.*] Well, Mr Thumb?

THUMB [*gets up*]: It's being held in reserve in case science should discover a term even more commonly used than the term 'whatever'.

LEAR: Correct, Mr Thumb. You get an A.

# SCENE THREE

*The Secretariat of the Translation Centre. It is something between an office and a waiting-room. A large desk, a typist's desk, a few straight chairs or armchairs, a small conference table. STROLL is seated on it, a paper bag full of peaches in his lap. He is consuming them with gusto.*

[GROSS *enters by B.D., his memorandum in hand.*]

GROSS: Good morning.

STROLL [*with his mouth full*]: Morning.

GROSS: I've dropped in to get acquainted with the activities of the Translation Centre. I'm the Managing Director.

STROLL [*with his mouth full*]: So you're the Managing Director?

GROSS: Yes. Josef Gross.

STROLL [*slowly lets himself down from the table, finishes his peach, wipes hands on handkerchief and walks over to GROSS*]: Very glad to meet you. Sorry I didn't recognize you. I've been here only a very short time and so I still haven't met everybody. My name's Stroll. Head of the Translation Centre. Do sit down.

[STROLL *folds his handkerchief and shakes hands with* GROSS. *Both sit down.* STROLL *lights a cigarette.* GROSS *tries all his pockets, but cannot find his.*]

STROLL: Everything here is still so to speak at the nappy stage.

GROSS: I understand.

STROLL: We're still grappling with a great many teething troubles.

GROSS: That's clear enough –

STROLL: It's no easy matter, you know.

GROSS: No, quite.

STROLL: Tell me, exactly what would you like to find out?

GROSS: I'd like to see how you've organized the process of making translations. Do you do them while one waits?

STROLL: We'll make a translation from Ptydepe while you wait for any member of our organization who is a citizen of our country and has an authorization to have a Ptydepe text translated.

GROSS: Does one need a special authorization?

[SAVANT *enters by S.D.*]

SAVANT: Morning, Otto. Have you heard that there's goose for lunch today?

STROLL [*jumps up*]: What! Did you say goose?

SAVANT: That's what the chaps in the Secretariat said. Pick you up on the way to the canteen, right?

STROLL: Right! The sooner the better!

[SAVANT *leaves by S.D.*]

STROLL: I love goose, you know! Now, what were we talking about?

GROSS: You were saying that one needs an authorization to get a translation made.

STROLL: Right. Well now, look here. We, the staff, do use Ptydepe, but we're no experts. Let's face it, we're no linguists, are we? So, naturally, the exploitation and development of Ptydepe cannot be left in our hands alone. If it were it might lead to unwelcome spontaneity, and Ptydepe might quite easily change under our very noses into a normal natural language and thus lose its whole purpose. [*Suddenly he halts, becomes preoccupied, then quickly gets up.*] Excuse me. [*Hurries out by S.D.*]

[GROSS *stares after him in surprise, then begins another search through his pockets, but finds no cigarettes. Pause.* HELENA *enters by S.D.*]

HELENA: Was Alex here?

GROSS: I don't know who that is.

HELENA: You're not part of this shop, love?

GROSS: On the contrary. I'm Managing Director.

HELENA: Are you, love? Well, you must do something about this snack-bar, I mean it! It's a bloody shame to see our girls traipse miles for a cup of tea, it really is. Does anyone think about people in this shop?

GROSS: And who, may I ask, are you?

HELENA: I'm the chairman. But you can call me Nellie.

GROSS: The chairman of what, if you'll forgive my asking?

HELENA: Of what? Don't know of what just yet. As a matter of fact we're having a meeting about that very thing this afternoon. But I'm already so bloody busy I don't know which way to turn. They don't give you time to have a proper look around and they expect you to start cleaning up their smelly little messes straight away. Well, see you. [*Leaves by S.D.*]

> [*Pause.* GROSS *again tries his pockets. Then looks at his watch. Waits. Pause.* STROLL *at last returns by S.D. Walks slowly. Buttons up his trousers while walking.*]

STROLL: You don't like goose?

GROSS: I do. You were saying that Ptydepe cannot be left only in your hands.

STROLL: Right. And that's why every department which starts to introduce Ptydepe is assigned a special methodician, a so-called Ptydepist, who, being a specialist, is supposed to ensure that Ptydepe gets used correctly.

> [MARIA *enters by B.D., carrying a string bag full of onions.*]

MARIA [*walking towards S.D.*]: Good morning.

GROSS: Good morning.

> [MARIA *leaves by S.D.*]

STROLL: Our Ptydepist fulfils this task by issuing for every translation a special authorization –

MARIA [*off stage*]: Here are the onions, Miss Helena.

STROLL: Which enables him to record all outgoing translations from Ptydepe.

HELENA [*off stage*]: Would you mind putting them over by the filing cabinet, that's a good girl.

STROLL: Thus he obtains all the necessary material for various statistics, on the basis of which he then directs the use of Ptydepe.

[MARIA *returns by S.D., carrying an empty string bag, puts it in the drawer, sits at typist's desk and begins to work.*]

GROSS: So, if I've understood you correctly, you'll give a translation only to those staff members who can produce an authorization from your Ptydepist.

STROLL: Right.

[SAVANT *enters by S.D., knife and fork in hand.*]

SAVANT: Are you ready?

STROLL [*to* MARIA]: Where are my tools?

[MARIA *takes knife and fork from a drawer and hands them to him.*]

GROSS: Who is your Ptydepist?

STROLL: Have they been washed?

MARIA: Of course.

STROLL [*to* GROSS]: What did you say?

GROSS: Who is your Ptydepist?

STROLL: Dr Savant here.

GROSS [*shakes hands with* SAVANT]: How do you do. I'm Josef Gross, the Managing Director.

SAVANT: How do you do. I'm Alex Savant, the Graduate Ptydepist. My degree is like a doctorate, you know.

GROSS: I'd like a word with you, Dr Savant.

STROLL: Are you going to ask for breast?

SAVANT: Sorry, Mr Gross, but we really must go and have our lunch now. Shouldn't want to miss it. [*To* STROLL] I prefer a leg.

[SAVANT *and* STROLL *leave by B.D.* GROSS *stands for a while in surprise, then slowly sits down. Pause. He looks at his watch. Waits. Again looks at his watch, puts it to his ear. Then tries all his pockets.*]

GROSS: Have you a cigarette, by any chance?

MARIA: I'm sorry, I don't smoke.

[*Pause.* GROSS *again looks at his watch. Then he notices a box on the desk.*]

GROSS: What's that?

MARIA: Cigars.

GROSS: May I take one?

MARIA: Oh no! They belong to Mr Stroll. He's counted them. He'd be very angry if you did.

[*Long pause.* GROSS *stretches, looks at his watch, finally gets up, slowly approaches* MARIA *and peers over her shoulder to see what she is doing.*]

MARIA: Reports —

GROSS: Mmnn —

[GROSS *slowly walks around the office, examining everything, then again sits down.* HELENA *quietly enters by S.D.* GROSS *sits with his back towards her.* HELENA *gestures to* MARIA *to keep quiet. Tiptoeing, she creeps up to* GROSS *and from behind puts her hands over his eyes.* GROSS *starts.*]

HELENA [*changing her voice to make it sound like a man's*]: Guess who?

GROSS: I beg your pardon!

HELENA: Guess who!

GROSS: Take your hands off at once!

HELENA: Come on, guess! Who am I?

GROSS [*hesitates a moment*]: The District Inspector.

HELENA: No.

GROSS: The Regional Inspector.

HELENA: No.

GROSS: The Inspector General.

HELENA: No.

GROSS: Ilon.

HELENA: No.

GROSS: Then it's Karel.

HELENA: No — no — no.

GROSS: Do stop it, Ilon! You're being very silly!

HELENA: Shall I tell you?

GROSS: Would you, please!

[HELENA *takes her hands away.* GROSS *turns.*]

HELENA: You're not Alex? Sorry. love. I thought it was Alex Savant. Hasn't he showed up yet?

GROSS: What charming manners!

MARIA: He's gone to lunch.

HELENA [*to* GROSS]: Starchy, aren't you? What the hell! It was just a bit of fun, that's all. Well, see you. [*Leaves by S.D.*]

[*Pause.* GROSS *once more tries his pockets.*]

GROSS: Have you a cigarette, by any chance?

MARIA: You've already asked, Mr Gross.

GROSS: I'm sorry, I must have forgotten.

[GROSS *looks at his watch, puts it to his ear, begins to be impatient. Again the same search, then gets up and wanders about the office. Stops behind* MARIA *and peers over her shoulder to see what she is doing.*]

MARIA: Reports –

GROSS: Mmnn –

[*Pause.* GROSS *again notices Stroll's box, slowly approaches, looks at it for a while, opens it quietly, takes a cigar, smells it.* MARIA *watches him.* GROSS *realizes he is being watched, replaces the cigar and returns to his seat. Pause.*]

GROSS [*loudly*]: Good God! It wouldn't hurt him, would it?

[STROLL *and* SAVANT *are returning by B.D. in lively conversation, they hand their knives and forks to* MARIA, *then sit down.*]

STROLL: That was simply delicious. The way it was cooked! Straight through!

SAVANT: I think it was better last time.

STROLL: Not juicy enough. The very best was the time before last.

GROSS: Dr Savant –

STROLL [*to* MARIA]: Would you go and see if Mr Langer is having his lunch today? If not, ask whether he'd mind sending me his voucher.

GROSS: Dr Savant –

[MARIA *quickly walks out by B.D.* SAVANT *watches her with greedy appreciation.*]

SAVANT [*turning to* GROSS]: Not bad, eh?

GROSS: Rather pleasant.

SAVANT: Sexy little thing, isn't she?

GROSS: Dr Savant –

STROLL: Her? Sexy? Come off it!

SAVANT [*to* GROSS]: Yes?

GROSS: I understand you can authorize the making of a translation from Ptydepe.

SAVANT: Yes, for those who bring me their documents.

GROSS: What do you mean? What sort of documents?

SAVANT: Personal registration.

[STROLL *offers a cigarette to* SAVANT.]

SAVANT [*taking it*]: Ta.

[STROLL *and* SAVANT *light their cigarettes.* GROSS *again tries his pockets, hesitates, then speaks up.*]

GROSS: I'm sorry – er – could you sell me a cigarette?

STROLL: I wish I could, but I've only three left.

GROSS: Oh, I see. I'm sorry. [*To* SAVANT] Why do you actually need the personal registration documents?

SAVANT [*to* STROLL]: She is sexy, you know. Just wait till someone catches her in the dark! [*To* GROSS] What did you say?

GROSS: Why do you actually need the personal registration documents?

SAVANT: Well, it's like this, you see. Although I've been employed by this organization, I'm no common or garden staff-member. I am, as you well know, a scholar of a new sort, of course, as everything about Ptydepe is new. And as such I naturally take certain – shall we say –

exceptions to some of the rather bureaucratic procedures of my staff colleagues. As a matter of fact, it's not really exceptions I take – it's more like objections. No, objections isn't the right word either. How shall I put it? I'm sorry. You see, I'm used to speaking in Ptydepe and so it's rather difficult for me to find the right words in a natural language.

GROSS: Please go on.

SAVANT: In Ptydepe one would say axajores. My colleagues sometimes ylud kaboz pady el too much, and at the same time they keep forgetting that etrokaj zenig ajte ge gyboz.

STROLL: Abdy hez fajut gagob nyp orka?

SAVANT: Kavej hafiz okuby ryzal.

STROLL: Ryzal! Ryzal! Ryzal! Varuk bado di ryzal? Kabyzach? Mahog? Hajbam?

SAVANT: Ogny fyk hajbam? Parde gul axajores va dyt rohago kabrazol? Fabotybe! They think they can simply send me a chap, I'll give him an O.K., and that'll be the end of it. Byzugat rop ju ge tyrak! If our statistics are to make any sense at all we must have concrete foundations to build on. We must have detailed information about everybody who comes in contact with Ptydepe, in order to get the greatest possible variety of sociological and psychological data.

GROSS: Wouldn't it be enough if a chap just told you himself everything you want to know about him?

SAVANT: That wouldn't guarantee that everything was hutput.

GROSS: I beg your pardon?

SAVANT: Hutput. Quite exact.

[MARIA *returns by B.D.*]

MARIA: I'm sorry, but it appears that Mr Langer will definitely be eating his lunch today.

STROLL: Pity.

[MARIA *sits at her desk and continues working.*]

GROSS: Excuse me, you were speaking about the uncertainties of verbal statements.

SAVANT: Ah, yes! Well now, all the particulars concerning each employee have long been recorded with the greatest precision and without any possible subjective zexdohyt – I'm sorry – point of view –

GROSS: I understand – [*Jokingly*] I've a completely hutput zexdohyt of it.

SAVANT: Zexdohyttet! You've forgotten that every noun preceded by the adjective hutput takes on the suffix 'tet' –

STROLL: Or tete.

SAVANT: Or tete. Quite. Many people make this mistake. Even Mr Wassermann in one of his letters –

GROSS: Excuse me, you were speaking about the advantages of the personal registration documents.

SAVANT: Ah, yes! Well now, the personal registration documents often record things which even the particular employee doesn't know about himself. [*To* STROLL] Nuzapom?

STROLL: Zapom. Yd nik fe rybol zezuhof.

SAVANT: Yd nik yd nek.

GROSS: To sum up. You'll authorize a translation only for those members of the staff who can produce their documents. All right, where does one get them?

[HELENA *enters by S.D.*]

HELENA: Hallo everybody!

SAVANT [*sings*]: Hallo everybody hallo –

HELENA: You know whose birthday it is? Eddi Kliment's!

SAVANT: Eddi's? Is it?

HELENA: There's a do going on for him next door. So drop everything and come along. [*To* MARIA] Seems the grocer's got limes. Would you mind running over and getting me eight?

[MARIA *hurries out by S.D.*]

SAVANT: What are they drinking?

HELENA: Vodka.

SAVANT: Did you hear that, Otto?

> [SAVANT *and* STROLL *hasten towards the S.D.*]

GROSS: You haven't told me yet where one gets those documents.

SAVANT: Why, right here from our chairman. From Nellie, of course.

> [SAVANT *and* STROLL *quickly walk out by S.D.* HELENA *is about to follow them.*]

GROSS: Miss Helena –

HELENA [*halts by the door*]: What?

GROSS: I'd like a word with you.

HELENA: Later, love. You'll have to wait.

GROSS: Here?

HELENA: Where else?

GROSS: You mean you don't mind leaving me here alone? With all the classified material and all that?

HELENA: You won't be alone, love. There's a chink in the wall. You're being watched by our Staff Watcher.

GROSS: Good gracious! A chink?

HELENA: Wouldn't be much good if he was actually in here. That way he'd be able to watch only one office, wouldn't he? This way he can watch five of them at once. You see, his cubicle is surrounded by offices and each is furnished with an observation chink. So all he has to do is to walk – at random, natch – from one to another and peer.

GROSS: Interesting idea.

HELENA: Isn't it, love? And it's my idea, too! My point was to stop visitors from having to hang about in the hall when the office is empty. Bloody nuisance, isn't it? Even in these piddling details one must be thinking of the good of the people! Well, see you. [*Runs out S.D.*]

> [GROSS *wanders about investigating the walls.*]

GEORGE [*after a while, off stage*]: Don't bother. The chink is well disguised.

GROSS: I should say it is! One might make use of this idea in other departments as well.

GEORGE [*off stage*]: Not likely. This kind of thing has to be planned for by the architect from the very start.

GROSS: I see what you mean. On the other hand, he couldn't very well have planned for it here.

GEORGE [*off stage*]: He didn't. He made a mistake in his calculations. And when this building was erected it was found that there was this space left over between the offices. So it was used in this way.

GROSS: A really stimulating idea!

[*Pause.* GROSS *sits down, looks impatiently at his watch, gets up, sits down, again looks at his watch, gets up, searches his pockets, again sits down.* MARIA *runs in by B.D.*]

GROSS: What's the matter?

MARIA: Forgot my purse. [*Opens drawer of typing desk and rummages in it hastily.*]

GROSS: Miss –

MARIA: Yes?

GROSS: Do you know Ptydepe?

MARIA: A bit.

GROSS: Can you translate it?

MARIA: I'm strictly forbidden to make any translations before I've passed my exams.

GROSS: But on my authority you might try to make a translation, mightn't you? It doesn't have to be perfect, you know. [MARIA *smiles.*] What's so funny about it?

MARIA: You wouldn't understand. It's impossible, that's all.

GROSS: What's your name?

MARIA: Maria.

GROSS: Maria! A pretty name.

MARIA: Do you like it?

GROSS: Very much. Maria – just for once! Nobody'll know about it.

MARIA: Mr Gross! Somebody might walk in any minute. Please be reasonable!

GROSS [*urgently*]: Go on, sweetheart!

MARIA: And what about the Staff Watcher?

GROSS [*whispers*]: You could whisper the translation to me.

MARIA: The limes will soon be sold out and Miss Helena will be angry. 'Bye. [*Having found her purse, she runs out by B.D.*]

[*Pause.* GROSS, *tired, sinks into his chair. He stares ahead, mechanically begins to try his pockets again. Then gets up and walks straight to the cigar box. When he is about to open it, he quickly takes his hand away and looks around cautiously.*]

GROSS: Mr Watcher – [*Pause.*] Mr Watcher – [*Pause.*] Listen, Mr Watcher, can you hear me? Have you got a cigarette? [*Pause.*] He must have fallen asleep. [*Carefully opens the box.*]

GEORGE [*off stage*]: What do you mean – fallen asleep!

GROSS [*jerks away from the box*]: Well, why didn't you answer me?

GEORGE [*off stage*]: I wanted to test you out.

GROSS: I beg your pardon! Do you realize who I am? The Managing Director!

GEORGE [*off stage*]: Habuk bulugan.

GROSS: I beg your pardon?

GEORGE [*off stage*]: Habuk bulugan, avrator.

GROSS: What did you mean by that?

GEORGE [*off stage*]: Nutuput.

GROSS [*looks at his watch, then walks quickly to B.D., turns by the door*]: I won't put up with any abuse from you! I expect you to come to me and apologize. [*Exit by B.D.*]

GEORGE [*off stage*]: Gotroch!

# SCENE FOUR

*The Director's office.*

[BALLAS *and* PILLAR *are silently waiting for* GROSS.
PILLAR *has a notebook in his hand.* HANA *is combing her hair.
Then* GROSS *hurries in by B.D., crosses to his desk, sits down
with studied casualness. For a while there is menacing silence.*]

BALLAS: Well?

GROSS: Well?

BALLAS: The hour has passed. Ready to be more sensible
now?

GROSS: Certainly not.

BALLAS: As you may have noticed, the introduction of
Ptydepe into our organization successfully proceeds.
What are you going to do about it?

GROSS: Put a stop to it.

HANA: Mr Gross, may I go and get the chocolates?

BALLAS: How?

GROSS: By issuing an order that the introduction of Ptydepe
be stopped and its use cancelled.

BALLAS: You cannot.

GROSS: Why not?

BALLAS: You never issued any order for its introduction
and use, so you're in no position to stop and cancel anything at all.

GROSS: Then you'll do it.

BALLAS: I haven't issued any such order either. Have I,
Mr P.?

[PILLAR *shakes his head.*]

HANA: Mr Gross, may I go and get the chocolates?

GROSS: What do you mean?

BALLAS: It was just a verbal directive, based on an

assurance that you'd validate it by a supplementary order.

GROSS: Then I'll simply not give any supplementary order.

HANA: Mr Gross, may I go and get the chocolates?

BALLAS: The introduction of Ptydepe is in full swing and it will naturally go on even without it. [*To* HANA] Run along.

[HANA *immediately stops combing her hair and is off by B.D.*]

GROSS: In that case I'll have to report the whole matter to the authorities.

BALLAS [*laughs*]: Did you hear that, Mr P.? He doesn't know that the authorities have taken a great fancy to Ptydepe.

GROSS: If that's the case, why haven't they made its use obligatory in all organizations?

BALLAS: Playing it safe. If Ptydepe succeeds, they'll have plenty of time to take the credit for it; if it fails, they'll be able to dissociate themselves from it and blame the departments.

GROSS: I hope you don't expect me to be a traitor to my beliefs.

BALLAS: I do.

GROSS: How do you propose to make me?

BALLAS [*points at* PILLAR'*s book*]: Do you see this book? Not long ago it was improperly authenticated by your order, although it had not been registered by the Purchasing Department and thus was your own property. Do you know what that constitutes? Abuse of authority.

GROSS: Good God! Don't you make yourself sick?

BALLAS: Do we make ourselves sick, Mr P.?

[PILLAR *shakes his head.*]

BALLAS: Of course we don't. When the good of Man is at stake, nothing will make us sick.

GROSS: But you yourself got me to sign it!

BALLAS: I did? I don't seem to remember –

GROSS: By your hints about the rumours concerning that damned rubber-stamp!

BALLAS: I wouldn't bring that up, if I were you.

GROSS: Why not?

BALLAS: Because it's no extenuating circumstance at all. Just the reverse, in fact.

GROSS: I don't know what you're talking about.

BALLAS: Don't you? Well, look here. If it weren't for the rubber-stamp affair, you might have claimed that you signed the authentication of this book moved by a sincere desire to help our clerical staff, which of course wouldn't have excused your conduct, but would at least have explained it somewhat on humanitarian grounds; while if you do bring up this motive now, you'll be admitting thereby that you signed it moved merely by petty cowardice, so as to silence legitimate inquiries into the circumstance of the rubber-stamp affair. Do you follow me? If, on the other hand, you hadn't signed it, you might have pretended that you were indeed taking the rubber-stamp home for reasons of work, but your signature proves that you were clearly aware of your guilt. As you see, both your errors are intertwined in such an original way that the one greatly multiplies the other. By publicizing the circumstances which you consider extenuating you would leave nobody in any doubt whatever about the real motives of your conduct. Well then, shall we come to an agreement?

GROSS: All right, I'll resign.

BALLAS: But we don't want you to.

GROSS: Well, what do you want me to do?

BALLAS: Sign the supplementary order for the introduction and the use of Ptydepe in our organization.

GROSS: But you said, didn't you, that Ptydepe will be used even without a supplementary order? Then why do you insist on it now?

BALLAS: That's our business.

[*A long pause.*]

GROSS [*quietly*]: Are you sure that Ptydepe will really make office communications more precise?

BALLAS: I'm glad our discussion is at last reaching a realistic level. Mr Pillar, would you offer Mr Gross some milk?

[PILLAR *hands* GROSS HANA'*s bottle of milk.* GROSS *drinks mechanically.*]

BALLAS: Look here. You yourself know best how many misunderstandings, suspected innuendoes, injustices and injuries can be contained in one single sentence of a natural language. In fact, a natural language endows many more-or-less precise terms, such as for example the term 'coloured', with so many wrong, let's say emotional, overtones, that they can entirely distort the innocent and eminently human content of these terms. Now tell me sincerely, has the word 'mutarex' any such overtones for you? It hasn't, has it? You see! It is a paradox, but it is precisely the surface inhumanity of an artificial language which guarantees its truly humanist function! After Ptydepe comes into use, no one will ever again have the impression that he's being injured when in fact he's being helped, and thus everybody will be much happier.

[HANA *returns by B.D., carrying a box of chocolates, puts it in her shopping bag, sits down and once more begins to comb her hair. Pause.*]

GROSS: You have convinced me. Have the supplementary order for the introduction of Ptydepe in our organization typed and bring it to me for signature.

BALLAS: Mr Gross, we're overjoyed that you've grasped the demands of the times. We look forward to our further work in the organization under your expert and enlightened leadership. [*He takes out a sheet of paper and puts it on the desk in front of* GROSS.] Here is the typed order you request.

> [GROSS *signs. When he finishes,* BALLAS *and* PILLAR *begin to applaud.* GROSS *also claps uncertainly a few times. They all shake hands and congratulate each other. Finally,* BALLAS *takes the signed document.*]

BALLAS: Well, that's that. Aren't you hungry, Mr P.?

> [PILLAR *shakes his head. Pause.*]

BALLAS: I believe that from now on we'll be working very closely together.

GROSS: We'll have to. Without your help it'd probably be rather hard for me to find my bearings in the new situation. Perhaps at the beginning we shan't be able to avoid directing the organization, so to speak, hand in hand.

BALLAS: I have a better idea. What about me being the director and you my deputy. Won't that make things much easier?

GROSS [*confused*]: But you said, didn't you, that you were looking forward to working under my expert and enlightened leadership?

BALLAS: You will be able to use your expertise and enlightenment just as well as a deputy. I'll go and get my things, while you, Mr Gross, will kindly move out of my desk!

GROSS: As you wish, Mr Ballas.

BALLAS: Mr P., let's go.

> [BALLAS *and* PILLAR *leave by S.D.* GROSS *collects his papers from his desk and stuffs them in his pockets, then carefully takes down the fire-extinguisher hanging on the wall.*]

GROSS: Things do seem to be moving rather fast.

HANA: Mr Gross –

GROSS: There was nothing else I could do. An open conflict would have meant that I'd be finished. This way – as Deputy Director – I can at least salvage this and that.

HANA: Mr Gross –

GROSS: Anyway, who knows, maybe this – Ptydepe – will turn out to be a good thing after all. If we grasp the reins firmly and with intelligence –

HANA: Mr Gross –

GROSS: What is it?

HANA: May I go and get my lunch?

GROSS: Run along!

[HANA *hastily takes her knife and fork, and hurries out by B.D.* BALLAS *and* PILLAR *enter by S.D.* BALLAS *is carrying a fire-extinguisher, identical with the one* GROSS *just took off the wall.* GROSS *halts in the centre and sadly stares ahead.*]

GROSS [*to himself*]: Why can't I be a little boy again? I'd do everything differently from the beginning.

[GROSS *lingers dejectedly for a second longer, then turns and slowly walks out by B.D., the fire-extinguisher clasped in his arms. Meanwhile,* BALLAS *has placed his own extinguisher in the emptied space,* PILLAR *has taken various papers from his pockets and spread them on the desk. Then they both sit down at the desk, make themselves comfortable, grow still, look at each other and smile happily.*]

# SCENE FIVE

*The Ptydepe classroom. Again* LEAR *lecturing to four* CLERKS.

LEAR: Historically, the natural languages originated in all probability through the development of the inarticulate shrieks by which a primitive creature expressed his basic reactions to the surrounding world. The very oldest group of words is thus the interjections. At the same time, the interjections form an unusually easy part of Ptydepe, which is quite obvious, as their frequency in inter-office communications is rather limited. This is why the interjections will form the first few lessons of your curriculum. Well then, let us proceed to the interjections. As you know, every word of a natural language – including the interjections – has several Ptydepe equivalents, which differentiate its several shades of meaning. To start with, for each interjection we shall learn only one, the most common, expression in Ptydepe. Nevertheless, as an example, I'd like to demonstrate to you through the Ptydepe renderings of the interjection 'boo', how rich and precise is Ptydepe, even in this marginal sphere.

[GROSS *enters by B.D., fire-extinguisher in his arms, walks towards S.D., hesitates, halts, thinks for a moment, then turns to* LEAR.]

GROSS: Sir –

LEAR: What is it?

GROSS: I do hate to interrupt you, but I happen to have with me a little Ptydepe text, and I was wondering if – just as a refresher, you know – it might not be a good thing to acquaint our colleagues here with the actual shape of Ptydepe. Perhaps if you read it aloud and then possibly translated it, it might be of interest to the class.

LEAR: As regards a sample of an actual Ptydepe text, I've prepared my own, authorized, specimen. However, for the sake of variety, I'm quite prepared to read your text as well, that is, provided you can show that your interest in Ptydepe is vital and you're not just trying to interfere with the class. You may sit down.

[GROSS, *surprised, mechanically sits in an empty chair, puts the extinguisher in his lap.*]

LEAR: Generally speaking, the interjection 'boo' is used in the daily routine of an office, a company, a large organization when one employee wants to sham-ambush another. In those cases where the endangerment of an employee who is in full view and quite unprepared for the impending peril is being shammed by an employee who is himself hidden, 'boo' is rendered by 'gedynrelom'. The word 'osonfterte' is used in substantially the same situation when, however, the imperilled employee is aware of the danger. 'Eg gynd y trojadus' is used when an employee who has not taken the precaution, or the time, or the trouble to hide wants to sham-ambush another employee who is also in full view, in case it is meant as a joke. 'Eg jeht kuz' is used in substantially the same situation when, however, it is meant in earnest. 'Ysiste etordyf' is used by a superior wishing to test out the vigilance of a subordinate. 'Yxap tseror najx' is used, on the contrary, by the subordinate towards a superior, but only on the days specially appointed for this purpose.

And now let me see if you've been paying attention. Who can tell us how one says 'boo' in Ptydepe when a hidden employee wants to sham-ambush another employee who is in full view and quite unprepared for the danger? Mr Thumb!

THUMB [*gets up*]: Gedynrelom. [*Sits down.*]

LEAR: Correct. And when the imperilled employee is aware of the danger? [*Points at* GROSS.]

GROSS [*gets up*]: Danger menacing an employee who is in full view?

LEAR: Yes.

GROSS: Who is aware of the danger?

LEAR: Yes.

GROSS: And the perpetrator is hidden?

LEAR: Yes.

GROSS: Aha – yes – I see. Well – in that case one says – damn it, it was on the tip of my tongue.

LEAR: Mr Thumb, do you know?

THUMB [*gets up*]: Osonfterte. [*Sits down.*]

LEAR: There you are. You see how easy it is! Well, let's take another case, shall we? For example, how would a superior say 'boo' when he wishes to test out the vigilance of a subordinate?

GROSS: A superior?

LEAR: Yes.

GROSS: The vigilance of a subordinate?

LEAR: Yes.

GROSS: I say, I think I know this one!

LEAR: Well, then tell us.

GROSS: We're translating the interjection 'boo', aren't we?

LEAR: Yes.

GROSS: I'm sure I know it – only – it has sort of slipped my mind.

LEAR: Well, Mr Thumb?

THUMB [*gets up*]: Ysiste etordyf. [*Sits down.*]

LEAR: Correct, Mr Thumb. Well, shall we try once more? Third time never fails, eh? Let's see if you can tell us, for example, how does an employee who has not taken the precaution, or the time, or the trouble to hide say 'boo' if he wants to sham-ambush another employee who is also in full view, when it is meant in earnest?

GROSS: I'm afraid I don't know.

LEAR: Let me help you. Eg –

GROSS: Eg – eg – eg –

LEAR: Jeht –

GROSS: Yes, I do remember now. Eg jeht.

LEAR: Wrong. Mr Thumb, would you mind telling him?

THUMB [*gets up*]: Eg jeht kuz. [*Sits down.*]

LEAR: Correct. Eg jeht doesn't mean anything at all. Those are only two sub-words of the word eg jeht kuz.

GROSS: The third sub-word escaped me.

LEAR: Unfortunately, the first two sub-words also escaped you, like all the other Ptydepe words which I was trying to teach you only a moment ago. When one considers that the interjections are the easiest part of Ptydepe and that my requirements have indeed been minimal, one cannot avoid concluding that in your case it is not merely a matter of average inattentiveness or negligence, but of that particular inability to learn any Ptydepe whatsoever which stems from a profound and well-disguised doubt in its very sense. Under these circumstances I don't see why I should oblige you by reading aloud and, what's more, translating an unauthorized text. Chozup puzuk bojt!

GROSS: Goodness! So much fuss about three little words! [*Clasps fire-extinguisher in his arms and leaves by S.D.*]

LEAR: Let us proceed. Mr Thumb, can you tell us how a subordinate says 'boo' to a superior in Ptydepe on the days specially appointed for this purpose?

THUMB [*gets up*]: Yxap tseror najx. [*Sits down.*]

LEAR: Correct, Mr Thumb. You get an A.

# SCENE SIX

*The Secretariat of the Translation Centre. The office is empty, only the noise of a party going on off stage can be heard: gay voices, laughter, clinking of glasses, singing of 'Happy birthday to you', drinking songs, etc. During the first part of the following scene the noise occasionally becomes very loud, then quietens down a little.* GROSS *hurries in by B.D. with fire-extinguisher still in his arms, halts in the centre, looks around, listens, then he puts extinguisher on the floor and tentatively sits down.* MARIA *enters by B.D., carrying a paper bag full of limes and walks towards S.D.* GROSS *gets up at once.*

GROSS: Good afternoon.

MARIA: Good afternoon. [*Leaves by S.D. Off stage*] Here are the limes, Miss Helena.

HELENA [*off stage*]: Would you mind putting them down by the coat-rack? That's a good girl.

    [MARIA *re-enters by B.D., sits at her desk and begins to work.*]

GROSS [*also sits down*]: Miss Helena is next door?

MARIA: Yes. They're celebrating Mr Kliment's birthday.

GROSS: Do you think she'd mind coming here for a moment?

MARIA: I'll ask – [*Exits by S.D. Returns after a short while.*] Mr Gross –

GROSS: Yes?

MARIA: You're no longer the Managing Director?

GROSS: I'm his deputy now.

MARIA: Oh! Forgive me for asking – but what happened?

GROSS: Oh, well, we just – we exchanged jobs, Mr Ballas and I.

MARIA: Well, Deputy Director is also a very responsible position.

GROSS: It is, isn't it? As a matter of fact, to some extent it's even more responsible than the director's! I can remember, for instance, that when I was the director, my deputy often solved some of the most important problems for me. Will Miss Helena come?

MARIA: You'll have to wait a little, I'm afraid.

[HELENA *looks in at S.D.* GROSS *quickly gets up.*]

HELENA [*to* MARIA]: Come here a moment, will you?

[MARIA *leaves with* HELENA *by S.D.* GROSS *slowly sits down again. Long pause. Loud voices and noise from next door. After a while all quietens down.*]

GROSS: Mr Watcher –

GEORGE [*off stage*]: What is it?

GROSS: We're friends again, aren't we?

GEORGE [*off stage*]: Oh, well – why not?

[*Pause. Noise of the party.*]

GROSS: Mr Watcher –

GEORGE [*off stage*]: What now?

GROSS: Aren't you celebrating?

GEORGE: I'm following the party through the chink.

GROSS: Does it look like being a long one?

GEORGE [*off stage*]: They've finished the vodka.

GROSS: Have they?

[*Pause. Singing off stage, changing into cheers.*]

VOICES [*off stage*]:

> For he's a jolly good fellow
> For he's a jolly good fellow
> For he's a jolly good fellow
> Which nobody can deny.

Hip – hip – hurrah!

[*Cheers and shouts culminate in laughter which, however, soon dies down, voices are beginning to recede, a few farewells, then all is quiet. The party is over.* STROLL *and* SAVANT *enter by S.D., absorbed in animated conversation.*]

STROLL: I bet she was shy!

SAVANT: To start with. But then —

STROLL: Then what?

SAVANT: You know what.

STROLL: Come off it! I bet you've made up that part about xachaj ybul!

SAVANT: Absolutely not! Literal truth! Down to the last letter.

STROLL: Come off it.

SAVANT: Mind you, if it hadn't been for kojufer bzal gaftre, we'd have certainly luhofr dyboroch!

STROLL: Does she actually —

SAVANT: I tell you. She's a wild 'un! [*Sings*] Cigarettes and whisky and wild wild women —

STROLL: How old is she?

SAVANT: Sixteen.

STROLL: I prefer them a teency weency bit younger.

HELENA [*enters by S.D.*]: Come on, everybody! Let's have some coffee!

STROLL: That's a thought! Where's Maria?

SAVANT: Our sexy little thing? Mr Gross might know.

GROSS: I?

SAVANT: Don't try to deny it! You lust after her!

GROSS: I beg your pardon!

SAVANT: You called her sweetheart. The Staff Watcher heard you.

GEORGE [*off stage*]: You talk too much, Alex.

SAVANT: Listen, why don't you shut up and do your watching!

STROLL: Now, now, friends! [*Calls*] Maria!

SAVANT [*sings*]: Maria — Maria — Maria!

HELENA: Leave her alone, love. She's ironing my slip. I'll make the coffee. [*Calls towards S.D.*] Where do you keep the percolator?

[MARIA *runs in by S.D., iron in one hand, with the other she takes percolator from drawer, and runs out again.*]

STROLL: You won't mind, Mr Gross, will you, if we don't offer you any coffee? We've very little left, you see. It'll just about make three cups.

GROSS: Never mind. I don't really care for any.

STROLL: Nellie, Mr Gross doesn't care for any coffee. Make it three cups, but make a double one for me, will you? [*To* SAVANT] I say, what about a cigar with the coffee?

SAVANT: That's a thought!

GROSS: Miss Helena –

HELENA [*calling towards S.D.*]: Where do you keep the coffee?

[MARIA *runs in by S.D. with the iron, takes tin of coffee from another drawer, runs out again. Meanwhile* STROLL *has taken cigar box off his desk. Offers one to* SAVANT.]

GROSS: Miss Helena –

STROLL: That's what I call a cigar!

SAVANT [*takes one*]: Ta.

[STROLL *also takes one. Both light them expertly.* GROSS *watches them. As usual, he first tries all his pockets, then takes out some money and offers it to* STROLL.]

GROSS: Excuse me – may I – if you'd –

STROLL: Sorry, Mr Gross, I wouldn't recommend it. I really wouldn't. They're awfully heavy, you're not used to them, they're sure to make you cough.

GROSS: Just one –

STROLL: I mean it. You'd be making a mistake.

[GROSS, *disappointed, puts his money back.* STROLL *and* SAVANT *smoke with gusto.*]

GROSS: Miss Helena –

HELENA: Why don't you call me Nellie, love? What is it?

GROSS: Miss Nellie, do you issue the documents one needs to get a translation authorized?

STROLL: Goose, vodka, and a cigar, that's what I call living.

SAVANT: And what a cigar!

GROSS: I said, do you issue the documents one needs to get a translation authorized?

HELENA [*calling towards S.D.*]: Where do you get water?

MARIA [*off stage*]: I'll get it. [*Runs in by B.D., iron in hand, grabs kettle, and runs out B.D.*]

HELENA [*to* GROSS]: What?

GROSS: Do you issue the documents one needs to get a translation authorized?

HELENA: Yes. To anybody who hasn't received a memo written in Ptydepe.

GROSS: Why?

SAVANT: Downright heady!

STROLL: I should say!

GROSS: I said, why?

HELENA [*calling towards S.D.*]: Where do you keep the cups?

MARIA [*off stage*]: Coming! [*Runs in by B.D., carrying iron and kettle full of water. Pours water into percolator, takes out cups and a spoon, hands them to* HELENA, *and runs out by S.D.*]

HELENA [*spoons out coffee into percolator*]: Why what?

GROSS: Why this condition?

HELENA: Because I cannot be expected to give the documents of personal registration to every Tom, Dick and Harry without making damned sure they don't conflict with the findings of the last inventory in his blessed memo!

GROSS: Why can't you look at his memo and see what it says?

STROLL: Poor Zoro Bridel used to smoke only these. And he was a real gourmet!

SAVANT: Pity he passed away!

GROSS: I said, why?

HELENA [*calling towards S.D.*]: Sugar!
[*Maria runs in, carrying iron, hands* HELENA *a paper bag of sugar and again runs out.*]

HELENA [*to* GROSS]: Why what?

GROSS: Why can't you look at his memo and see what it says?

HELENA: I'm forbidden to translate any Ptydepe texts. [*Towards S.D.*] It's almost empty.

MARIA [*off stage*]: There's another bag in the drawer.

GROSS: Good gracious! What can a staff member do in such a case?

SAVANT: Mr Bridel loved goose, didn't he?

STROLL: Zoro? Simply mad about it!

HELENA [*calling towards S.D.*]: Water's boiling.

[MARIA *runs in by S.D., puts iron on floor, unplugs percolator, pours coffee into cups.*]

HELENA [*to* GROSS]: What?

GROSS: What can a staff member do in such a case?

HELENA: He can have his memo translated. Listen, everybody! Today your coffee's hyp nagyp!

[MARIA *passes cups to* STROLL, SAVANT *and* HELENA, *then takes iron and runs out S.D.*]

SAVANT: Nagyp avalyx?

HELENA: Nagyp hayfazut!

[STROLL, SAVANT *and* HELENA *pass the spoon around, offer sugar to each other, sip their coffee with gusto, absorbed in their Ptydepe conversation.* GROSS, *growing more and more desperate, turns from one to the other.*]

GROSS: Mr Stroll –

STROLL: Hayfazut gyp andaxe. [*To* GROSS] Yes?

SAVANT: Andaxe bel jok andaxu zep?

GROSS: In order to make a translation from Ptydepe, you require an authorization from Mr Savant –

HELENA: Andaxe zep.

STROLL: Ejch tut zep. Notut?

GROSS: Dr Savant –

SAVANT: Tut. Gavych ejch lagorax. [*To* GROSS] Yes?

HELENA: Lagorax nagyp.

GROSS: In order to grant the authorization, you require the documents from Miss Helena?

STROLL: Lagorys nabarof dy Zoro Bridel cef o abagan.

SAVANT: Mavolde abagan?

GROSS: Miss Helena –

HELENA: Abagan fajfor! [*To* GROSS] Yes?

STROLL: Fajfor? Nu rachaj?

GROSS: In order to issue the documents, you require that a staff member have his memorandum translated.

SAVANT: Rachaj gun.

HELENA: Gun znojvep?

STROLL: Znojvep yj.

SAVANT: Yj rachaj?

HELENA: Rachaj gun!

STROLL: Gun znojvep?

SAVANT: Znojvep yj.

HELENA: Yj rachaj?

STROLL: Rachaj gun!

SAVANT: Gun znojvep?

GROSS [*shouts*]: Quiet!

[*At once all three become silent and quickly get up. Not on account of* GROSS, *of course, but because* BALLAS *and* PILLAR *have just quietly entered by B.D.* GROSS's *back is turned towards* BALLAS *and* PILLAR, *thus he does not see them.*]

GROSS: I'm the Deputy Director and I insist that you show me some respect! You may sit down.

[*Naturally they remain standing. Pause.* MARIA, *unaware of what has been happening, enters by S.D. carrying the ironed slip over her arm. Seeing the situation, she crumples the slip behind her back and stands like the others.*]

GROSS: As I've just discovered, any staff member who has recently received a memorandum in Ptydepe can only be granted a translation of a Ptydepe text after his memorandum has been translated. But what happens if the Ptydepe text which he wishes translated is precisely that memorandum? It can't be done, because it hasn't yet been translated officially. In other words, the only way to learn what is in one's memo, is to know it already. An extraordinary paradox, when you come to think of it. Ladies and gentlemen, do you come to think of it? I ask you, what must an employee of our organization – whoever he may be – do in order to escape this vicious, vicious circle?

[*For a second there is dead silence.*]

BALLAS: He must learn Ptydepe, Mr Gross. [*To the others*] You may sit down.

[*They all sit down at once.* MARIA, *still hiding the slip behind her, runs fearfully to her desk.*]

GROSS [*faintly*]: Are you here?

BALLAS: Yes, we are.

GROSS: Have you been here long?

BALLAS: Not long.

GROSS: I didn't hear you come in.

BALLAS: We entered quietly.

GROSS: Excuse me, I –

BALLAS: There are things, Mr Gross, that cannot be excused. And when, at the very time in which the whole organization is conducting a courageous struggle for the introduction and establishment of Ptydepe, an official, referring to the activities of our employees, speaks with such malicious innuendo and mean irony about – I quote – 'a vicious, vicious circle', then it cannot be excused at all.

GROSS: I'm sorry, Mr Ballas, but the circumstance I've allowed myself to point out is simply a fact.

BALLAS: What of it? We won't be bullied by facts!

[*Long pause.*]

GROSS [*in a quiet, broken voice*]: I plead guilty. I acknowledge the entire extent of my guilt, while fully realizing the consequences resulting from it. Furthermore, I wish to enlarge my confession by the following self-indictment. I issued an illegal order which led to the fraudulent authentication of my own, personal notebook. By this action I abused my authority. I did this in order to avert attention from the fact that I'd appropriated a bank endorsement stamp improperly for my private use. I request for myself the most severe punishment.

BALLAS: I think that under these circumstances it is no longer possible for him to remain in our organization. What do you say, Mr P.?

[PILLAR *shakes his head.*]

BALLAS: Certainly not. Come to my office tomorrow morning. We'll settle the formalities connected with your dismissal. [*Calls*] George, come out of there! You'll be my deputy. [*To the others*] You may leave now. Mr P., let's go.

[BALLAS *and* PILLAR *leave by B.D.,* STROLL, SAVANT *and* HELENA *by S.D.* GROSS *remains standing in the centre. Motionless, he stares ahead.* MARIA *watches him in silence. It seems she would like to help him in some way. Then she takes the cigar box and shyly offers one to* GROSS. GROSS *does not see her.* HELENA *looks in at S.D.*]

HELENA [*to* MARIA]: Seems the grocer's got fresh cantaloupes. Would you mind running over and getting me ten? If you're quick about it, I'll give you a taste!

[HELENA *disappears.* MARIA *hastily replaces cigar box, snatches her string bag and runs out B.D.* GROSS *hangs his head, takes the fire-extinguisher, and slowly, sadly leaves by B.D. Just then a small secret door opens in one of the side walls and* GEORGE *backs out of it on all fours. When he is quite out, he straightens, stretches, arranges his clothes with a dash of vanity, takes a cigar from the box and haughtily struts out by B.D.*]

Interval

# SCENE SEVEN

*The Director's office.* BALLAS *and* PILLAR *enter by B.D., take off their coats, sit at the desk.* BALLAS *begins to go through the morning mail, like* GROSS *at the beginning of the play. One letter suddenly arrests his attention, he glares at it, then starts to read it aloud.*

BALLAS [*reads*]: Ak ok utuh d utoked yle umobert ehusome, ragedv dy, orts uner re kyrg ydnek, vylaz edyvz uzed, ladnyvk ref unyked yles – [*Puts down the letter, hesitates, turns to* PILLAR.] You don't know Ptydepe, do you?
    [PILLAR *shakes his head.*]
BALLAS: You might have learned it by now!
STROLL [*looks in at S.D.*]: I hope I'm not interrupting. [*To* PILLAR] Ferry, would you come here a moment?
    [PILLAR *gets up at once and leaves with* STROLL *by S.D.* BALLAS *looks after them in surprise. Meanwhile* GROSS *quietly enters by B.D., fire-extinguisher clasped in his arms.*]
BALLAS [*to himself*]: Ferry?
    [BALLAS, *puzzled, shakes his head, then again stares at his letter.* GROSS *after a while speaks up timidly.*]
GROSS: Good morning.
BALLAS: You're here?
GROSS: I haven't been here long.
BALLAS: What do you want?
GROSS: I was supposed to come to your office today concerning my dismissal from our organization, Mr Ballas.
BALLAS: I'm busy now. Come back in a while –
GROSS: I'm sorry. Thank you. I'll come later.
    [GROSS *quickly backs out by B.D.* PILLAR *returns by S.D. and sits at his place.*]

BALLAS: What did he want?

[PILLAR *gestures that it was nothing important.* BALLAS *shakes his head doubtingly, and again stares at his letter.* HANA *enters by B.D., wearing a coat and carrying a vast shopping bag.*]

HANA: Good morning.

BALLAS [*without looking up*]: Morning.

[HANA *hangs coat on coat-rack, sits at her desk and begins to comb her hair. After a moment,* BALLAS *turns to her.*]

BALLAS: Hana –

HANA: Yes, Mr Ballas?

BALLAS: You know Ptydepe, don't you?

HANA: I'm sorry, I don't.

BALLAS: Why not? I thought you'd been going to the Ptydepe classes.

HANA: I used to, but I had to give them up. May I go and get the milk?

BALLAS: Why?

HANA: It was too hard for me. May I go and get the milk?

BALLAS: Aren't you ashamed? The secretary to the Managing Director and Ptydepe's too hard for her!

HANA: May I go and get the milk?

BALLAS: Run along.

[HANA *takes milk bottle and hurries out by B.D.*]

BALLAS: I hope you won't end up like her!

[PILLAR *makes an embarrassed face.*]

SAVANT [*looks in at S.D.*]: Morning, Jan! Can you spare Ferry a minute?

BALLAS: By all means –

SAVANT: Ta. Cheerio!

[SAVANT *gestures to* PILLAR. PILLAR *gets up at once and both leave by S.D.* BALLAS *looks angrily after them. Meanwhile* GROSS *quietly enters by B.D., extinguisher in his arms.*]

233

BALLAS [*to himself*]: Ferry! Ferry! Ferry! [*Again stares at his letter.*]

GROSS: Good morning.

BALLAS: You're here again?

GROSS: You said, Mr Ballas, that I should come back in a while.

BALLAS: By which I didn't mean such a short while!

GROSS: Sorry. I'll come later. Sorry – [*He is backing towards B.D.*]

BALLAS: Listen –

GROSS: Yes, Mr Ballas?

BALLAS: Nothing.

GROSS: Did you want something?

BALLAS: No, no. You may go.

[GROSS *backs out by* B.D. PILLAR *returns by S.D. and sits down at his place.*]

BALLAS: What did he want?

[PILLAR *puts on a vague expression.*]

BALLAS: I don't like the way they keep addressing you. Much too familiar.

[PILLAR *shrugs, embarrassed.* HANA *returns by B.D., drinks, then continues combing her hair. Pause.*]

BALLAS [*to* HANA]: Is Ptydepe so difficult to learn?

HANA: It makes great demands on one's memory, Mr Ballas.

BALLAS: Others can learn it –

HANA: Very few can, Mr Ballas. Most of the staff have had to give it up.

BALLAS: Even when all give up, you should persevere!

HANA: But you also dropped out, Mr Ballas, after the first lesson.

BALLAS: That's different. I had to interrupt my studies for reasons of work. You think it's child's play to be at the helm of this colossus? And, what's more, in these times? Come and try it and you'd see.

HANA: But Ptydepe really makes great demands on people. Besides, they say it's based on doubtful principles. May I go and get the rolls?

BALLAS: Who says that?

HANA: Mr Pillar here.

BALLAS: Surely not Mr Pillar! And if, by any chance, he did say such a thing, it was just in fun. Who of the staff actually knows Ptydepe?

HANA: Only the teacher and the personnel of the Translation Centre. May I go and get the rolls?

BALLAS: There you are! And then you tell me that it's beyond human powers to learn it!

HANA: May I go and get the rolls?

BALLAS: Run along.

[HANA *takes string bag and leaves by B.D. As soon as she is out,* BALLAS *turns furiously against* PILLAR.]

BALLAS: You talk too much! Far too much!

HELENA [*looks in by S.D.*]: Hallo everybody! Ferry, love – would you?

[PILLAR *gets up at once.*]

HELENA: Well, see you.

[HELENA *and* PILLAR *leave by S.D.* BALLAS *jumps up furiously. He does not notice that* GROSS *has again entered with his fire-extinguisher by B.D.*]

BALLAS [*to himself*]: I'll teach you a lesson! Ferry!

[BALLAS *sits down. Again stares at his letter. Pauses. Then* GROSS *speaks up.*]

GROSS: Good morning.

BALLAS: You're here again?

GROSS: You said, Mr Ballas, that I should come back in a while.

BALLAS: By which I didn't mean such a short while!

GROSS: Sorry. I'll come later. Sorry – [*He is backing towards B.D.*]

BALLAS: Listen –

GROSS: Yes, Mr Ballas?

BALLAS: Nothing.

GROSS: Did you want something?

BALLAS: I just wanted to say that I seem to have overdone it a bit yesterday. You know, there were so many people about, I wasn't sure who might be among them – my nerves were a bit ruffled after all that happened –

GROSS: Thank you. You're very kind. Thank you. But the dismissal stands, doesn't it?

BALLAS: Dismissal? Well, for the moment, perhaps we needn't take such drastic measures. You can't be my deputy, of course –

GROSS: Of course –

BALLAS: But there is an opening.

GROSS: Is there? To do what?

BALLAS: The position of Staff Watcher has become free.

GROSS: Do you think I could handle it?

BALLAS: Well, why don't you give it a try for a while? We'll see how it works out.

GROSS: Very kind of you, Mr Ballas. When may I start?

BALLAS: At once, if you like.

GROSS: Thank you, Mr Ballas. Thank you very much.

[GROSS *backs out by B.D.* PILLAR *returns by S.D. and sits down at his place.*]

BALLAS: What did she want?

[PILLAR *puts on a vague expression.*]

BALLAS: Don't you play games with me!

[HANA *returns by B.D., her string bag full of rolls. She puts them in her shopping bag, sits down and combs her hair.*]

BALLAS [*to* HANA]: Who else says that Ptydepe is based on doubtful principles?

HANA: All except you, Mr Ballas.

BALLAS: Don't exaggerate!

HANA: Really.

BALLAS: What else do they say?

HANA: That it's only a matter of time before you find it out too.

BALLAS: Indeed. This is the reward one gets for all one has done for them! [*Hands his letter to* HANA.] Couldn't you at least make out what this is about?

HANA [*skims the letter*]: It could be either a memorandum concerning the last audit –

BALLAS: Hardly –

HANA: Or a protest.

BALLAS: What sort of protest?

HANA: I don't know.

BALLAS: Why should it be a protest, of all things?

HANA: It's being rumoured that protests written in Ptydepe get preferential treatment.

BALLAS: Where did you hear all this?

HANA: Oh, in the dairy shop this morning.

BALLAS: If anybody thinks he can come and protest here I'll – I'm off to lunch. [*He grabs his letter and leaves by B.D.*]

HANA [*calls after him*]: You'll like it, Mr Ballas. They have goulash in the canteen today!

# SCENE EIGHT

*The Ptydepe classroom. All is as before, with the exception that*
LEAR *is lecturing to only one clerk,* THUMB. *All other chairs are*
*empty.*

LEAR: And now I shall name, just for the sake of pre-
liminary orientation, some of the most common Ptydepe
interjections. Well then, our 'ah!' becomes 'zukybaj',
our 'ouch!' becomes 'bykur', our 'oh!' becomes 'hayf
dy doretob', English 'pish!' becomes 'bolypak juz', the
interjection of surprise 'well!' becomes 'zyk', however,
our 'well, well!' is not 'zykzyk', as some students
erroneously say, but 'zykzym' –
  [GROSS *with his fire-extinguisher enters by B.D., crosses*
  *the room and leaves by S.D.*]
LEAR: 'Aow!' becomes 'varylaguf yb de solas', or sometimes, though much more rarely, 'borybaf', 'bang!' as
the symbol of a shot or explosion becomes 'hetegyx
ujhoby', 'bang' as a colloquial expression for sudden
surprise is 'maluz rog'. Our 'eek!' becomes 'hatum' –
THUMB [*raises his hand*]: Sir –
LEAR: What is it?
THUMB [*gets up*]: Would you mind telling us how one says
'oops' in Ptydepe?
LEAR: 'Mykl'.
THUMB: Thank you. [*Sits down.*]
LEAR: 'Psst!' becomes 'cetudap', 'mmnn' becomes
'vamyl', the poetic 'oh!' is rendered in Ptydepe by
'hrulugyp'. The 'hoooo' of a ghost is translated mostly
as 'lymr', although I'd prefer the expression 'mryb
uputr'. Our very important 'hurrah!' becomes in

Ptydepe 'frnygko jefr dabux altep dy savarub goz texeres'. And now a little test of your memory. Aow?

[THUMB *raises his hand.*]

LEAR: Mr Thumb!

THUMB [*gets up*]: Varylaguf yb de solas. [*Sits down.*]

LEAR: Eek?

[THUMB *raises his hand.*]

LEAR: Mr Thumb!

THUMB [*gets up*]: Hatum. [*Sits down.*]

LEAR: Psst?

[THUMB *raises his hand.*]

LEAR: Mr Thumb!

THUMB [*gets up*]: Cetudap. [*Sits down.*]

LEAR: Bang?

THUMB: As the symbol of a shot?

LEAR: No, as the colloquial expression for sudden surprise.

[THUMB *raises his hand.*]

LEAR: Mr Thumb!

THUMB [*gets up*]: Maluz rog.

LEAR [*correcting his pronunciation*]: Maluz –

THUMB: Maluz –

LEAR: M–a–l–u–z –

THUMB: M–a–l–u–z –

LEAR: Listen carefully: m–a–l–u–z –

THUMB: M–a–l–u–z –

LEAR: Your pronunciation isn't too good. How do you say well?

THUMB: Zyk.

LEAR: And well, well?

THUMB: Zykzyk.

LEAR: Zykzym!!

THUMB: I'm sorry, I forgot.

LEAR: Mr Thumb! Mr Thumb! Yippee!

THUMB: We haven't learned yippee yet, sir.

LEAR: Don't try to excuse yourself. You simply don't know it. Hurrah!

THUMB: Frnygko jefr dabux altep dy savarub gop texeres.

LEAR: Goz texeres!!

THUMB: I mean, goz texeres.

LEAR: Such an important word! No, no. Mr Thumb! It won't work this way. I've placed so many hopes in you, and you have what? Well? You have disappointed me! Yes, disappointed! No, no, this way we can't do what? Well? Carry on. Certainly not. This way our class would soon turn into what? Well? Go on, answer me!

THUMB: I don't know.

LEAR: Then try.

THUMB: A kindergarten?

LEAR: No.

THUMB: A borstal?

LEAR: No.

THUMB: Bedlam?

LEAR: Quite correct! Bedlam! No, no! Under these circumstances I can't let you carry on with your studies. You'd only slow down the class and hold up the other students. Please leave the classroom!

[THUMB *takes his briefcase and sadly leaves by B.D.*]

LEAR [*addressing the empty classroom*]: Let us proceed. 'Hallo!' becomes 'trevunt', 'gosh!' is translated as 'kavlyz ubahaj kupit', the American 'gee!' becomes 'hofro gaborte', 'pooh!' is translated as –

# SCENE NINE

*The Secretariat of the Translation Centre. The room is empty, then*
MARIA *enters by B.D., carrying a string bag full of onions,*
*crosses the room and leaves by S.D.*

MARIA [*off stage*]: Here are the onions, Miss Helena.
HELENA [*off stage*]: Would you mind putting them by the
   filing cabinet? That's a good girl.
   [MARIA *returns by S.D., carrying an empty string bag, sits*
   *at the typist's desk and works for a while, then looks about her*
   *a few times, takes a mirror from drawer, props it up in front of*
   *her, carefully takes out a new hat and tries it on in front of the*
   *mirror.*]
GROSS [*off stage*]: It suits you.
   [MARIA *starts, tears the hat off her head, shoves it hastily*
   *into the drawer, hides the mirror, and fearfully looks about.*]
GROSS [*off stage*]: Don't worry. It's only me, Gross.
MARIA [*heaves a sigh of relief*]: Oh! But where are you?
GROSS [*off stage*]: I'm the Staff Watcher now.
MARIA: You? Oh, no!
GROSS [*off stage*]: Yes. Mr Ballas dropped my dismissal and
   he's letting me work here for a trial period.
MARIA: You? Staff Watcher?
GROSS [*off stage*]: Very much so. And in the given circum-
   stances it really seems the best solution for me. I only
   wish I could get used to the lack of space.
MARIA: Goodness! And I've found a job for you.
GROSS [*off stage*]: Have you? What sort of job?
MARIA: With a theatre group.
GROSS [*off stage*]: But I can't act.
MARIA: You could always manage a bit part. There's
   always bit parts cropping up, you know, a butler, a

241

messenger, a workman, that sort of thing. Well, anyway, if worse came to worst you could prompt the actors.

GROSS [*off stage*]: Yes, perhaps. Are you somehow connected with the theatre?

MARIA: My brother works with this group.

GROSS [*off stage*]: You're kind. [*Pause.*] Maria –

MARIA: Yes?

GROSS [*off stage*]: Isn't it odd? I have to look at you all the time.

MARIA: Oh, Mr Gross!

HELENA [*looks in at S.D.*]: Seems the grocer's got limes. Would you mind running over and getting me eight? [*Disappears.*]

> [MARIA *takes string bag from drawer and runs out by B.D. Short pause, then* BALLAS *stalks in energetically by B.D., his letter in hand. Looks about, tries his pockets, but finds no cigarettes. Turns towards secret door.*]

BALLAS: Are you there?

GROSS [*off stage*]: But of course, Mr Ballas.

BALLAS: Well, how goes it?

GROSS [*off stage*]: Very well, thank you.

BALLAS: Many strangers?

GROSS [*off stage*]: Only three visitors in number five.

BALLAS: Alone in the office?

GROSS [*off stage*]: One, for a moment.

BALLAS: Behaved?

GROSS [*off stage*]: Decently.

BALLAS: Good. I think you'll manage. Anything else?

GROSS [*off stage*]: Sorry, but what else, precisely?

BALLAS: Well, for example, what sort of things are being said about Ptydepe among the staff?
> [*Pause.*]

GROSS [*off stage*]: I'm sorry, Mr Ballas, but I – how should I put it? – I – I'm not an – you know what I mean.

BALLAS: I know. You still haven't shaken off the shackles of outdated prejudices. But you must understand that it's for a good cause. What's more, it is, in a certain sense, your moral duty.

[STROLL *enters by S.D. and swiftly walks towards B.D.*]

BALLAS [*to* STROLL]: Just a moment!

[STROLL *halts.*]

BALLAS [*towards secret door*]: Is that quite clear?

GROSS [*off stage*]: Quite clear, Mr Ballas.

BALLAS [*to* STROLL]: I say, old boy! How goes the translating?

STROLL: Very well, thank you.

BALLAS: Tell me, how many texts have you translated so far?

STROLL: Into Ptydepe or from Ptydepe?

BALLAS: Well, let's say into Ptydepe.

STROLL: One. I'm just working on the second one now.

BALLAS: So few?

STROLL: That's not so few.

[SAVANT *enters by S.D. and quickly walks towards B.D.*]

BALLAS [*to* SAVANT]: Just a moment!

[SAVANT *halts.*]

BALLAS [*to* STROLL]: Slow work, isn't it?

STROLL: Indeed it is. Every expression has several variants in Ptydepe and so one must consult the author of the submitted text regarding each separate word, in order to find out precisely how it was meant and which of the Ptydepe variants to use. Am I not right, Alex?

SAVANT: Quite right. Often the authors themselves aren't sure. They simply don't know such precision from their mother tongue.

STROLL: The shades of meaning of individual words in Ptydepe are so subtle that most of the staff can't grasp them at all.

BALLAS: Why don't you get some help?

STROLL: Help? But you know how things are! Am I not right, Alex?

SAVANT: So far, nobody has really managed to learn Ptydepe. Only Pekarek, and then he left for steam-navigation.

BALLAS: Well, what you'll have to do is to speed up your translating. The world won't come to an end if an occasional little word isn't exactly right.

[PILLAR *looks in at B.D.* BALLAS *does not see him.* PILLAR *stares questioningly at* STROLL, *who gestures to him that he is ready to go.*]

STROLL: Sorry, Mr Ballas, I have a meeting now –

BALLAS: Well then, go along.

[PILLAR *disappears.* STROLL *hurries out by B.D.* SAVANT *is about to follow.*]

BALLAS: Wait, Alex! Just one more little thing. Tell me how is Ptydepe actually making out? From the expert's point of view, I mean.

SAVANT: Hard to say. I still have no basis for my statistics, so I can't form any real opinion.

[HELENA *enters by S.D. and briskly walks towards B.D.*]

BALLAS [*to* HELENA]: Just a moment!

[HELENA *halts.*]

BALLAS [*to* SAVANT]: What about the results in other organizations?

SAVANT: They're all right, I suppose. Except that wherever Ptydepe has started to be used more widely, it has automatically begun to assume some of the characteristics of a natural language: various emotional overtones, imprecisions, ambiguities. Correct, Nellie?

HELENA: Correct. And you know what? They say that the more one uses Ptydepe the more it gets soiled by these characteristics.

BALLAS: Did you say emotional overtones? But in that case Ptydepe is losing its very purpose!

SAVANT: One could put it that way.

[PILLAR, *unnoticed by* BALLAS, *looks in at* B.D., *silently beckons to* SAVANT *who gestures back that he is ready.*]

BALLAS: What can be done about it?

SAVANT: Practically nothing. I'm sorry, Mr Ballas, do you mind if I go now? I have a meeting –

BALLAS: Well then, go along.

[PILLAR *disappears.* SAVANT *hurries out by* B.D. HELENA *is about to follow.*]

BALLAS: Wait, Nellie!

HELENA: What is it, Jan?

BALLAS: Listen, we two have always been able to talk as man to man. Now, tell me quite frankly, I mean really quite frankly, do you get the impression that Ptydepe isn't doing as well as it might be, or, to put it bluntly, that it's sort of got stuck?

HELENA: I do, love.

BALLAS: Thank you, Nellie.

[PILLAR *looks in at* B.D.]

HELENA: May I go now?

BALLAS: Run along.

[PILLAR *disappears.* HELENA *runs out by* B.D. BALLAS *thoughtfully paces up and down. Then sits and again talks towards the secret door.*]

BALLAS: Mr Gross –

GROSS [*off stage*]: Yes, Mr Ballas.

BALLAS: I hope you aren't taking seriously what occurred yesterday. You do realize, don't you, it was just a bit of a show for the sake of the others? Listen, why don't I call you Jo, shall I?

GROSS [*off stage*]: But of course, Mr Ballas, I'll be delighted.

BALLAS: I say, old boy – come out of there! You don't want to be doing that sort of work! You! I don't see why you shouldn't carry on as my deputy.

GROSS [*off stage*]: After what happened?

BALLAS: We must take some risks, damn it! I won't hear of your being abused in this way, Jo! We're having some difficulties at present. Ptydepe isn't doing as well as it might be –

GROSS [*off stage*]: Yes, I've heard.

BALLAS: The way things are now, I simply need you here, Jo!

[GROSS *emerges from the secret door, scrambling out backwards on all fours.*]

BALLAS: Sit down.

[GROSS *sits down.*]

BALLAS: Where's the enthusiasm we all felt when we were launching Ptydepe! I worked at it as stubbornly as a mule! You know, drank only water, ate only purple hearts, went without sleep, just slaved and organized; when the cause was at stake, I was quite ruthless. Well, you remember, don't you?

GROSS: I do remember.

BALLAS: That was the best time of my life! And now see how it's all turned out! This isn't what we wanted, is it?

GROSS: Well, perhaps things will mend themselves again somehow.

BALLAS: Listen, Jo! You and I, between us, we'll pull things together again! You have your experience, you know how things were done in the past when everything worked; I know how they ought to be done so they'll work in the future; if we two work hand in hand, I'll bet anything you like, we'll hammer out something damn well astonishing! Are you free tonight?

GROSS: Yes.

BALLAS: Good. Now look, let's meet quietly at some pub, have a glass of beer and really think things out! We'll map out a little plan, so we know how to go about it all. Who should I rely on here if not on you, old boy!

GROSS: But I –

BALLAS [*cuts in*]: And now fetch George and tell him to march back into his cubicle. He's already proved himself in the job and he must see that what we need now above all in the high positions is specialists.

[GROSS *leaves by B.D. Long pause.* BALLAS *searches his pockets, no cigarettes. Looks at his watch.* STROLL *enters by B.D., carrying a folder, and briskly walks towards S.D.*]

BALLAS: Otto!

[STROLL *halts.*]

BALLAS: You still haven't told me about your translations from Ptydepe.

STROLL: So far, I haven't translated anything from Ptydepe.

[SAVANT *enters by B.D., carrying a folder, and walks towards S.D.*]

BALLAS: Alex!

[SAVANT *halts.*]

BALLAS [*to* STROLL]: Why not?

STROLL: Up till now nobody has brought me any authorization from Alex.

BALLAS: Alex! Why do you refuse to authorize translations?

SAVANT: But I can't authorize them without personal registration documents.

[HELENA *enters by B.D., carrying a folder, and walks towards S.D.*]

BALLAS: Nellie!

[HELENA *halts.*]

BALLAS [*to* SAVANT]: You mean in all this time nobody has brought you any documents from Nellie?

SAVANT: That's right.

BALLAS: Nellie! Why do you refuse to issue those damned documents?

HELENA: Oh, for heaven's sake, love! I can't issue them until I've made sure they don't conflict with the findings in the memos, and I can't learn the findings, because the blessed memos are written in Ptydepe and, as you bloody well know, I'm forbidden to make any translations whatsoever. Hasn't the girl brought my limes yet?

BALLAS: Then why doesn't Otto translate the memos?

STROLL: I can translate only after getting an authorization from Alex!

BALLAS: Then Alex will have to start granting the authorizations!

SAVANT: I can't, if nobody has the documents from Nellie!

BALLAS: Do you hear that, Nellie? You'll have to start giving people the documents regardless!

HELENA: But I'm not permitted to translate!

BALLAS: Why doesn't Otto do the translating?

STROLL: I can translate only after getting an authorization from Alex!

BALLAS: Then Alex will have to start granting the authorizations!

SAVANT: I can't, when nobody has the documents from Nellie!

BALLAS: Do you hear that, Nellie? You'll have to start giving people the documents regardless!

HELENA: But I'm not permitted to translate!

BALLAS: Why doesn't Otto do the translating?

STROLL: I can translate only after getting an authorization from Alex!

BALLAS: Then Alex will have to start granting the authorizations!

SAVANT: I can't, when nobody has the documents from Nellie!

BALLAS: Do you hear that, Nellie? You'll have to start giving people the documents regardless!

HELENA: But I'm not permitted to translate!

BALLAS: I'd like to know who thought up this vicious circle.

STROLL  
SAVANT } [*in chorus*]: You did, Mr Ballas!  
HELENA

BALLAS: Well, what of it! The situation was entirely different at that time. Then it had a profound significance! But we've progressed since then, and that's why I propose the following simplifications in the procedure of translating all Ptydepe texts. These will come into effect at once. First: Helena is permitted to issue the personal registration documents without knowing the contents of the memos. Second: Alex is permitted to authorize all translations without the personal registration documents. Third: Otto is permitted to translate without an authorization from Alex. Is that quite clear? The fact that we can afford these measures is one more eloquent proof of the rightness of our way! [*Hands his letter to* STROLL.] And now – translate this for me!

STROLL [*reads*]: A protest. We, the undersigned staff of the Accounts Department, protest most emphatically against the transfer of our offices to the cellar and we announce hereby that we can no longer work under these deplorable conditions –

BALLAS [*interrupts*]: That's enough! You may carry on with your work.

> [BALLAS *leaves by B.D.* STROLL, SAVANT *and* HELENA *stand about for a moment or two in silence, then B.D. opens a crack,* PILLAR *appears and beckons them to follow him. They all leave by B.D. Pause. Then* GROSS *and* GEORGE *enter by B.D.* GEORGE *is livid, frowns, and furiously kicks the coat-rack, then the desk, spits, kneels down and climbs on all fours through the secret door into the observation cubicle. After a moment he indignantly throws out* GROSS's *fire-extinguisher,* GROSS *takes it and walks towards B.D. Just*

*then* MARIA *enters by B.D., carrying a paper bag full of limes. When she sees* GROSS *she halts in surprise.*]

MARIA: Do you realize what would happen to you if anybody saw you here?

GROSS: I'm no longer the Staff Watcher.

MARIA: Oh?

GROSS: Mr Ballas has made me his deputy again.

MARIA: Congratulations!

GROSS: Good gracious, what for? Frankly, I'd rather have remained the Staff Watcher.

MARIA: I know. You'll have to cope with some pretty nasty bits of business now, I expect.

GROSS: Never mind. Well, Maria, have a good time here. And do come and see me in my office one day. [*Slowly starts towards B.D.*]

MARIA: Mr Gross –

GROSS [*stops*]: Yes?

MARIA: Has anybody translated for you that – you know – the thing you wanted to have translated yesterday?

GROSS: The memorandum? No. And according to current regulations, nobody can. Well, it's probably better that way.

MARIA: Do you think it's a negative one?

GROSS: I've learned always to expect the worst.

MARIA: Was any irregularity found during the audit in your department?

GROSS: Not that I know of. I did take the rubber-stamp home just then, but I took it for reasons of work and not, as some people seemed to suggest, for my children to play with. My little Martin might have played with it at most twice in all that time.

MARIA: If your conscience is clear, you've nothing to worry about. Your innocence will be proved, but you have to fight for it! I believe that if one doesn't give way, truth must always come out in the end.

GROSS [*walks to Maria, sadly smiles at her and strokes her cheek*]: What do you know about the world, dear child! Still, I wish you could always stay like this! You're right, one really ought always to stand firm. The trouble is, I've never been very firm, more of an intellectual, always hesitant, always full of doubts, too considerate, a dreamer rather than a man of action – and that's my bad luck.

[*Pause.*]

GROSS: When I think back, I see that I muddled up many things in my life myself. I often gave in too soon, yielded to threats, and I trusted people too much.

[*Pause.*]

GROSS: If I ever have any influence on the course of things again, I'll do everything differently. More real deeds and fewer clever words! I've never been sufficiently matter-of-fact, cool-headed, proud, severe and critical – especially with myself.

[*Pause.*]

GROSS: It may be partly because I belong to an odd, lost generation. We've given ourselves out in small change, we invested the best years of our lives in things which turned out not to be worth it. We were so busy for so long talking about our great mission that we quite forgot to do anything great. In short, we were a mess!

[*Pause.*]

GROSS: But I believe that now I can at least face all this frankly, without hysteria and without self pity; that I'll manage to recover from all the upheavals; that I'm still able to forget the past and make a quite new and quite different beginning.

MARIA [*moved*]: Have you the memo with you?

GROSS: You mean – surely you wouldn't –

MARIA: I'm quite grown up, thank you, Mr Gross. I know what I'm doing. Give it to me!

251

[GROSS *takes out his memo, hands it to* MARIA, *who reads it with growing excitement.*]

MARIA [*reads*]: Dear Sir, the last audit in your department has shown that the allegation of a repeated appropriation of the bank endorsement stamp for improper use is in your case entirely unfounded. On the contrary, we feel obliged to emphasize the very positive findings of the audit, which clearly prove that you have been conscientious and responsible in the directing of your organization and that you therefore merit full confidence. This is further confirmed by your stand as regards Ptydepe, which has been quite unequivocal from the beginning. Our view of the Ptydepe campaign has always been entirely negative, for we understand it to be a profoundly harmful attempt to place office communications on a confused, unrealistic, anti-human basis. We suggest that you liquidate with the greatest possible resolution and speed any attempt to introduce Ptydepe into your organization, and that you severely punish all those who have been propagating Ptydepe for their own personal advantage and in disregard of the consequences. Wishing you all success in your future work, we remain, yours faithfully, signature illegible.

GROSS [*after a moment, seriously*]: Thank you, Maria. Now at last I have an opportunity to prove that I have more civil courage than I've shown so far. I promise you that this time I shall not give way to anything or anybody, even at the risk of my position! [*Grabs his fire-extinguisher and starts energetically towards B.D.*]

MARIA [*shyly bursts out*]: I like you –

GROSS: First I must deserve your sympathy, dear child! [*Leaves by B.D.*]
    [*Pause.*]

GEORGE [*off stage*]: That was a stupid thing to do, Maria.

MARIA [*frightened*]: Oh God! Are you there?

GEORGE [*off stage*]: I came back a moment ago. And I'm not sorry I did. I hope you realize why!

HELENA [ *off stage*]: Listen – what about those limes?

MARIA [*softly*]: I'm afraid I do.

# SCENE TEN

*The Director's office.* BALLAS *is sitting at his desk, vainly searching his pockets for cigarettes.* HANA *is combing her hair.* GROSS *enters energetically by B.D., carrying his fire-extinguisher.*

GROSS: Mr Ballas, your era is over! My memorandum has just been translated to me and its contents make it perfectly clear that I'm not only quite innocent as regards the rubber-stamp, but above all that I'm the only legitimate director of this organization. Furthermore, I'm requested by this memorandum to make an end of Ptydepe with the greatest possible resolution and speed –

BALLAS: Hana –

HANA: Yes, Mr Ballas?

BALLAS: Isn't it time for you to get your chocolates?

HANA [*looks at her watch*]: Oh yes, it is!

BALLAS: Well then, run along! And while you're there get me some cigarettes. The usual.

[HANA *runs out by B.D.*]

BALLAS: Sorry. What did you say?

GROSS: Furthermore, I'm requested by it to make an end of Ptydepe with the greatest speed and to punish severely all those who were engaged in its introduction for their own advantage. In other words, history has proved me right and I, on the basis of the authority which is rightfully mine –

[PILLAR *looks in at S.D.*]

BALLAS: In a minute, Mr P.!

[PILLAR *disappears, leaving the door ajar.*]

BALLAS: What did you say?

GROSS: In other words, history has proved me right and I, on the basis of the authority which is rightfully mine,

254

shall draw due consequences from what has occurred. The way in which you seized the entire organization and forced Ptydepe on it cries for vengeance. I'm a humanist and my concept –

[HANA *re-enters by B.D., carrying box of chocolates and packet of cigarettes. Hands cigarettes to* BALLAS, *puts chocolates in the shopping bag, sits down and resumes combing her hair.*]

BALLAS: Thanks, Hana. [*Lights cigarette with gusto.*] What did you say?

GROSS: I'm a humanist and my concept of directing this organization derives from the idea that every single member of the staff is human and must become more and more human. This is why I cannot but fight anyone who tries to spit upon this idea. I place the struggle for the victory of reason and of moral values –

[PILLAR *looks in at S.D.*]

BALLAS: In a minute, Mr P., in a minute!

[PILLAR *disappears, leaving the door ajar.*]

BALLAS: What did you say?

GROSS: I place the victory of reason and of moral values above a peace bought by their loss. And I will carry on to the bitter end a struggle against all the misdeeds you've committed here. I think that under these circumstances it is no longer possible for you to remain in our organization. Kindly move out of my desk!

BALLAS [*offering* GROSS *a cigarette*]: Have one!

GROSS: I said, kindly move out of my desk!

BALLAS: Do have one, they're superb.

GROSS: Move out of my desk!

BALLAS: Let's say after lunch. All right?

GROSS: I'm glad you aren't putting up any resistance. After lunch will be all right.

BALLAS: I don't see why I should put up any resistance.

GROSS: You mean you agree with me?

BALLAS: Of course.

GROSS [*astounded, puts fire-extinguisher on the floor*]: Good gracious! How so?

BALLAS: I've seen the light.

GROSS: Have you?

BALLAS: Absolutely. I've come to the conclusion that Ptydepe is all nonsense. I believed in it, I fought for its establishment, but it was all a mistake. Subjectively I meant well, but objectively the effect was negative and so now I must accept, whether I like it or not, all the severe consequences of my activity.

[PILLAR *looks in at S.D.*]

BALLAS: One more minute, Mr P.!

[PILLAR *disappears, leaving the door ajar.*]

GROSS: Are you being sincere? You ought not to be so calm about it. It's very confusing.

BALLAS: I'm calm, because your severe but just words express what I've been tragically feeling for a long time, and so they fill me with relief that I won't be obliged to continue any longer work which I don't believe in, and that finally all my mistakes will be put right. I wish you all the luck in your liquidation of the disastrous consequences of Ptydepe, and I firmly trust that your work will succeed at least as much as mine has failed. I'll help you to the limits of my humble abilities. [*Offers* GROSS *a cigarette.*] Do have one!

GROSS: No, thanks. You seem to have come to your senses.

BALLAS: I have.

GROSS: Perhaps you were indeed sincerely mistaken –

BALLAS: I was.

GROSS: How do you mean you'll help me?

BALLAS: Are you quite sure you won't have one?

GROSS: Thanks. Not now. How do you mean you'll help me?

BALLAS: But they're really superb!

GROSS: I'm sure they are. How do you mean you'll help me?

BALLAS: Look, old boy, if you don't take one, I'll be hurt! Well, as your deputy, of course.

GROSS: You must have misunderstood me. I said you'll leave the organization.

BALLAS: You wouldn't want to take such drastic measures, would you?

GROSS: I'm sorry, but I've made up my mind not to give way this time. I don't propose to repeat my old mistakes.

BALLAS: Come, come! Didn't I let you stay on as my deputy?

GROSS: That was different. Rightfully I should have remained the director, and truth was on my side.

BALLAS: I know that too, now!

GROSS: I've known it from the beginning.

BALLAS: It's always easy to be against a thing from the beginning! What is much harder is to be for a thing, even at the risk of getting your teeth kicked in!

GROSS: That doesn't change by one iota the fact that you are the chief culprit and so you must get the severest punishment. You'll simply have to pack up and get out!

BALLAS: And if I don't?

GROSS: You will!

BALLAS: Take it easy, old boy! [*Produces a sheet of paper and shows it to* GROSS.] Recognize this? It's the supplementary order for the introduction of Ptydepe and, if I'm not mistaken, it's signed by you, not by me. Or were you not the Managing Director at the time? Well then, who is the chief culprit?

[PILLAR *looks in at S.D.*]

BALLAS: Yes, Mr P. – Give me another minute, will you?

[PILLAR *disappears, leaving the door ajar.*]

BALLAS: Well?

257

GROSS: That one signature is insignificant. It's nothing in comparison with what you've done.

BALLAS: Trouble is, history only knows such signatures.

GROSS: Besides, it was you who got me to sign it.

BALLAS: I did? I don't seem to remember.

GROSS: By your trick about the authentication of the notebook.

BALLAS: I wouldn't bring that up if I were you.

GROSS: Why not?

BALLAS: Because it's no extenuating circumstance at all. Just the reverse, in fact.

GROSS: I don't know what you're talking about.

BALLAS: Don't you? Well, look here, old boy. If it weren't for the notebook affair, you might have claimed that you signed the order moved by a sincere belief in your principles, which, of course, wouldn't have excused your conduct, but would at least have explained it somewhat on humanitarian grounds; while if you do bring up this motive now, you'll be admitting thereby that you signed the order moved merely by petty cowardice; so as to avoid a piddling punishment for the notebook you didn't hesitate to plunge the whole organization into the jaws of the present catastrophe. Do you follow me? Now look. If, on the other hand, you hadn't signed the order, you might have pretended that you hadn't quite realized the impropriety of your action regarding the notebook; but your signature proves that you were clearly aware of this and that you panicked, because you were afraid of being punished. As you see, both your errors are intertwined in such an original way that the one greatly multiplies the other. If on top of your guilt in introducing Ptydepe you should now also volunteer an admission of your guilt regarding the notebook, you'd leave nobody in any doubt whatever about the real culprit responsible for all that's happened. Well then, shall we come to an agreement?

GROSS: All right, let's both resign.

BALLAS: As far as I'm concerned, I don't see why I should. [*Pause.*]

GROSS [*faintly*]: And you would really honestly help me in everything?

BALLAS: I'm glad our discussion is at last reaching a realistic level. Of course I would. [*Offers him a cigarette.*] Take one.

[GROSS *takes it.* BALLAS *gives him a light.*]

GROSS: You have a great deal of experience. You can work as stubbornly as a mule. Would you also work like a mule against Ptydepe?

BALLAS: I can't do things any other way.

[PILLAR *looks in at S.D.*]

BALLAS: Yes, Mr P. Nearly ready.

[PILLAR *disappears, leaving the door ajar.*]

GROSS [*hesitantly*]: But somebody has to get the axe. You know how people are –

BALLAS: Leave that to me. [*Calls towards S.D.*] Ready, Mr P.!

[PILLAR *enters by S.D., followed by* STROLL, SAVANT *and* HELENA, *all three carrying the folders they had in the last scene. They line up in a row and open the folders, as though about to sing in chorus.*]

BALLAS: You may begin.

[PILLAR *gives them a hand signal and they all start solemnly reading.*]

STROLL, SAVANT, HELENA [*together*]: Dear Sir: The delegation which, under the leadership of Mr Pillar, now comes to you consists of people who until the very last sincerely believed in Ptydepe and were in the vanguard of its introduction. All the more difficult it is therefore for us, your loyal colleagues, to approach you now as a delegation whose mission it is to warn you against the consequences of any further propagation of Ptydepe. But precisely because we have done so much for Ptydepe we feel obliged to be the first to point out to you the insoluble problems connected with its establishment.

BALLAS [*gestures them to stop*]: Dear friends. I know only too well, perhaps even better than you, how desperate is the situation we've reached with Ptydepe, and I assure you that it has cost me many a sleepless night. As your former Managing Director I also accept the greatest share of the blame for the whole affair. We meant well, but we did wrong. In short, we sinned and now we must accept, courageously and without any feeling of being sinned against, the full consequences of our activities, and with a redoubled energy struggle to remedy the damage we've done. In accordance with directives from the authorities I have taken certain first steps, with which I shall now acquaint you, because they are already specifically aimed towards a bold solution of the very problem which you have now come here to point out to me. First of all, I've resigned as your Managing Director and I've passed this position to the man who, as you'll surely agree, is the best qualified for it, Mr Josef Gross. Mr Gross who, throughout the era of Ptydepe, remained loyal to and even suffered for his convictions. I myself have received with gratitude from the hands of Mr Gross the position of his deputy. I've received it in order above all to have an opportunity to show by diligent work my willingness to serve the new cause and thus to repair all the harm which, with the best intentions, I committed. And now let me give the platform to Mr Gross.

GROSS [*embarrassed*]: What can I add? I'm not angry with you. I know that you meant well. The proof of it is also this your delegation, which comes in the name of reason and of moral values. Well, we should let bygones be bygones. Let us lose no more words over it. What is at stake now is the future.

[STROLL, SAVANT and HELENA *look questioningly at* PILLAR. *He gestures for them to turn the page. They begin to read further.*]

STROLL, SAVANT, HELENA [*together*]: We are sorry, but we cannot be satisfied with such a brief explanation. We threw our whole lives into the struggle for the wrong thing and we want to know who was responsible and who took advantage of it. We were deceived and we have the right to know who has deceived us.

GROSS [*softly to* BALLAS]: Will you answer this point?

BALLAS [*softly to* GROSS]: Yes. [*Louder*] Friends! We are all guilty.

HELENA [*at* PILLAR'S *signal*]: That is only a hollow phrase!

STROLL [*at* PILLAR'S *signal*]: We want to know the actual persons!

SAVANT [*at* PILLAR'S *signal*]: The names.

BALLAS: All right then, I'll tell you. You've all surely noticed that for some time now there has been prowling about our offices a mysterious, silent man whose real function in our organization has never been known to us. I myself have come to know this man very well, because I've been under his direct surveillance. Inexhaustible was the well of methods by which he has been forcing us to do things we disagreed with. He pried into every nook and cranny, was always present, always subtly disguised in the cloak of inconspicuousness and of silent participation. And it is no accident that this grey eminence of Ptydepe, so diligently trying never to be publicly compromised in any way, has penetrated today – when the cause he served with such sycophancy is quite lost – to the head of your delegation, abusing your honest trust and averting from himself all suspicion by assuming the mask of a critical attitude towards Ptydepe.

[PILLAR, *growing more and more desperate, turns from* STROLL *to* SAVANT, *from* SAVANT *to* HELENA *and even*

HANA, *but they all turn away from him. Dead silence.*
PILLAR *runs in panic across the room, but stops at B.D.*]

PILLAR [*shouts*]: Death to all artificial languages! Long
live natural human speech! Long live Man!

[PILLAR *runs out by B.D. An embarrassed pause. Then
somebody knocks on B.D. All turn towards the sound. Pause.
More knocking. Quizzical looks. More knocking.*]

GROSS: Come in.

[COLUMN *enters by B.D.*]

BALLAS: Welcome, Mr C.! Come in! This is Mr Column.

[COLUMN *bows to them, then sits in* PILLAR's *place. General
relief.*]

GROSS: Now then, let me conclude. What is at stake is the
future. I appeal to you to put all your best efforts into the
struggle for the re-establishment of natural human
language, of our beloved mother tongue –

BALLAS [*interrupts*]: Wait a minute, Jo! Our colleagues are
surely tired by now. We can talk tomorrow about what
happens next. Now, let me suggest that we all go and
have lunch together. Who's in favour?

[STROLL, SAVANT, HELENA, COLUMN *and* HANA *at
once raise their hands.*]

STROLL: That's an idea!

SAVANT: Bravo!

HELENA: Hurrah!

BALLAS: Let's all meet in a quarter of an hour at the
Translation Centre!

[STROLL, SAVANT *and* HELENA *hurry out by B.D.*]

BALLAS: Well, that's that. Are you quite comfortable,
Mr C.?

[COLUMN *nods, walks to the desk, begins to collect the
papers lying on it and to shove them in his pockets.* BALLAS
*crosses to fire-extinguisher hanging on the wall and takes it
down. Then* BALLAS *and* COLUMN *leave by S.D.*]

GROSS: Things do seem to be moving rather fast.

HANA: Mr Gross –

GROSS: There was nothing else I could do. An open conflict would have meant that I'd be finished. This way, as the Managing Director, I can at least salvage this and that.

HANA: Mr Gross –

GROSS: Anyway, who knows, maybe this – Ballas – will turn out to be quite a good man after all. If I use him in the right place –

HANA: Mr Gross –

GROSS: What is it?

HANA: May I go and get my lunch?

GROSS: Run along.

[HANA *hastily takes her knife and fork and hurries out by B.D.* GROSS *halts in the centre and sadly stares ahead.* BALLAS *and* COLUMN *enter by S.D., both carrying their knives and forks, and walk towards B.D.*]

GROSS [*to himself*]: Why can't I be a little boy again? I'd do everything differently from the beginning.

BALLAS: You might begin differently, but you'd end up exactly the same – so relax!

[BALLAS *and* COLUMN *leave by B.D.* GROSS *lingers dejectedly for a second longer, then takes his fire-extinguisher, hangs it in its original place, takes his knife and fork from the drawer and slowly walks out B.D.*]

# SCENE ELEVEN

*The Ptydepe classroom. All four* CLERKS *are back in their chairs, including* THUMB.

[LEAR *is lecturing.*]

LEAR: The basic mistake of Ptydepe was its uncritical over-estimation of the significance of redundancy. Redundancy turned into a veritable campaign, it became the slogan of the day. But it was overlooked that side by side with a useful redundancy, which indeed lowered the danger of incorrect interpretations of texts, there existed also a useless redundancy, consisting merely in a mechanical prolongation of texts. In the pursuit of maximum redundancy some eager clerks inserted within Ptydepe words – already long enough, thank you – even further so-called empty texts, thus blindly increasing the percentage of redundancy, so that the length of inter-office communications grew out of all proportion and sense.

[BALLAS *and* COLUMN *enter by B.D., carrying their knives and forks, cross the room,* BALLAS *pats* LEAR *appreciatively on the shoulder, then both leave by S.D.*]

LEAR: Let me give you an example. I've heard of a case where a brief summons to military H.Q. filled thirty-six typed pages single spaced.

[THUMB *giggles.*]

LEAR: Another disastrous manifestation is to be seen in certain stylistic habits which came into being during the Ptydepe era. The straining after maximum dissimilarity between what preceded and what followed within a given text, out of which the habit grew, was limiting more and more the possibilities for the further continuation of texts, until in some instances either they could continue only in one specific direction, so that the authors lost all influence over what they were trying to communicate, or they couldn't be continued at all.

[GROSS *enters by B.D., carrying his knife and fork, starts towards S.D., but when he hears* LEAR, *he stops and listens.*]

LEAR: All these mistakes have served as a sound lesson in the creation of the new synthetic language – Chorukor – which no longer attempts to limit the unreliability of a text by a strenuous pursuit of words as dissimilar from each other as possible; on the contrary it achieves this by a purposeful exploitation and organization of their similarity; the more similar the words, the closer their meaning; so that a possible error in the text represents only a slight deviation from its sense.

[GROSS *hurries out S.D.*]

LEAR: This method has many advantages, among them the fact that Chorukor is very easy to learn. Often it is enough to know only one word from within a certain radius of meaning in order to guess many other words of that group. We can do that unaided and without any further study.

THUMB [*raises his hand*]: Sir!

LEAR: Yes?

THUMB [*gets up*]: Would you please demonstrate this to us with an example? [*Sits down.*]

LEAR: Certainly. Monday becomes in Chorukor 'ilopagar', Tuesday 'ilopager', Wednesday 'ilopagur', Thursday 'ilopagir', Friday 'ilopageur', Saturday 'ilopagoor'. Now, what do you think Sunday is? Well?

[*Only* THUMB *raises his hand.*]

LEAR: Well, Mr Thumb.

THUMB [*gets up*]: Ilopagor. [*Sits down,*]

LEAR: Correct, Mr Thumb. You get an A. It is easy, isn't it?

[THUMB *nods.*]

LEAR: There you are! And at the same time the danger of an error can be entirely disregarded. For example, if a typist makes a mistake and instead of 'ilopageur' writes in the announcement of a meeting 'ilopager', the subject of the meeting is not at all distorted thereby. The most that can happen is that the staff will meet on Tuesday, instead of on Friday, and the matter under consideration will thus even be expedited.

# SCENE TWELVE

*The Secretariat of the Translation Centre.* MARIA *is standing dejectedly by her desk.* BALLAS *and* COLUMN *are there, both with their knives and forks. Noise of a party off stage can be heard, as in Scene Six* MARIA *begins to sob.* BALLAS *looks at her.*


BALLAS: I'm sorry. I've promised Mr Gross that I shall work like a mule and I don't want to break my promise by compromising on the very first day. What's going on next door?

MARIA [*sobbing*]: It's Mr Wassermann's birthday, so his colleagues are giving him a party.

BALLAS: Paul Wassermann? Do you hear that, Mr C.? It's Paul's birthday!

[BALLAS *and* COLUMN *start towards S.D. Just then* GROSS *runs in by B.D., holding knife and fork in his hand.*]

GROSS [*excitedly*]: Mr Ballas!

BALLAS: Yes?

GROSS: What on earth does it mean?

BALLAS: What?

GROSS: Another artificial language is being taught here!

BALLAS: Chorukor.

GROSS: But we agreed, didn't we, that office communications are again to be conducted in our mother tongue!

BALLAS: I don't recall we agreed on anything of the sort.

GROSS: But my memorandum states quite clearly –

BALLAS: As far as I remember, it states nothing about what language is now to be used here. Making an end of Ptydepe doesn't mean that we must automatically give up all attempts at finally introducing some precision and order into office communications. If we did, we would –

so to speak – throw out the baby with the bath water. Am I not right, Mr C.?

[COLUMN *nods*.]

GROSS: But I understood that –

BALLAS: You understood wrong. It is evident that you've lived for a long time in an isolation which tragically marked you through the loss of a living contact with reality. I don't want to meddle in the business of the Managing Director, but when I see that you're clearly fumbling and could easily come into conflict with the opinion of most of our staff, then I'm sorry but I have to interfere.

GROSS: Look, wouldn't it make things easier if you carried on as the Managing Director and I as your deputy?

BALLAS: Not on your life! I've already been foolish enough to try that once already and I don't propose to do it again! Let's each do what suits him best. I have certain organizational talents which I can put to excellent use as your deputy, while you can better bear the weight of responsibility connected with the position of the Managing Director. [*To* COLUMN] They're still at it over there! Let's go!

[BALLAS *and* COLUMN *leave by S.D. The noise of the party grows louder, then quietens down.*]

MARIA: Josef –

GROSS: Yes?

MARIA: You didn't tell me the Watcher had come back.

GROSS: Well?

MARIA: He saw and heard everything!

GROSS: Everything? What?

MARIA: That I translated your memo.

GROSS: Well?

MARIA: He told on me and I was fired on the spot, because I'd translated an important Ptydepe text before passing my exams.

GROSS: But the use of Ptydepe has been cancelled –

MARIA: Mr Ballas said that's beside the point. A rule is a rule, he said. What guarantee is there, he said, that I wouldn't some day make an improper translation from Chorukor as well. He said he had promised you to work like a mule and he didn't want to break his promise the very first day by a compromise.

GROSS: What are you going to do?

MARIA: Well, I hate to bother you, but couldn't you perhaps reverse his decision? Or perhaps at least put in a kind word for me?

GROSS: Dear Maria! We're living in a strange, complex epoch. As Hamlet says, our 'time is out of joint'. Just think, we're reaching for the moon, and yet it's increasingly hard for us to reach our selves; we're able to split the atom, but unable to prevent the splitting of our personality; we build superb communications between the continents, and yet communication between Man and Man is increasingly difficult.

[Short pause. Noise of the party.]

GROSS: In other words, our life has lost a sort of higher axis, and we are irresistibly falling apart, more and more profoundly alienated from the world, from others, from ourselves. Like Sisyphus, we roll the boulder of our life up the hill of its illusory meaning, only for it to roll down again into the valley of its own absurdity. Never before has Man lived projected so near to the very brink of the insoluble conflict between the subjective will of his moral self and the objective possibility of its ethical realization. Manipulated, automatized, made into a fetish, Man loses the experience of his own totality; horrified, he stares as a stranger at himself, unable not to be what he is not, nor to be what he is.

[Again a short pause. Noise of the party.]

GROSS [turns directly to MARIA and continues with urgency]:

Dear Maria! You can't begin to guess how happy I would be if I could do for you what you've just asked me to do. The more am I frightened therefore that in reality I can do next to nothing for you, because I am in fact totally alienated from myself: the desire to help you fatefully encounters within me the responsibility thrust upon me – who am attempting to salvage the last remains of Man's humanity – by the permanent menace to our organization from the side of Mr Ballas and his men; a responsibility so binding that I absolutely may not risk the loss of the position on which it is based by any open conflict with Mr Ballas and his men.

[*Pause. The noise off stage culminates in unintelligible singing which changes into cheers.*]

VOICES [*off stage*]: Hip, hip, hurrah!

[*Cheers culminate in laughter which, however, soon dies down. The party is over. While* GROSS *continues speaking,* STROLL, SAVANT, HELENA, HANA, BALLAS, COLUMN, LEAR, THUMB *and three* CLERKS *enter by* S.D. GEORGE *scrambles out of the secret door. All have their knives and forks. All stand in the background, waiting for* GROSS *to join them to go to lunch.*]

GROSS: Besides, there is no point in further complicating my already complicated situation by taking too tragic a view of your prospects. Let's try to be quite matter-of-fact about it, shall we? You're still young, you have a whole life ahead of you, you have lost nothing so far. Just think! How many people today are able to say with any degree of honesty they have a brother with a theatre group? A minuscule minority! For all we can tell, one day you might come to be thankful to Mr Ballas for a career as a famous actress. What matters now is that you must not lose your hope, your love of life and your trust in people! Chin up, my girl! Keep smiling! I know it is absurd,

dear Maria, but I must go and have lunch. So – goodbye!
Be good! [*Joins the others in the background.*]

[*Pause. They all look at* MARIA.]

MARIA [*softly*]: Nobody ever talked to me so nicely before.
[*They all slowly leave in a solemn, funeral-like procession by
B.D., clutching their knives and forks.* MARIA *takes her bag,
collects her things, puts on her new hat, looks about for the last
time and then – happy – she also leaves.*]

# THREE SOVIET PLAYS

*Vladimir Mayakovsky:* The Bedbug
*Isaac Babel:* Marya
*Yevgeny Schwartz:* The Dragon

No Soviet play can escape from being 'Soviet', from register-
ing the facts of living in a country which has undergone and
is undergoing an experience too overwhelming to be ignored
in any serious drama. But not all the plays produced since
the Russian Revolution have been written obediently in the
'boy-meets-tractor' manner. A handful have been produced
by writers safe enough or brave enough to approach the
Russian experience with open minds and a sense of humour,
with imaginative power, originality, and unconcern with
the deadening ephemera of ideology. The three plays in
this volume are a selection from that handful.

# THREE EUROPEAN PLAYS

*Jean Anouilh:* Ring Round the Moon
*Ugo Betti:* The Queen and the Rebels
*Jean-Paul Sartre:* In Camera

This volume contains plays by three of the most brilliant and
accomplished contemporary European writers. Anouilh,
well-known for *Antigone*, is here represented by his ebullient
comedy *Ring Round the Moon*. In it he draws vivid and en-
tertaining portraits of human idiosyncrasies with a total
disregard for accepted moral values. The Italian dramatist
Ugo Betti's reputation now rivals that of Pirandello; his
deep concern with morality and religion is apparent in
*The Queen and the Rebels*, a serious political drama of our own
times written in the classical tradition. Sartre's *In Camera*, an
obsessive intellectual drama, is a study of three of life's
victims, who come to realize that 'hell is other people'.